D0970309

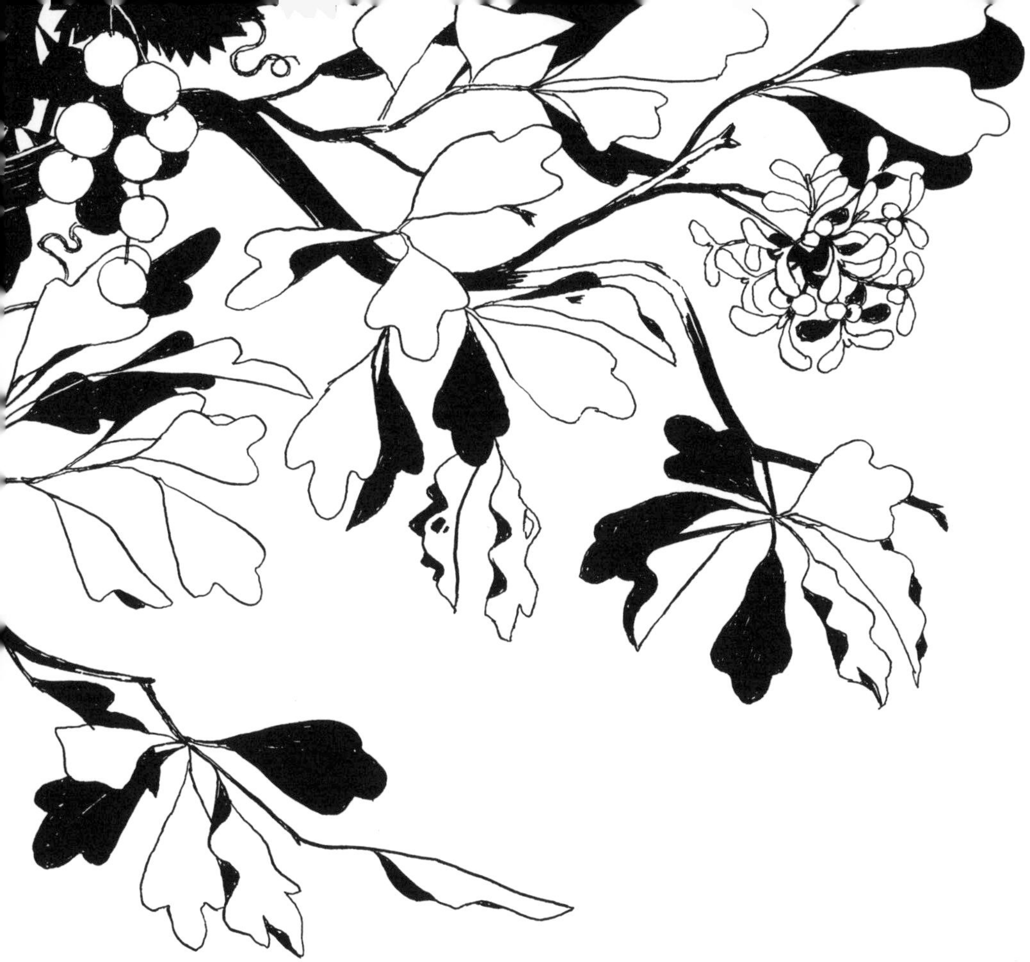

THE HARD
TOMORROW

For Drew

Thank you Kate Guillen. Thank you Lacey Jon Davis and Maggie Akstin. Thank you Leta Davis, Adam Aylard, ST, Athens for Everyone, and the whole team at D+Q. Thank you Lori and Jeremy Weing.

Thank you Drew Weing for helping me—beyond reason—with every line I draw.

Thank you to my dad and mom, Ed and Ann Davis, for all of it.

Thank you, in advance, to the person I hope to give birth to three months from when I write this. I look forward to meeting you. I don't know what your future will look like. I hope you will forgive us for bringing you into this beautiful and terrible world.

—*Eleanor Davis, April 2019*

drawnandquarterly.com I doing-fine.com

978-1-77046-373-8 I First edition: October 2019 I Printed in Bosnia and Herzegovina 10 9 8 7 6 5 4 3 2 1 I Cataloguing data available from Library and Archives Canada

Published in the USA by Drawn & Quarterly, a client publisher of Farrar, Straus and Giroux. Published in Canada by Drawn & Quarterly, a client publisher of Raincoast Books. Published in the United Kingdom by Drawn & Quarterly, a client publisher of Publishers Group UK

Eleanor Davis

THE HARD
TOMORROW

Drawn & Quarterly

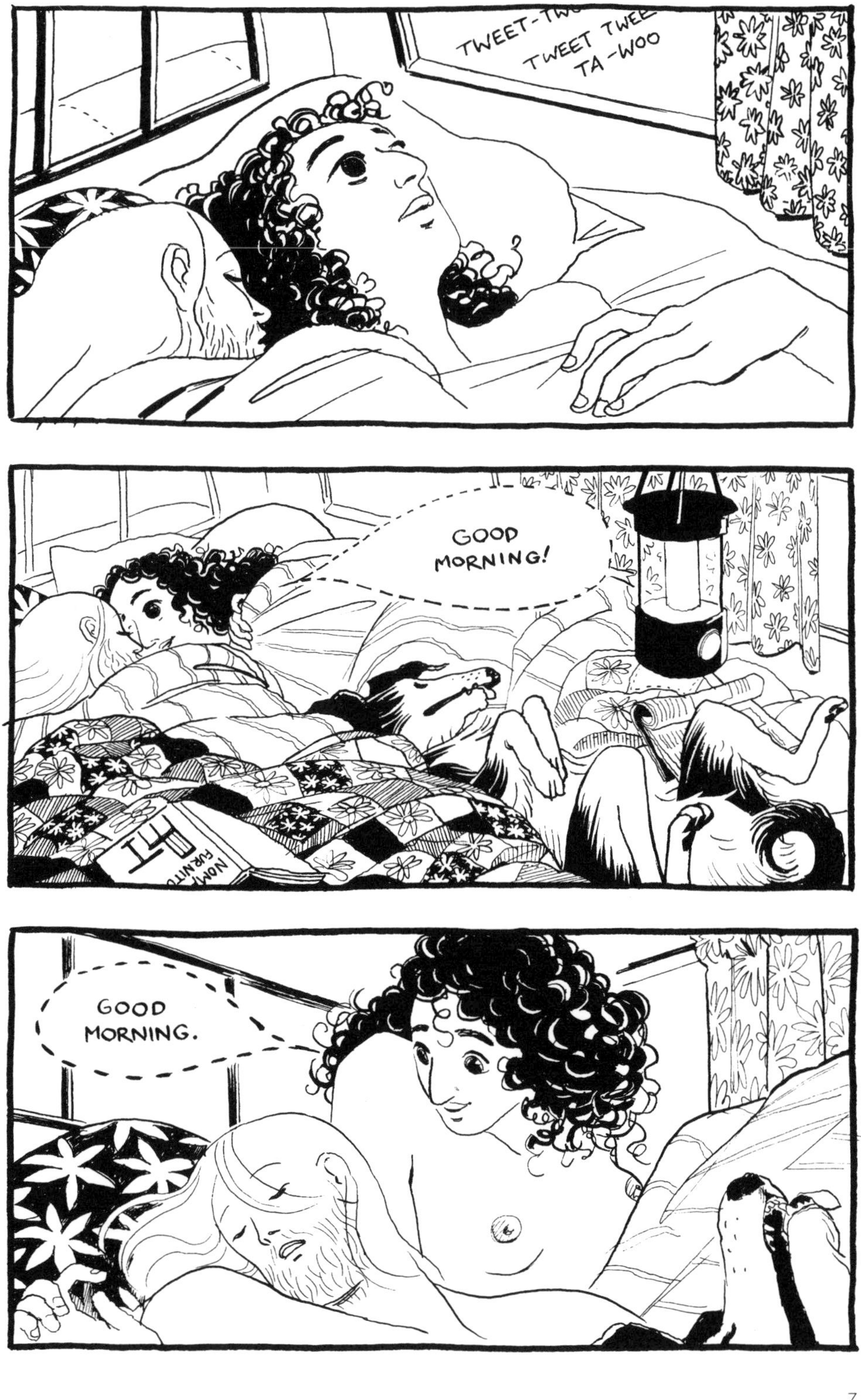
TWEET-TW
TWEET TWEE
TA-WOO
GOOD MORNING!
GOOD MORNING.

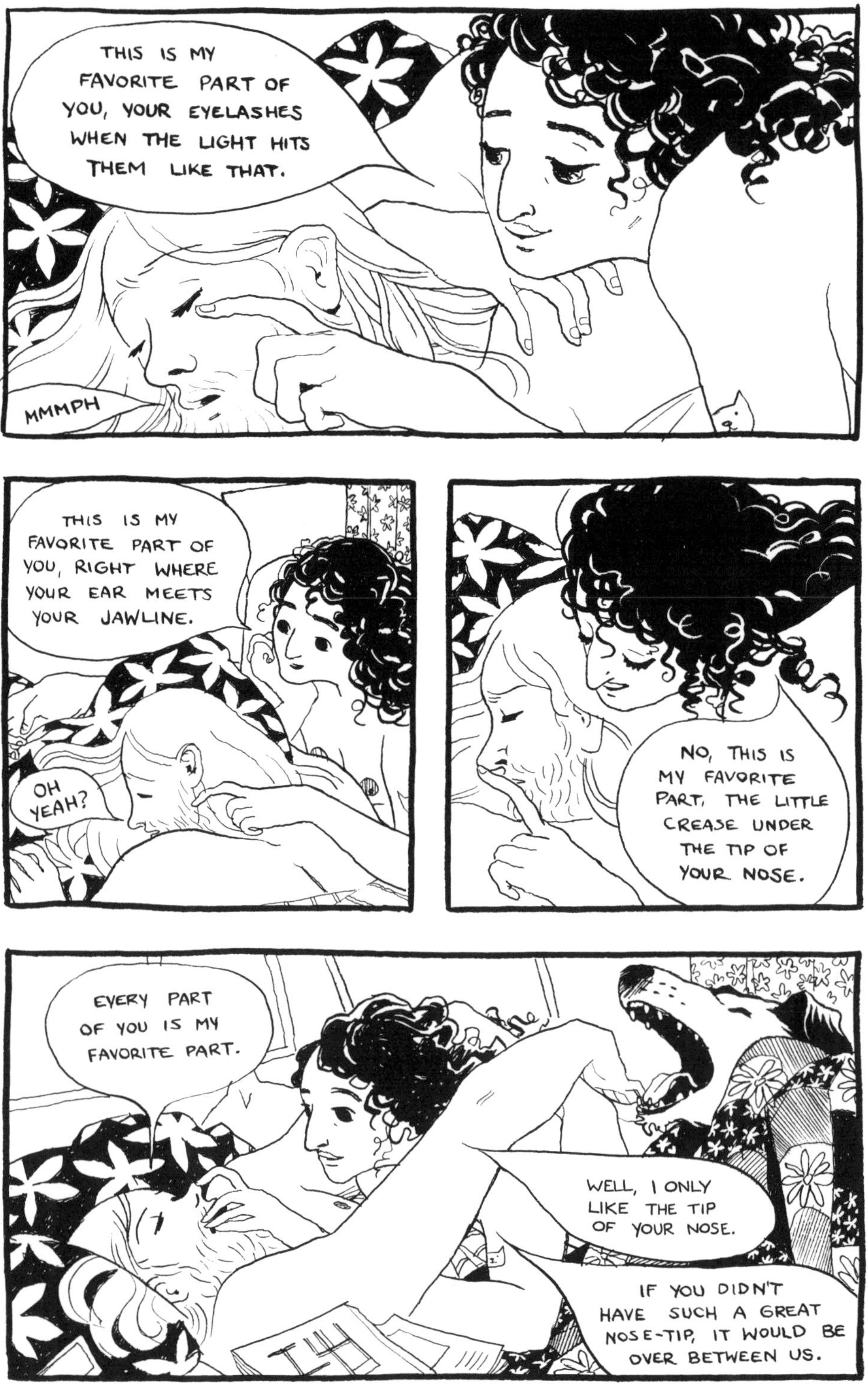
THIS IS MY FAVORITE PART OF YOU, YOUR EYELASHES WHEN THE LIGHT HITS THEM LIKE THAT.
MMMPH
THIS IS MY FAVORITE PART OF YOU, RIGHT WHERE YOUR EAR MEETS YOUR JAWLINE.
OH YEAH?
NO, THIS IS MY FAVORITE PART, THE LITTLE CREASE UNDER THE TIP OF YOUR NOSE.
EVERY PART OF YOU IS MY FAVORITE PART.
WELL, I ONLY LIKE THE TIP OF YOUR NOSE.
IF YOU DIDN'T HAVE SUCH A GREAT NOSE-TIP, IT WOULD BE OVER BETWEEN US.

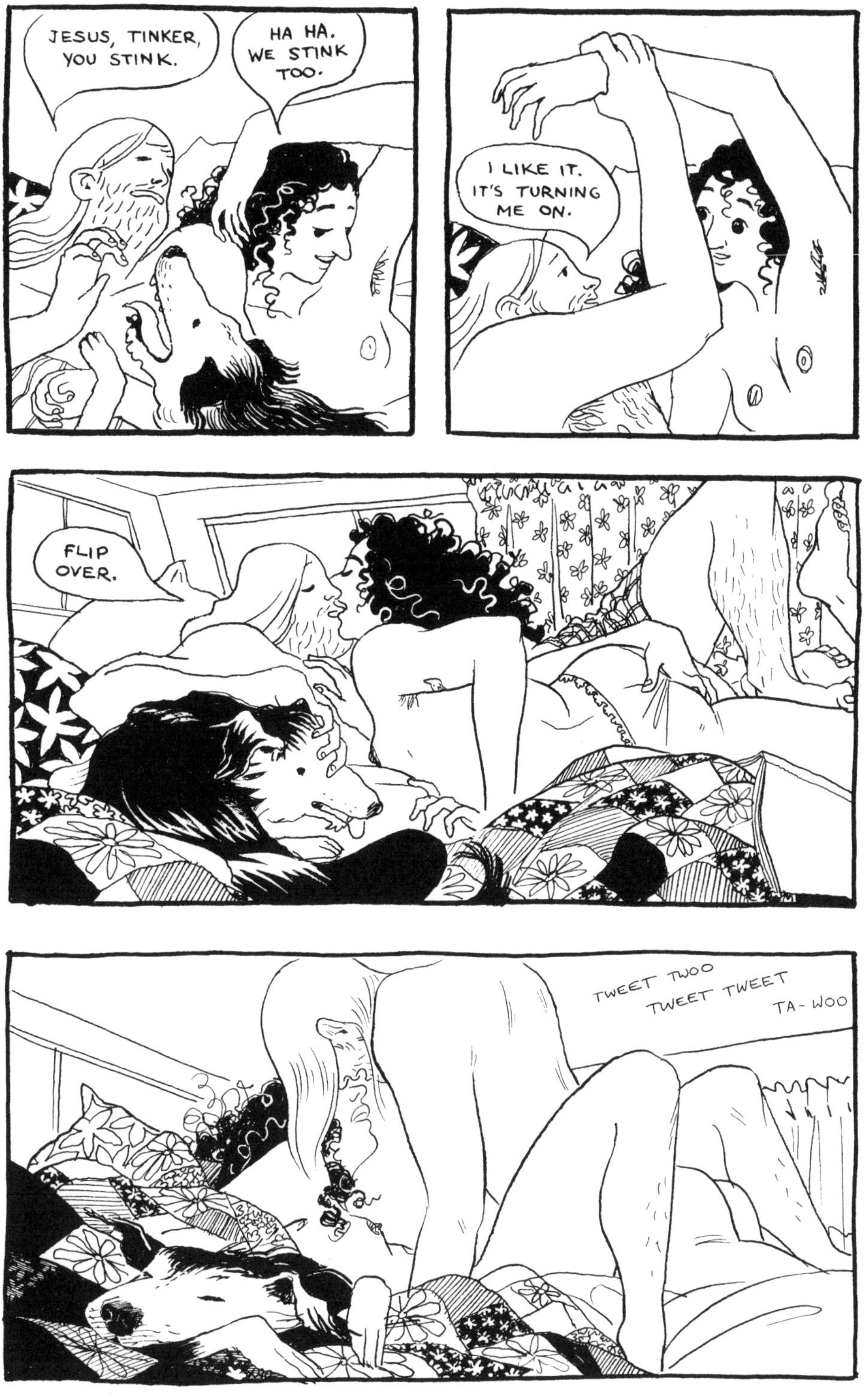
JESUS, TINKER, YOU STINK.
HA HA. WE STINK TOO.
I LIKE IT. IT'S TURNING ME ON.
FLIP OVER.
TWEET TWOO TWEET TWEET TA-WOO

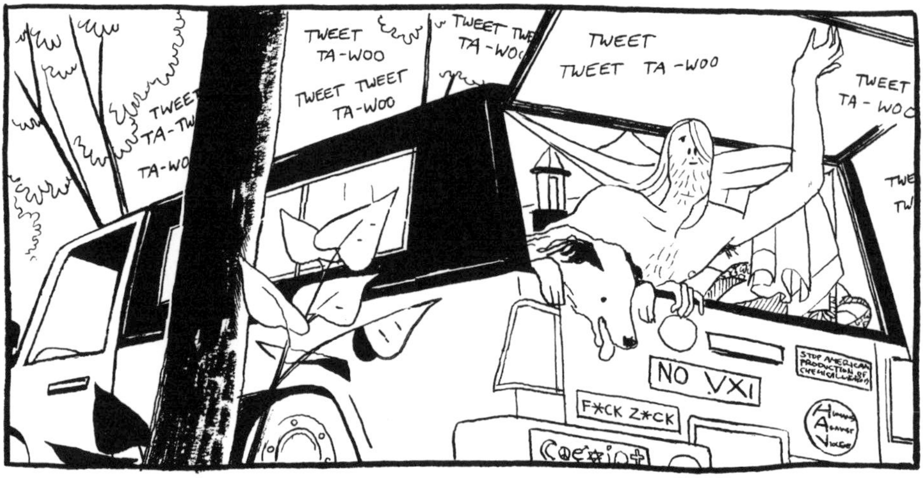
TWEET
TA-WOO
TWEET TWEET
TA-WOO
TWEET
TWEET TA-WOO
NO VXI
F*CK Z*CK

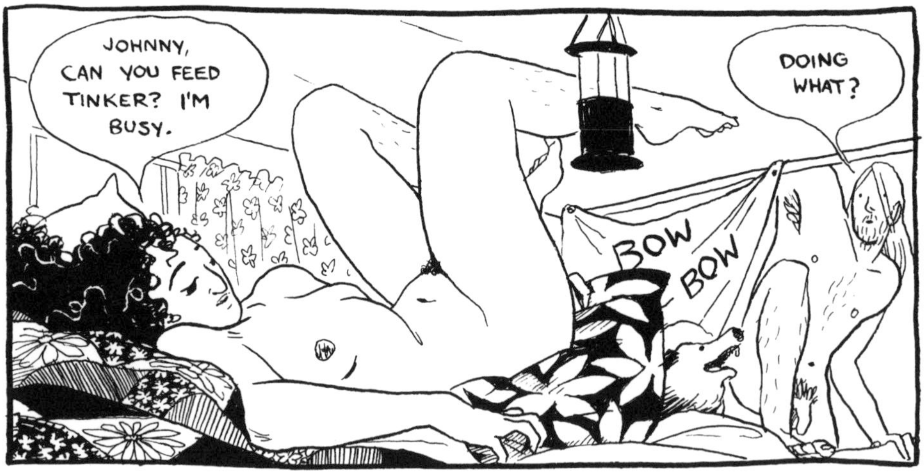
JOHNNY, CAN YOU FEED TINKER? I'M BUSY.
DOING WHAT?
BOW BOW

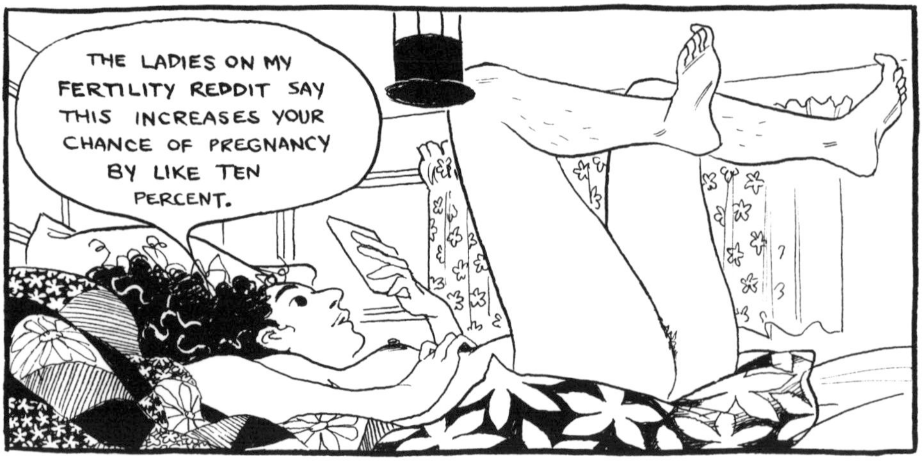
THE LADIES ON MY FERTILITY REDDIT SAY THIS INCREASES YOUR CHANCE OF PREGNANCY BY LIKE TEN PERCENT.

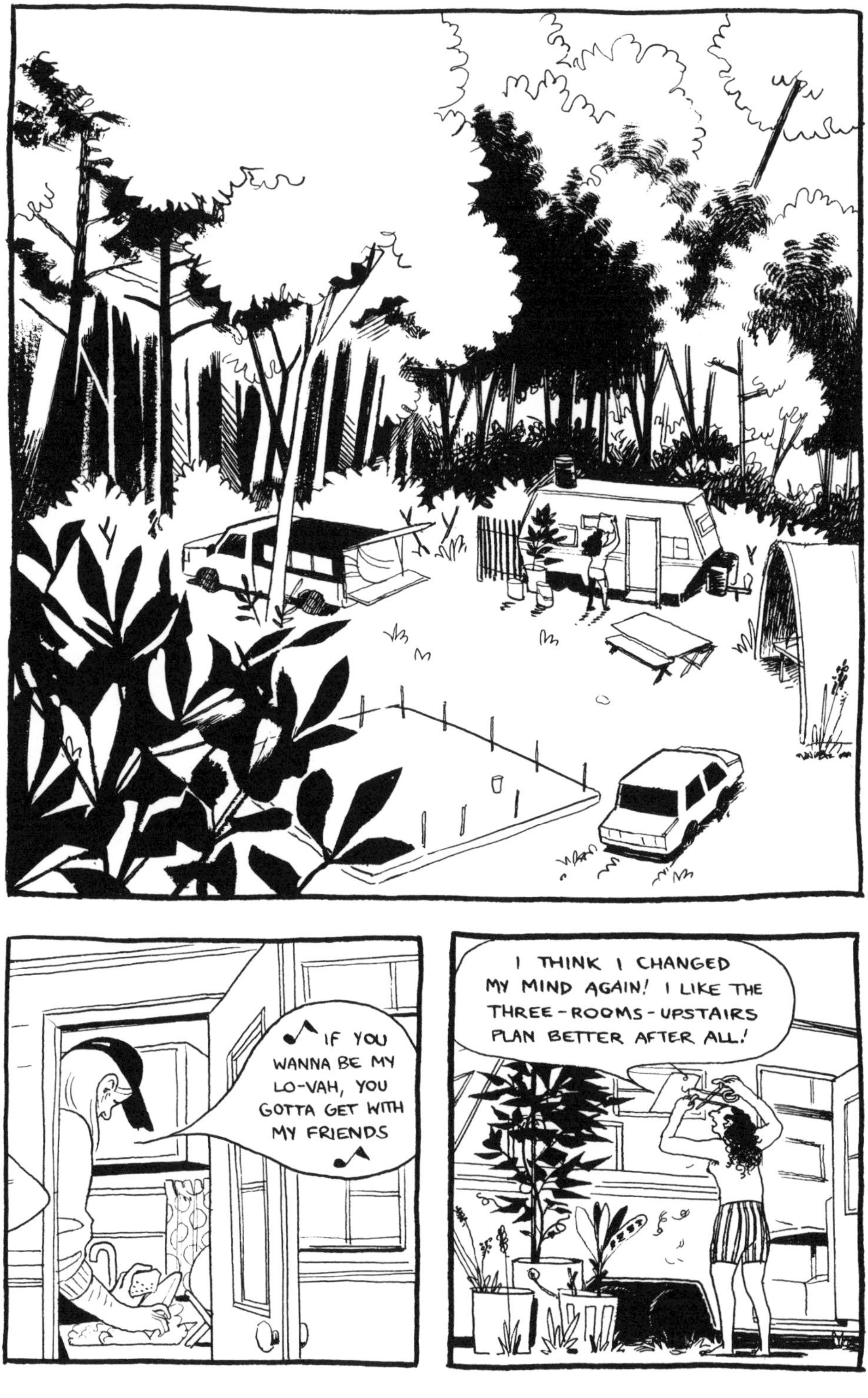
IF YOU WANNA BE MY LO-VAH, YOU GOTTA GET WITH MY FRIENDS
I THINK I CHANGED MY MIND AGAIN! I LIKE THE THREE-ROOMS-UPSTAIRS PLAN BETTER AFTER ALL!

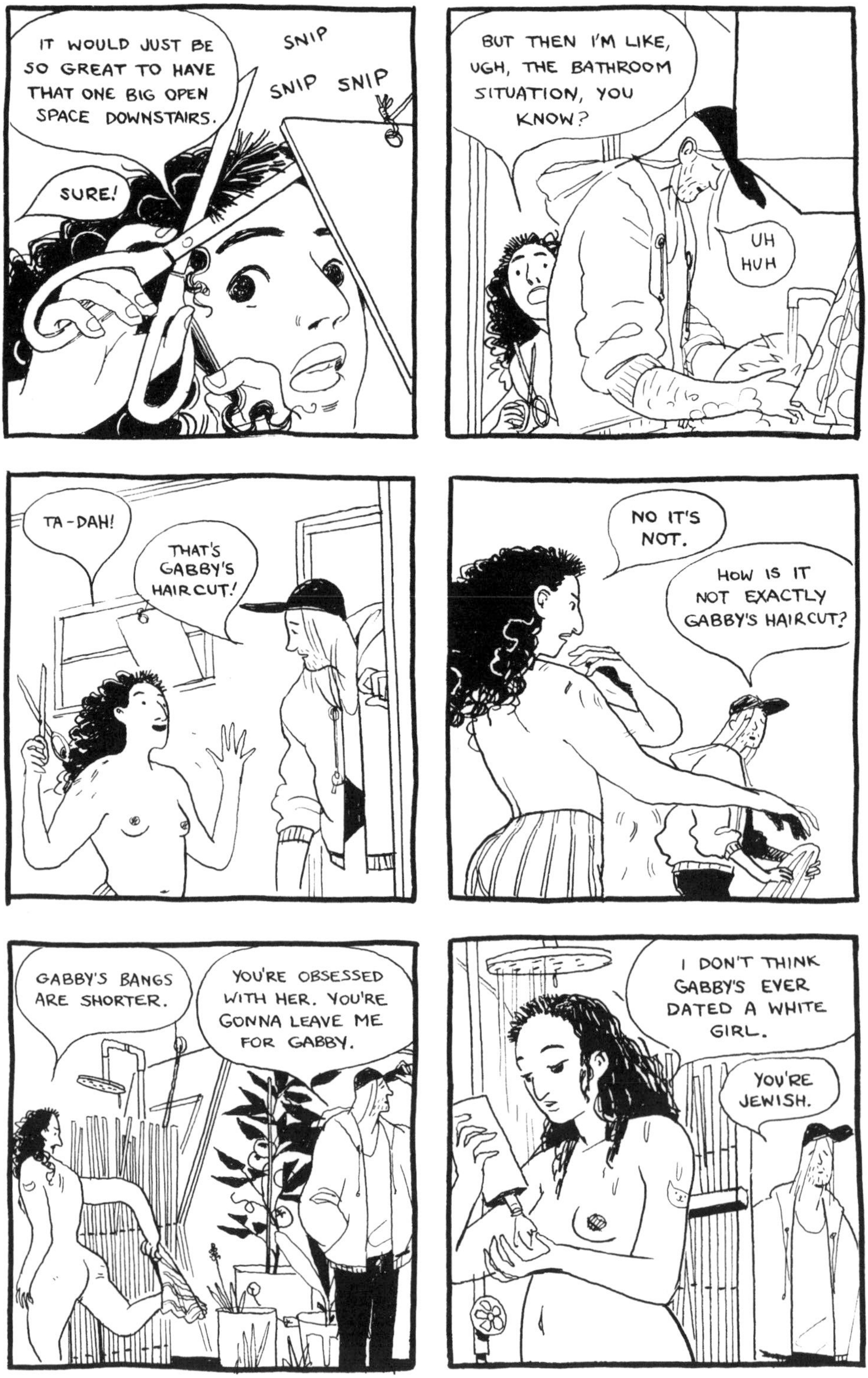
IT WOULD JUST BE SO GREAT TO HAVE THAT ONE BIG OPEN SPACE DOWNSTAIRS.
SNIP
SNIP SNIP
SURE!
BUT THEN I'M LIKE, UGH, THE BATHROOM SITUATION, YOU KNOW?
UH HUH
TA-DAH!
THAT'S GABBY'S HAIRCUT!
NO IT'S NOT.
HOW IS IT NOT EXACTLY GABBY'S HAIRCUT?
GABBY'S BANGS ARE SHORTER.
YOU'RE OBSESSED WITH HER. YOU'RE GONNA LEAVE ME FOR GABBY.
I DON'T THINK GABBY'S EVER DATED A WHITE GIRL.
YOU'RE JEWISH.

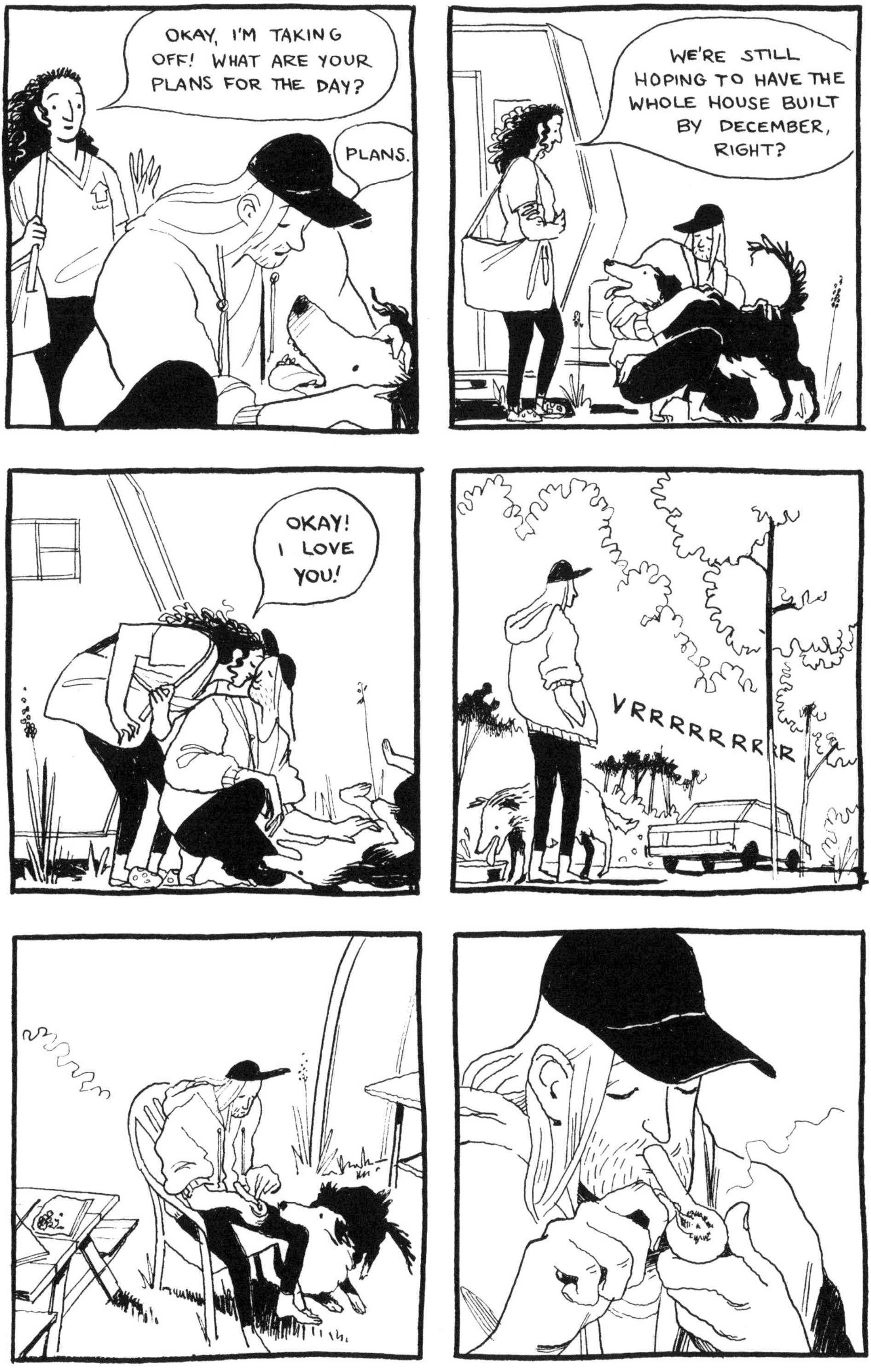
OKAY, I'M TAKING OFF! WHAT ARE YOUR PLANS FOR THE DAY?
PLANS.
WE'RE STILL HOPING TO HAVE THE WHOLE HOUSE BUILT BY DECEMBER, RIGHT?
OKAY! I LOVE YOU!
VRRRRRRRRRR

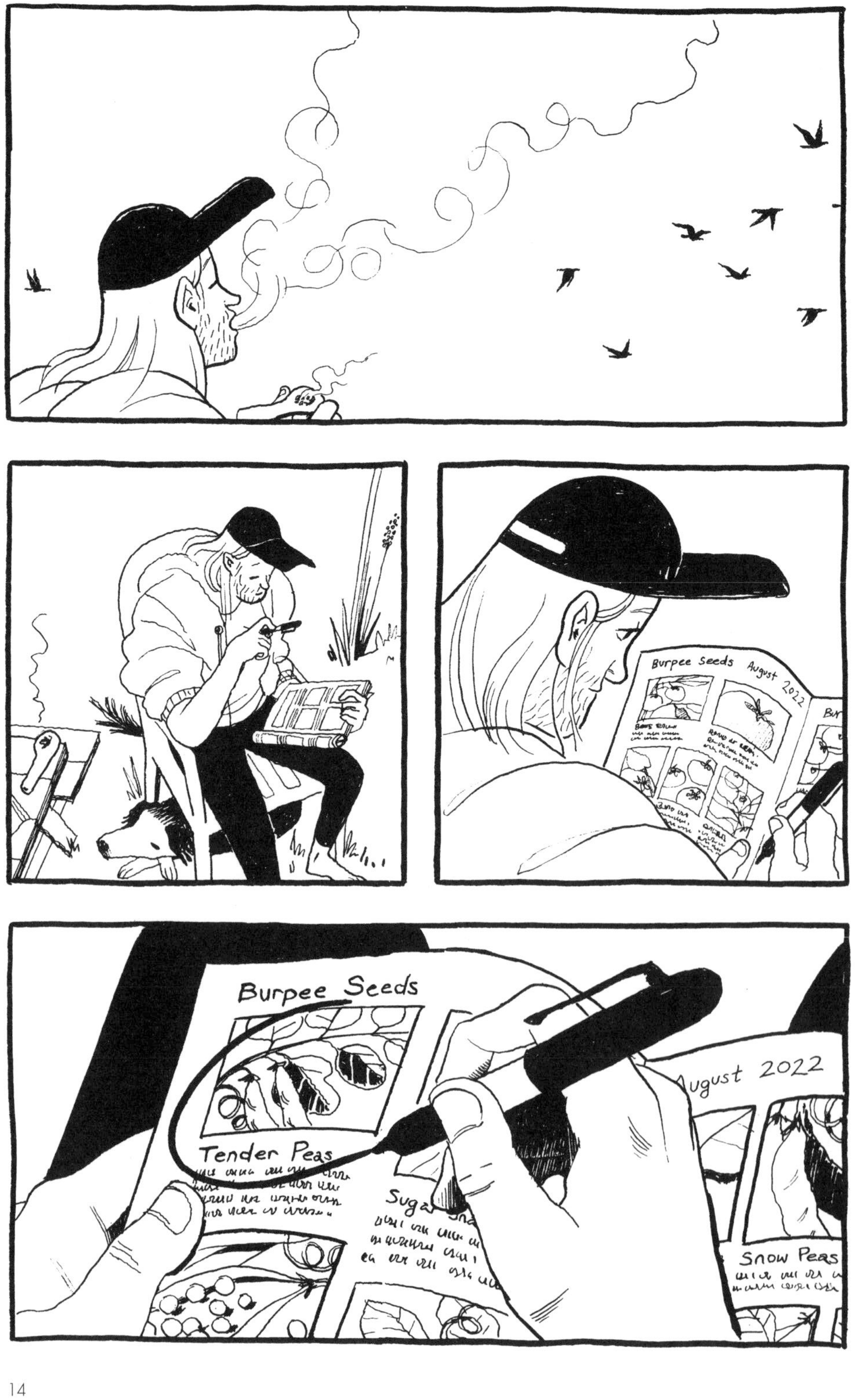
Burpee Seeds
August 2022
Burpee Seeds
August 2022
Tender Peas
Snow Peas

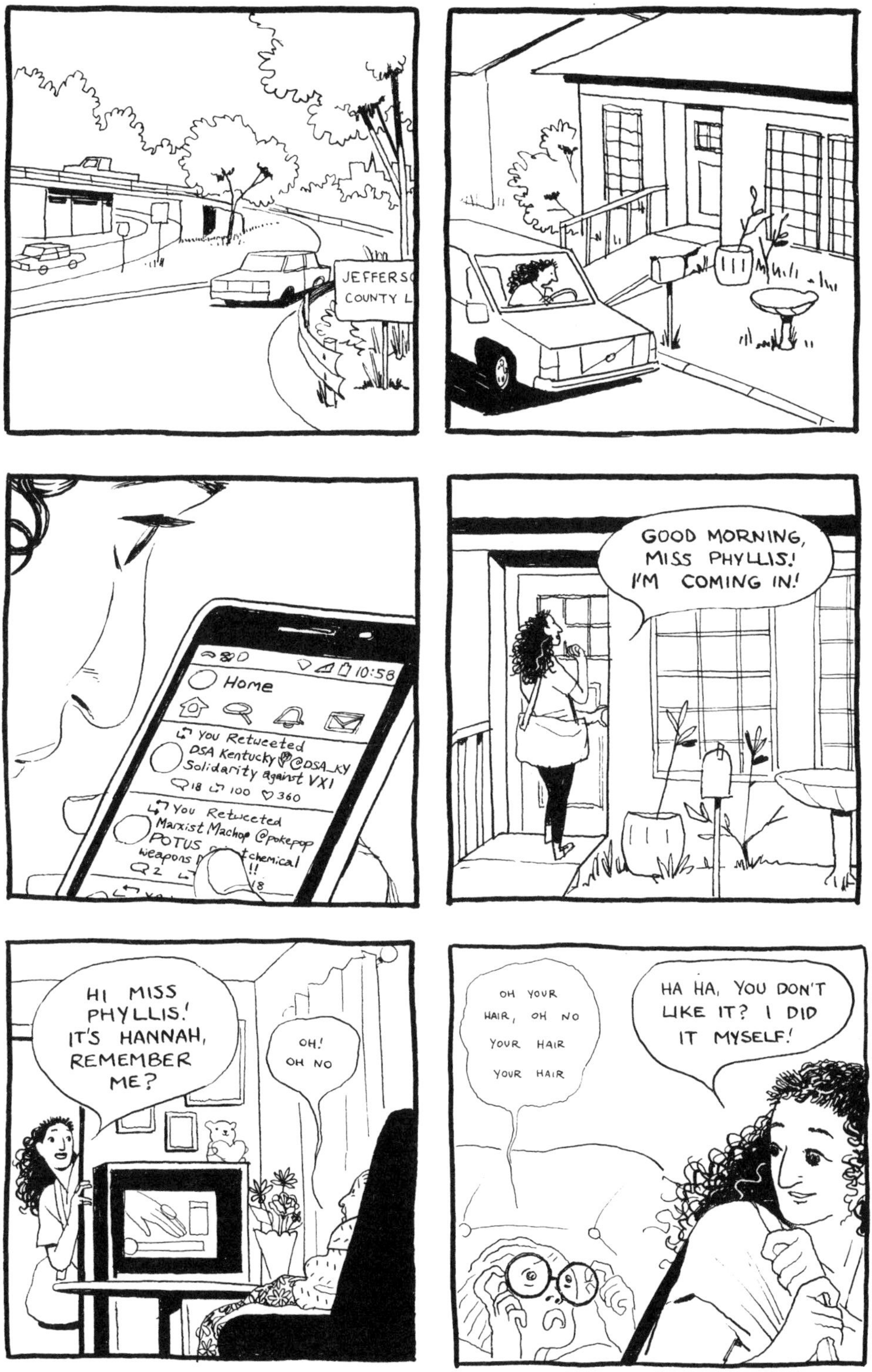
JEFFERS
COUNTY L
10:58
Home
You Retweeted
DSA Kentucky @DSA_KY
Solidarity against VXI
18 100 360
You Retweeted
Marxist Machop @pokepop
GOOD MORNING, MISS PHYLLIS! I'M COMING IN!
HI MISS PHYLLIS! IT'S HANNAH, REMEMBER ME?
OH! OH NO
OH YOUR HAIR, OH NO YOUR HAIR YOUR HAIR
HA HA, YOU DON'T LIKE IT? I DID IT MYSELF!

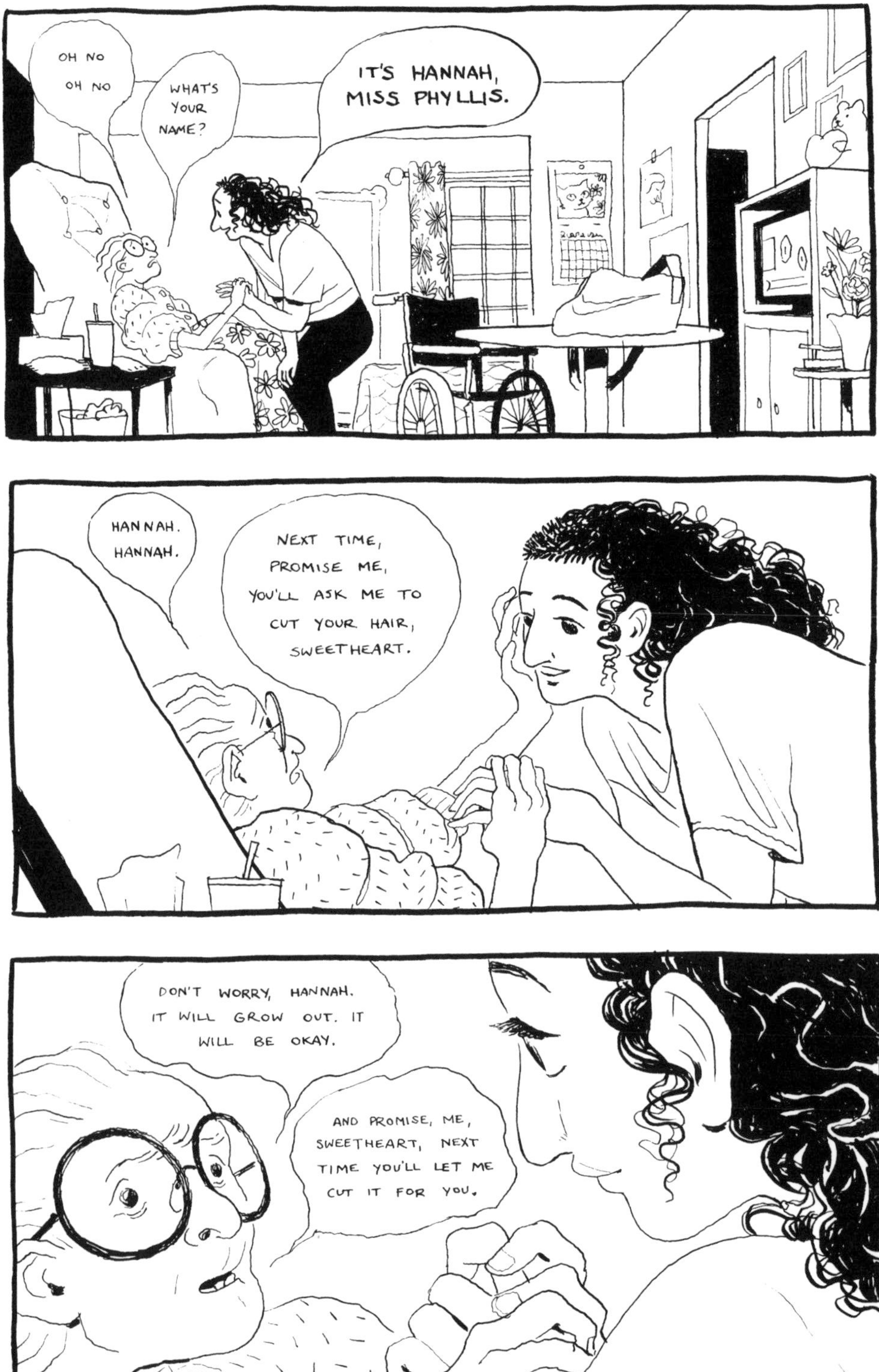
OH NO
OH NO
WHAT'S YOUR NAME?
IT'S HANNAH, MISS PHYLLIS.
HANNAH. HANNAH.
NEXT TIME, PROMISE ME, YOU'LL ASK ME TO CUT YOUR HAIR, SWEETHEART.
DON'T WORRY, HANNAH. IT WILL GROW OUT. IT WILL BE OKAY.
AND PROMISE, ME, SWEETHEART, NEXT TIME YOU'LL LET ME CUT IT FOR YOU.

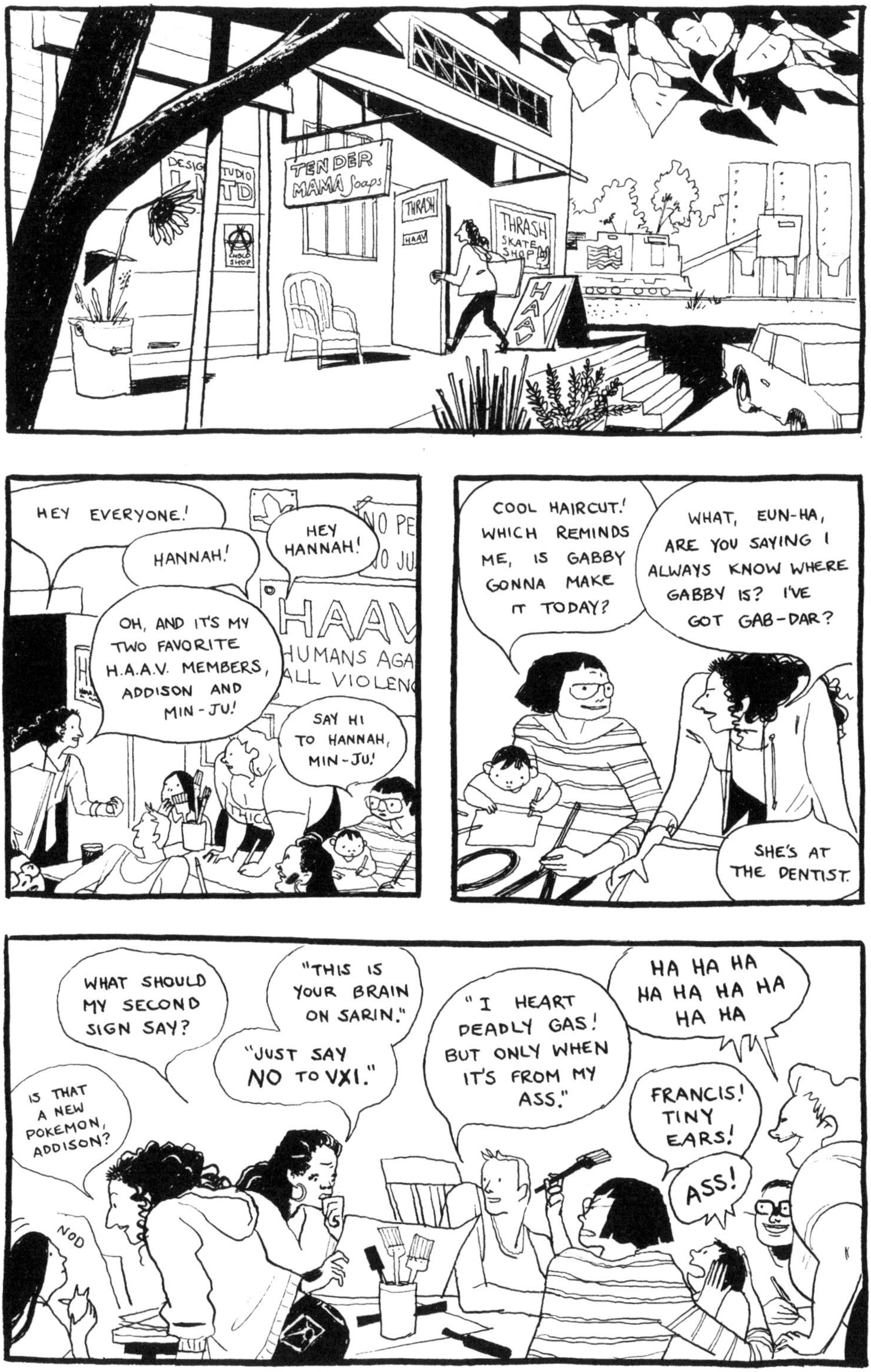
TENDER MAMA Soaps
THRASH
HAAV
THRASH SKATE SHOP
HEY EVERYONE!
HANNAH!
HEY HANNAH!
OH, AND IT'S MY TWO FAVORITE H.A.A.V. MEMBERS, ADDISON AND MIN-JU!
SAY HI TO HANNAH, MIN-JU!
COOL HAIRCUT! WHICH REMINDS ME, IS GABBY GONNA MAKE IT TODAY?
WHAT, EUN-HA, ARE YOU SAYING I ALWAYS KNOW WHERE GABBY IS? I'VE GOT GAB-DAR?
SHE'S AT THE DENTIST.
WHAT SHOULD MY SECOND SIGN SAY?
"THIS IS YOUR BRAIN ON SARIN."
"JUST SAY NO TO VXI."
"I HEART DEADLY GAS! BUT ONLY WHEN IT'S FROM MY ASS."
HA HA HA HA HA HA HA HA HA
IS THAT A NEW POKEMON, ADDISON?
NOD
FRANCIS! TINY EARS!
ASS!

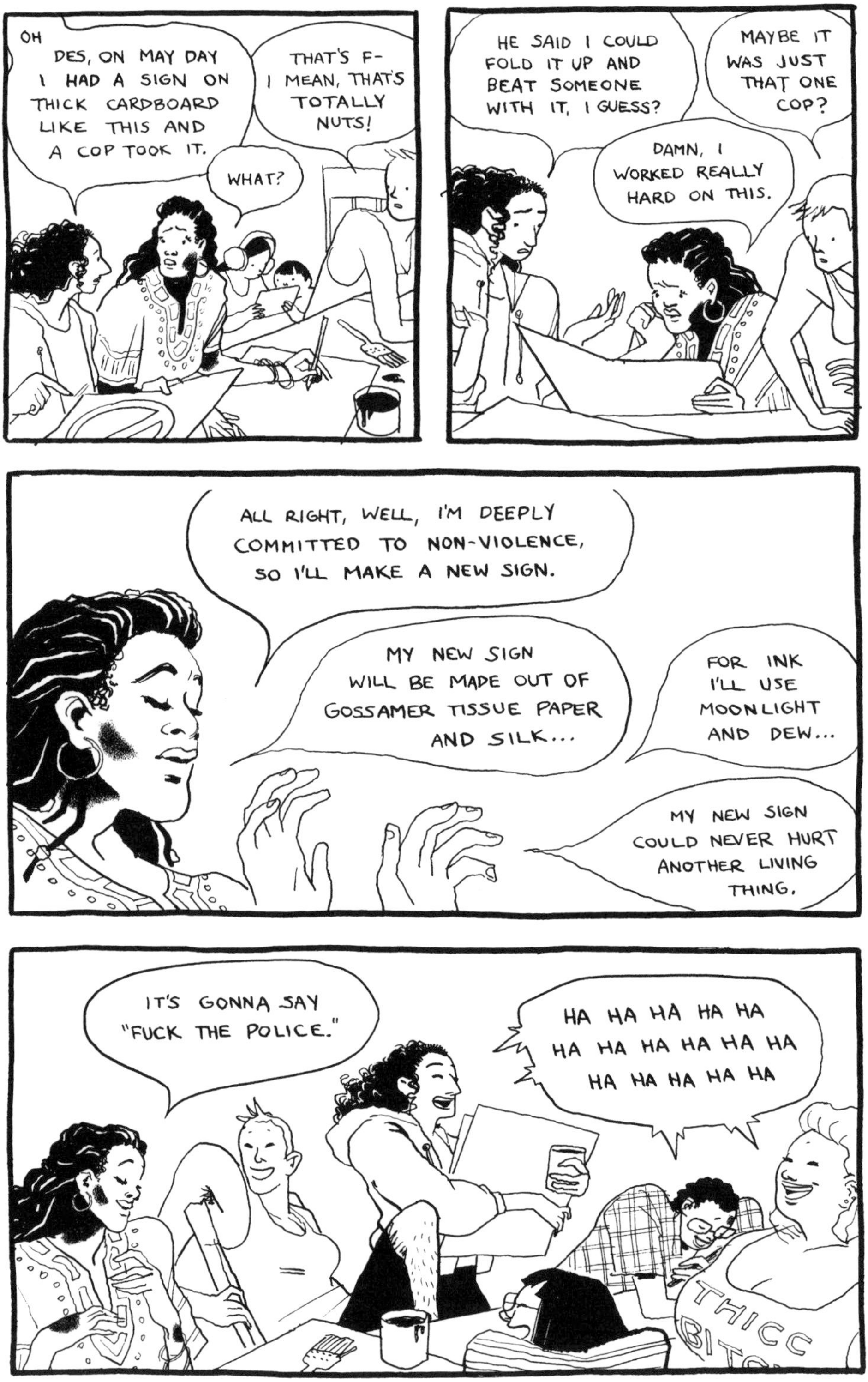
OH
DES, ON MAY DAY I HAD A SIGN ON THICK CARDBOARD LIKE THIS AND A COP TOOK IT.
WHAT?
THAT'S F- I MEAN, THAT'S TOTALLY NUTS!
HE SAID I COULD FOLD IT UP AND BEAT SOMEONE WITH IT, I GUESS?
MAYBE IT WAS JUST THAT ONE COP?
DAMN, I WORKED REALLY HARD ON THIS.
ALL RIGHT, WELL, I'M DEEPLY COMMITTED TO NON-VIOLENCE, SO I'LL MAKE A NEW SIGN.
MY NEW SIGN WILL BE MADE OUT OF GOSSAMER TISSUE PAPER AND SILK...
FOR INK I'LL USE MOONLIGHT AND DEW...
MY NEW SIGN COULD NEVER HURT ANOTHER LIVING THING.
IT'S GONNA SAY "FUCK THE POLICE."
HA HA HA HA HA HA HA HA HA HA HA HA HA HA HA HA
THICC

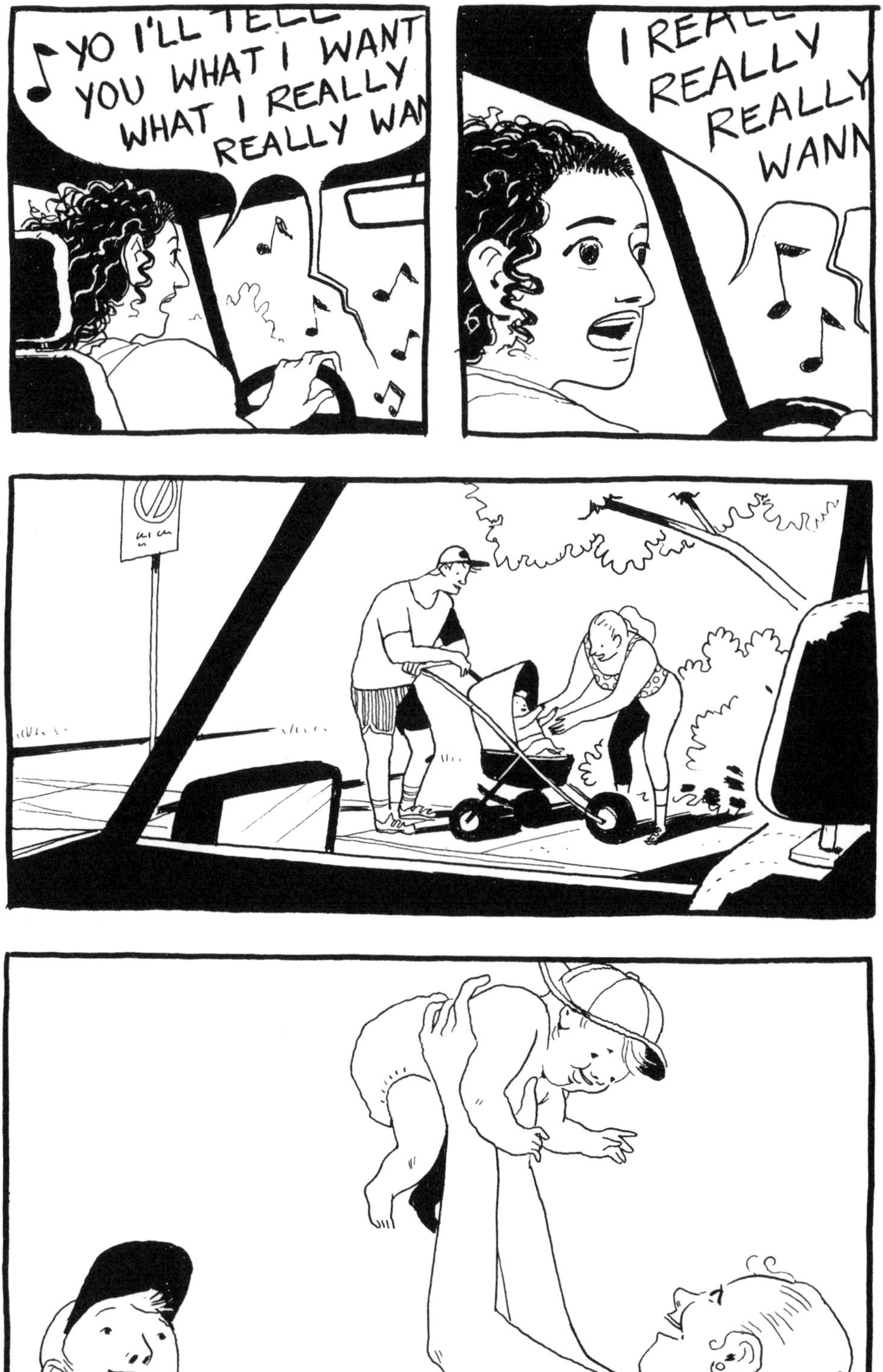
♪ YO I'LL TELL YOU WHAT I WANT WHAT I REALLY WHAT I REALLY WAN
I REALL REALLY REALLY WANN

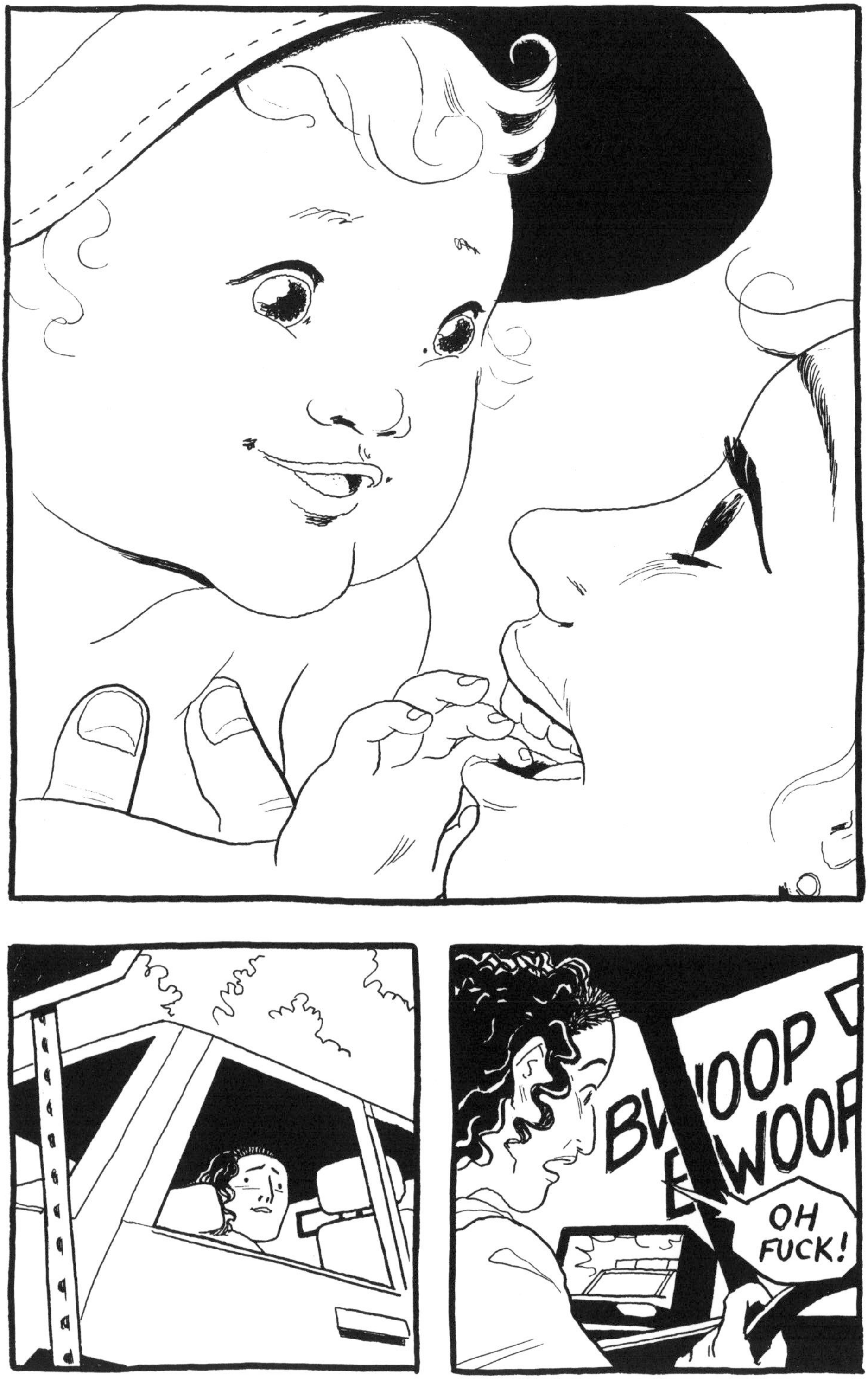
OH FUCK!

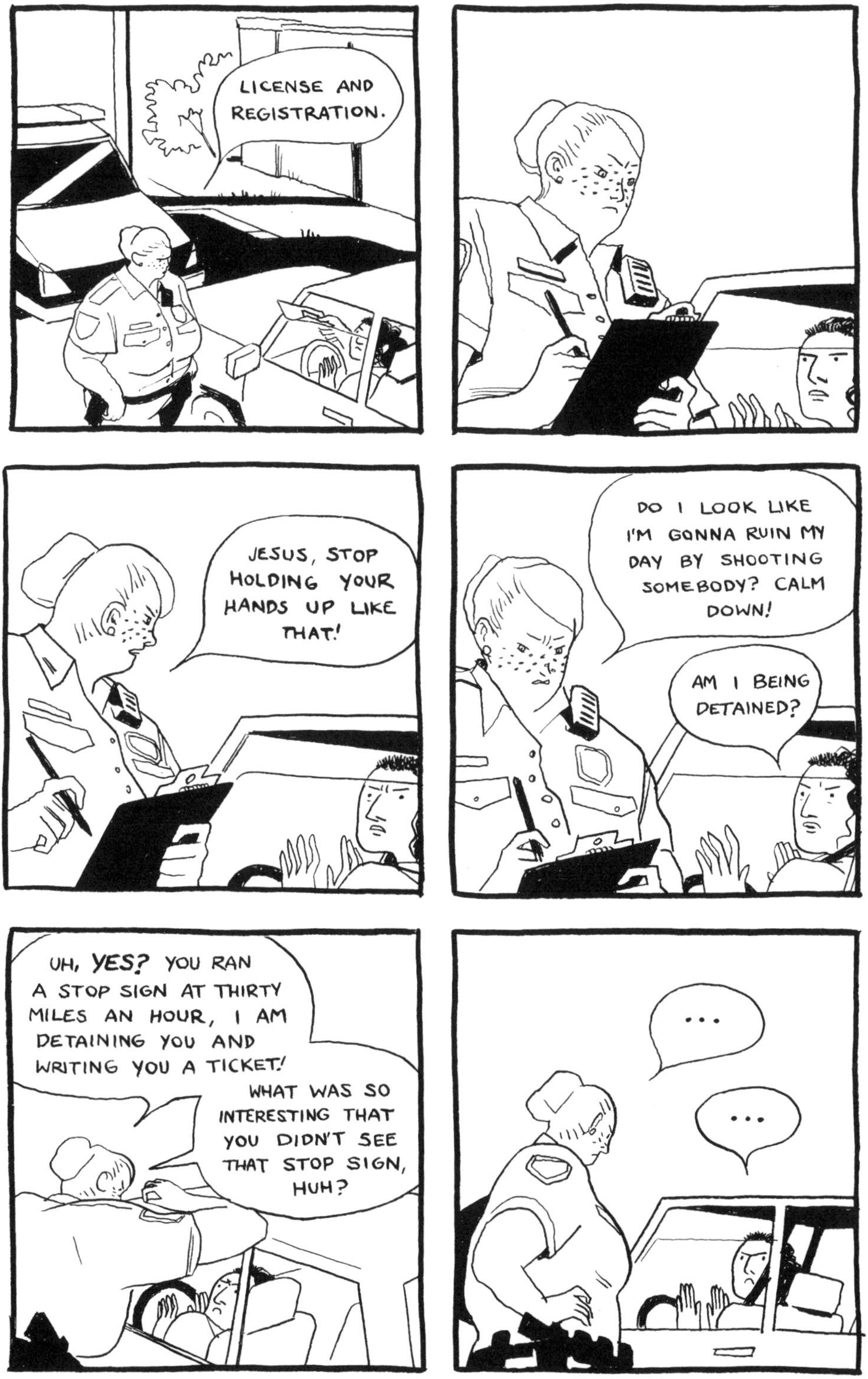
LICENSE AND REGISTRATION.
JESUS, STOP HOLDING YOUR HANDS UP LIKE THAT!
DO I LOOK LIKE I'M GONNA RUIN MY DAY BY SHOOTING SOMEBODY? CALM DOWN!
AM I BEING DETAINED?
UH, YES? YOU RAN A STOP SIGN AT THIRTY MILES AN HOUR, I AM DETAINING YOU AND WRITING YOU A TICKET!
WHAT WAS SO INTERESTING THAT YOU DIDN'T SEE THAT STOP SIGN, HUH?
...
...

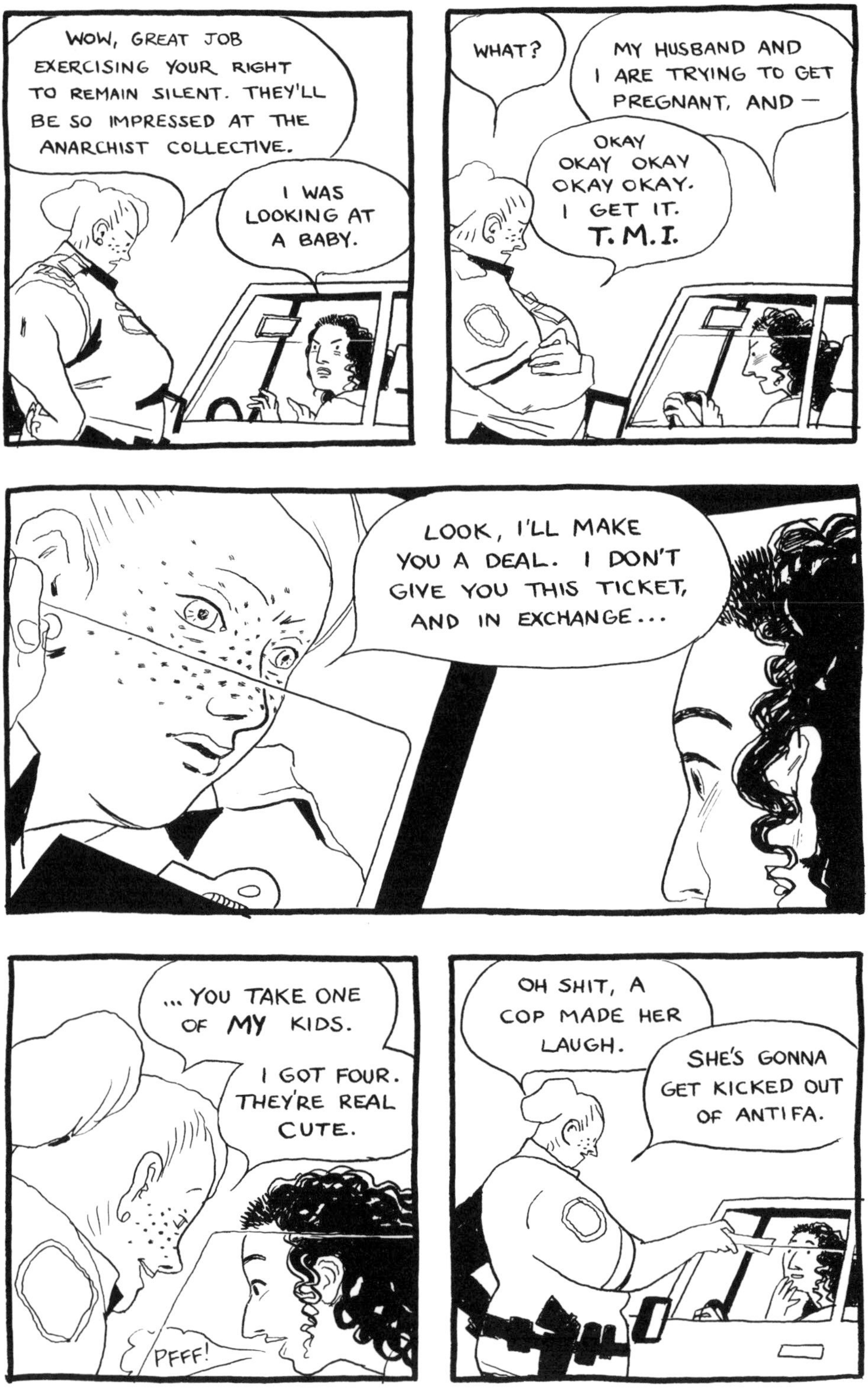
WOW, GREAT JOB EXERCISING YOUR RIGHT TO REMAIN SILENT. THEY'LL BE SO IMPRESSED AT THE ANARCHIST COLLECTIVE.
I WAS LOOKING AT A BABY.
WHAT?
MY HUSBAND AND I ARE TRYING TO GET PREGNANT, AND—
OKAY OKAY OKAY OKAY OKAY. I GET IT. T.M.I.
LOOK, I'LL MAKE YOU A DEAL. I DON'T GIVE YOU THIS TICKET, AND IN EXCHANGE...
...YOU TAKE ONE OF MY KIDS.
I GOT FOUR. THEY'RE REAL CUTE.
PFFF!
OH SHIT, A COP MADE HER LAUGH.
SHE'S GONNA GET KICKED OUT OF ANTIFA.

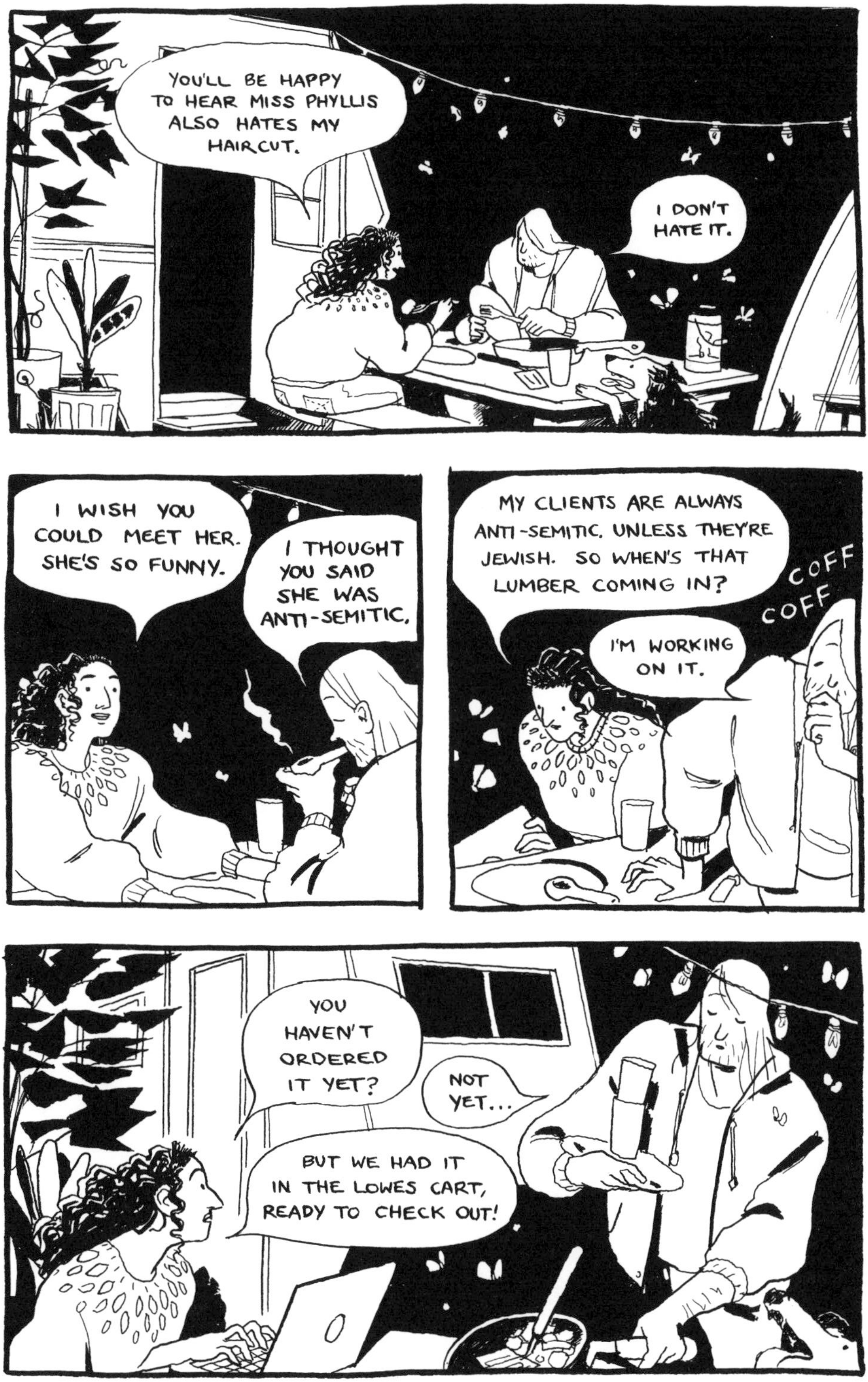

YOU'LL BE HAPPY TO HEAR MISS PHYLLIS ALSO HATES MY HAIRCUT.
I DON'T HATE IT.
I WISH YOU COULD MEET HER. SHE'S SO FUNNY.
I THOUGHT YOU SAID SHE WAS ANTI-SEMITIC.
MY CLIENTS ARE ALWAYS ANTI-SEMITIC. UNLESS THEY'RE JEWISH. SO WHEN'S THAT LUMBER COMING IN?
COFF COFF
I'M WORKING ON IT.
YOU HAVEN'T ORDERED IT YET?
NOT YET...
BUT WE HAD IT IN THE LOWES CART, READY TO CHECK OUT!

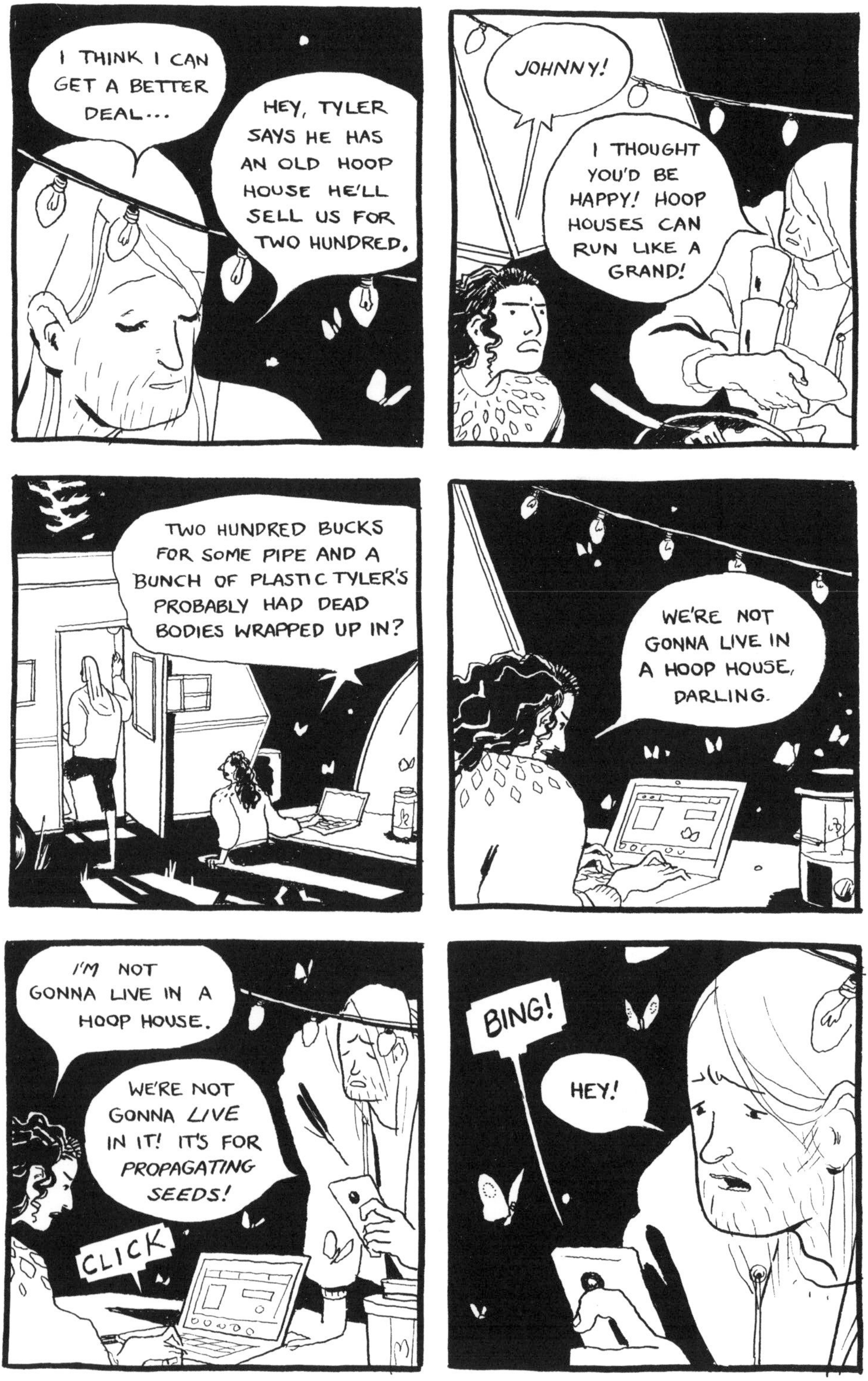
I THINK I CAN GET A BETTER DEAL...
HEY, TYLER SAYS HE HAS AN OLD HOOP HOUSE HE'LL SELL US FOR TWO HUNDRED.
JOHNNY!
I THOUGHT YOU'D BE HAPPY! HOOP HOUSES CAN RUN LIKE A GRAND!
TWO HUNDRED BUCKS FOR SOME PIPE AND A BUNCH OF PLASTIC TYLER'S PROBABLY HAD DEAD BODIES WRAPPED UP IN?
WE'RE NOT GONNA LIVE IN A HOOP HOUSE, DARLING.
I'M NOT GONNA LIVE IN A HOOP HOUSE.
WE'RE NOT GONNA *LIVE* IN IT! IT'S FOR *PROPAGATING SEEDS!*
CLICK
BING!
HEY!

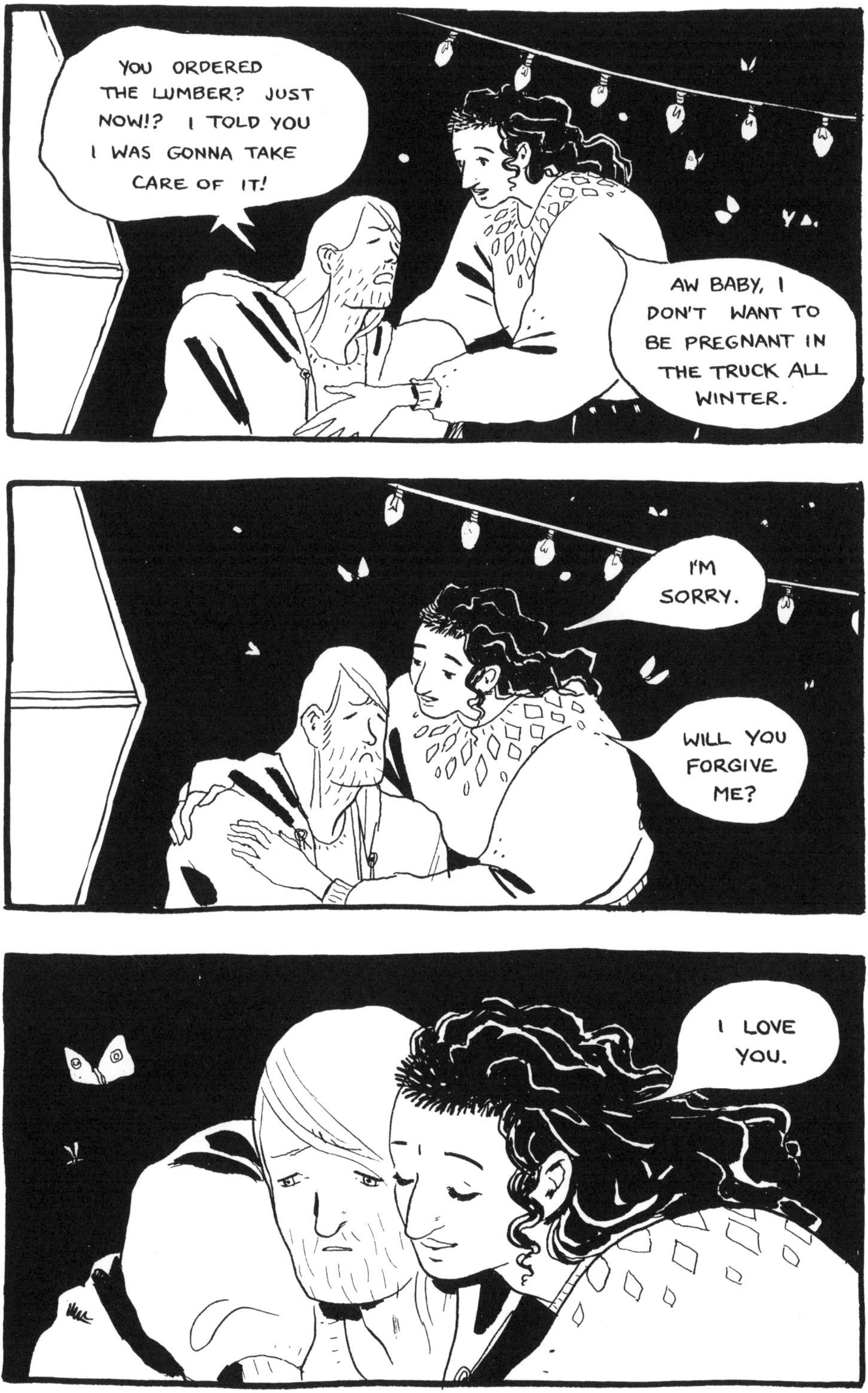
YOU ORDERED THE LUMBER? JUST NOW!? I TOLD YOU I WAS GONNA TAKE CARE OF IT!
AW BABY, I DON'T WANT TO BE PREGNANT IN THE TRUCK ALL WINTER.
I'M SORRY.
WILL YOU FORGIVE ME?
I LOVE YOU.

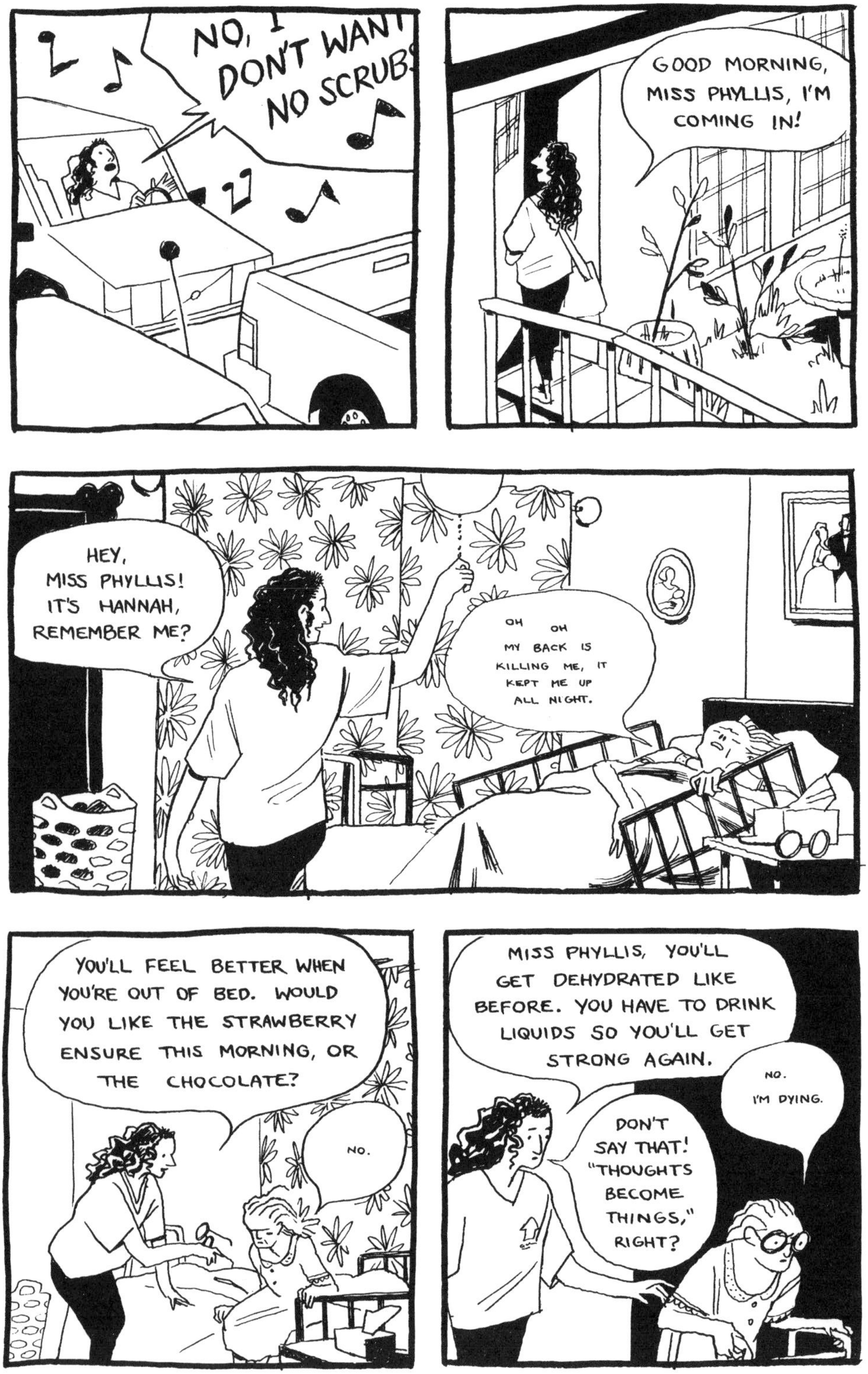
NO, I DON'T WANT NO SCRUBS
GOOD MORNING, MISS PHYLLIS, I'M COMING IN!
HEY, MISS PHYLLIS! IT'S HANNAH, REMEMBER ME?
OH OH MY BACK IS KILLING ME, IT KEPT ME UP ALL NIGHT.
YOU'LL FEEL BETTER WHEN YOU'RE OUT OF BED. WOULD YOU LIKE THE STRAWBERRY ENSURE THIS MORNING, OR THE CHOCOLATE?
NO.
MISS PHYLLIS, YOU'LL GET DEHYDRATED LIKE BEFORE. YOU HAVE TO DRINK LIQUIDS SO YOU'LL GET STRONG AGAIN.
NO. I'M DYING.
DON'T SAY THAT! "THOUGHTS BECOME THINGS," RIGHT?

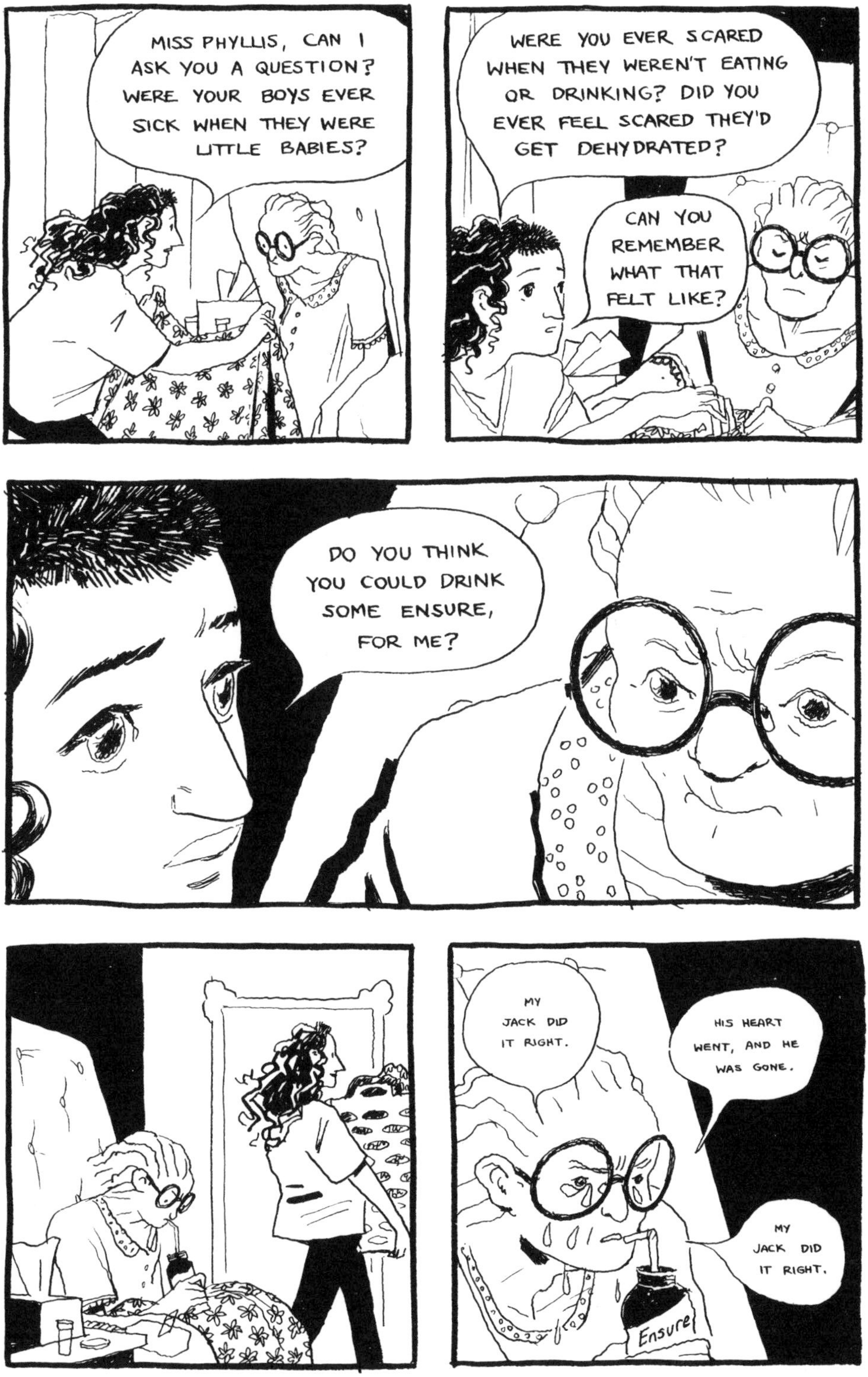
MISS PHYLLIS, CAN I ASK YOU A QUESTION? WERE YOUR BOYS EVER SICK WHEN THEY WERE LITTLE BABIES?
WERE YOU EVER SCARED WHEN THEY WEREN'T EATING OR DRINKING? DID YOU EVER FEEL SCARED THEY'D GET DEHYDRATED?
CAN YOU REMEMBER WHAT THAT FELT LIKE?
DO YOU THINK YOU COULD DRINK SOME ENSURE, FOR ME?
MY JACK DID IT RIGHT.
HIS HEART WENT, AND HE WAS GONE.
MY JACK DID IT RIGHT.
Ensure

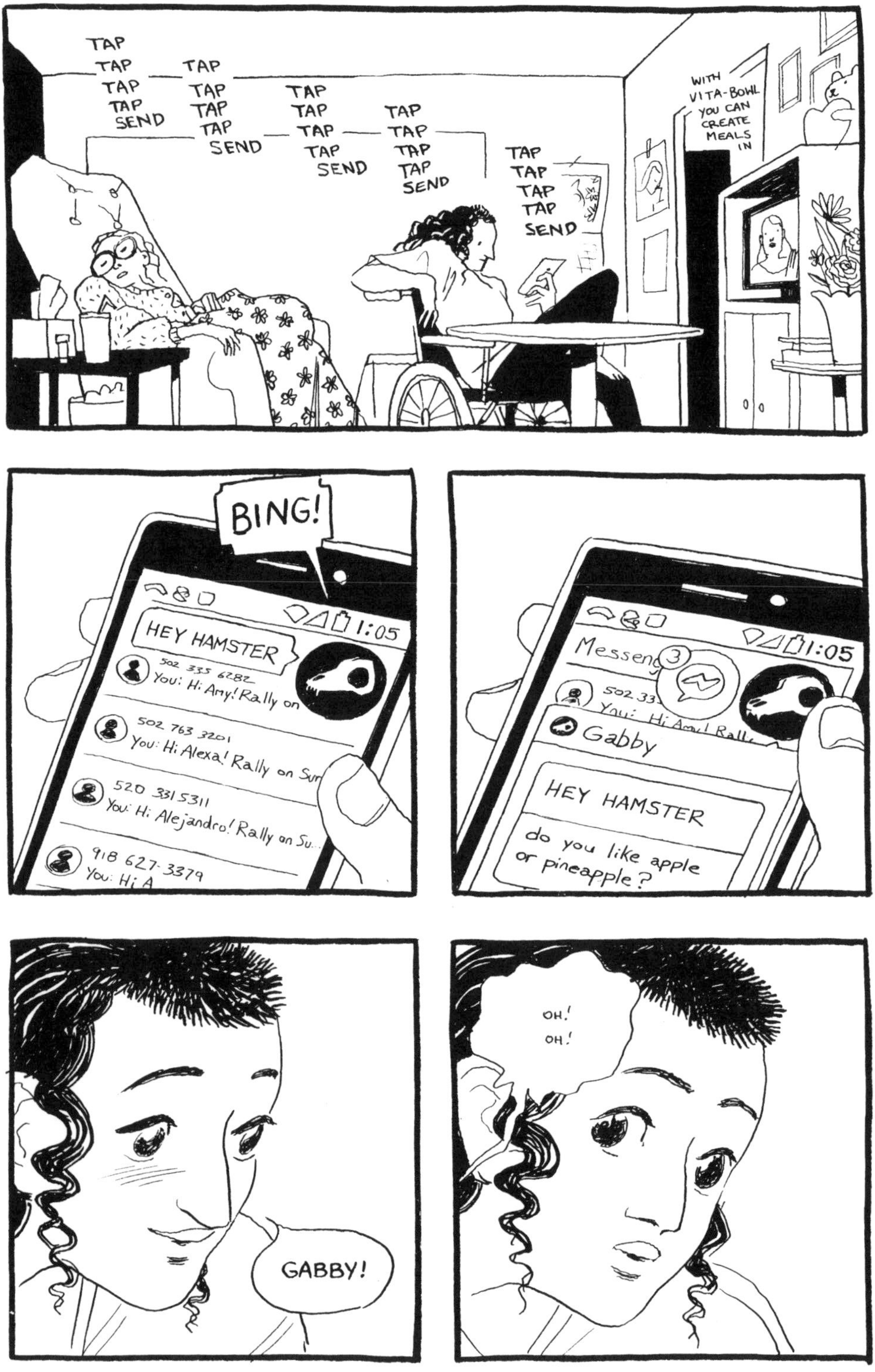
TAP
TAP
TAP
TAP
SEND
TAP
TAP
TAP
TAP
SEND
TAP
TAP
TAP
TAP
SEND
TAP
TAP
TAP
TAP
SEND
TAP
TAP
TAP
TAP
SEND
WITH VITA-BOWL YOU CAN CREATE MEALS IN
BING!
HEY HAMSTER
502 335 6282
You: Hi Amy! Rally on
502 763 3201
You: Hi Alexa! Rally on Sun
520 331 5311
You: Hi Alejandro! Rally on Su...
918 627-3379
You: Hi A
1:05
Messeng
3
1:05
502 33
You: Hi Amy! Rall
Gabby
HEY HAMSTER
do you like apple or pineapple?
GABBY!
OH!
OH!

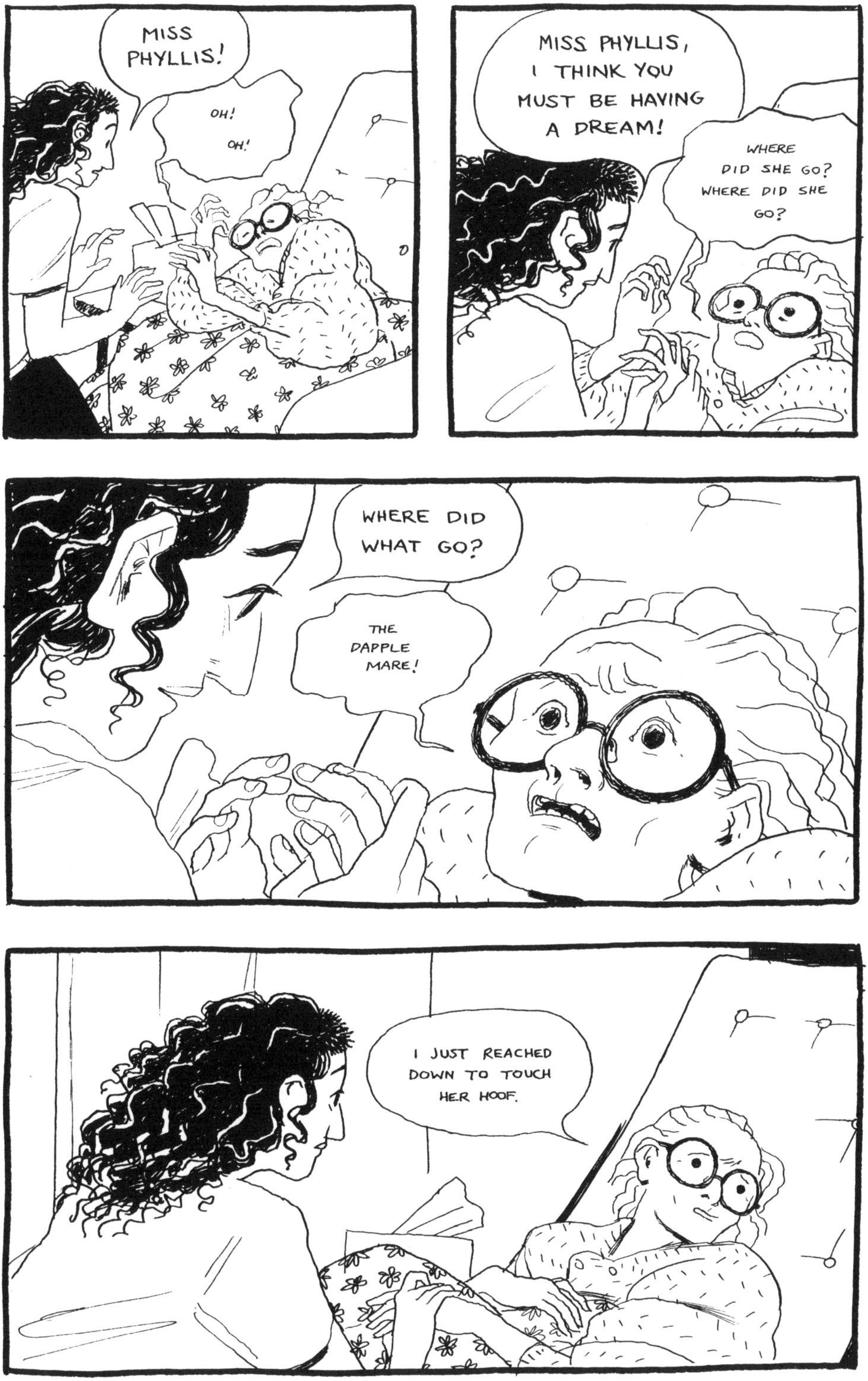
MISS PHYLLIS!
OH! OH!
MISS PHYLLIS, I THINK YOU MUST BE HAVING A DREAM!
WHERE DID SHE GO? WHERE DID SHE GO?
WHERE DID WHAT GO?
THE DAPPLE MARE!
I JUST REACHED DOWN TO TOUCH HER HOOF.

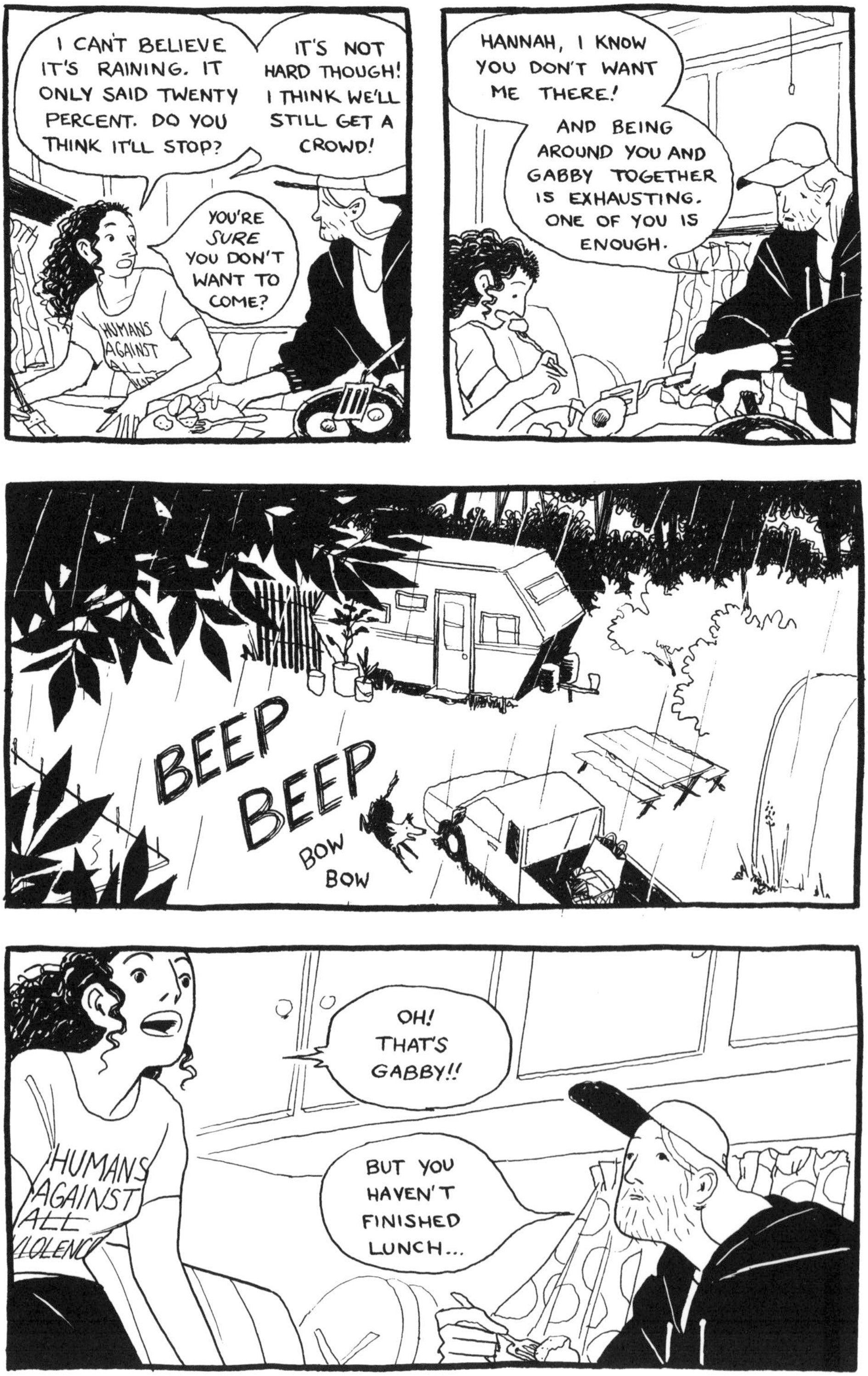
I CAN'T BELIEVE IT'S RAINING. IT ONLY SAID TWENTY PERCENT. DO YOU THINK IT'LL STOP?
IT'S NOT HARD THOUGH! I THINK WE'LL STILL GET A CROWD!
YOU'RE *SURE* YOU DON'T WANT TO COME?
HUMANS AGAINST
HANNAH, I KNOW YOU DON'T WANT ME THERE!
AND BEING AROUND YOU AND GABBY TOGETHER IS EXHAUSTING. ONE OF YOU IS ENOUGH.
BEEP BEEP
BOW BOW
OH! THAT'S GABBY!!
HUMANS AGAINST ALL
BUT YOU HAVEN'T FINISHED LUNCH...

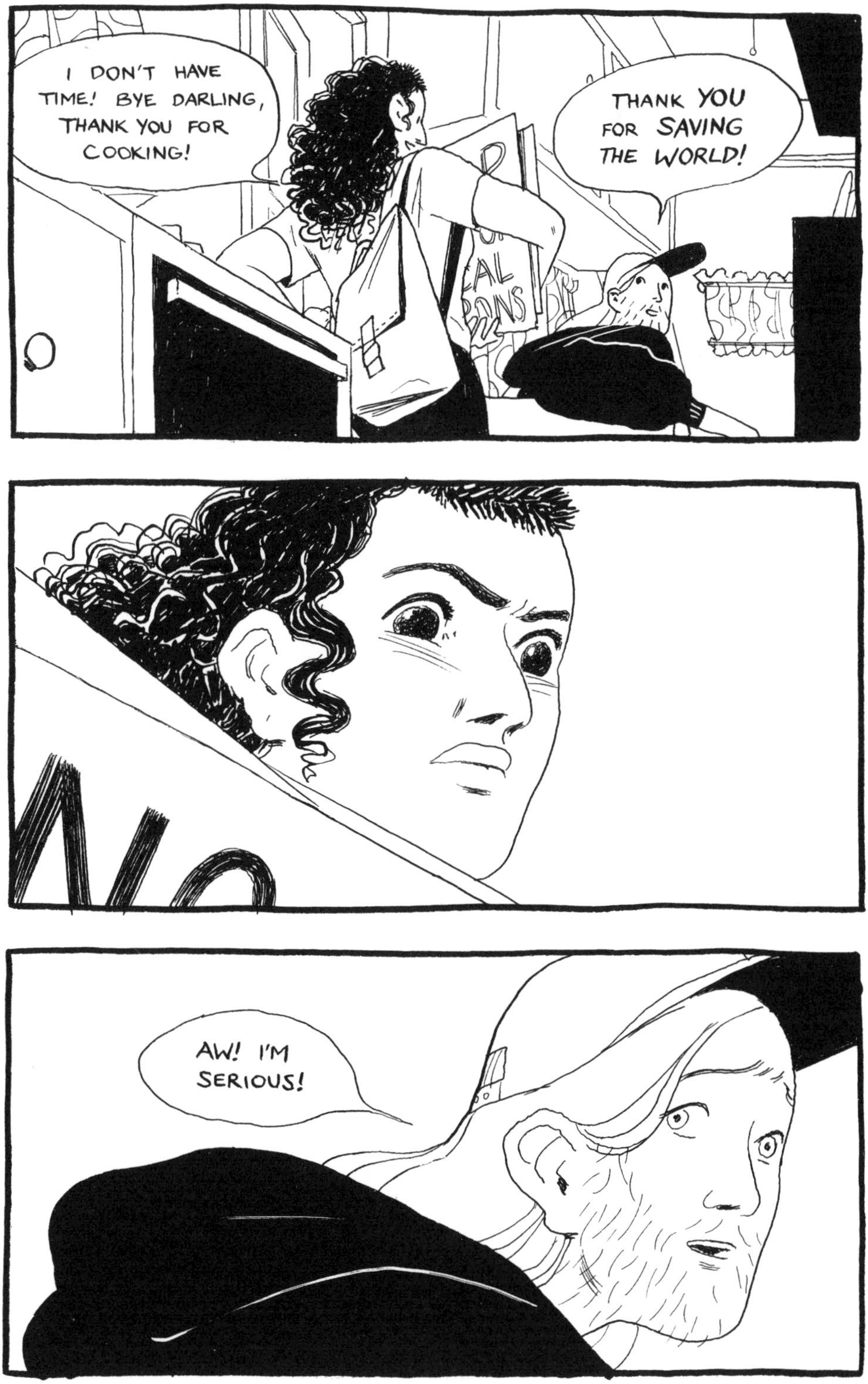
I DON'T HAVE TIME! BYE DARLING, THANK YOU FOR COOKING!
THANK YOU FOR SAVING THE WORLD!
AW! I'M SERIOUS!

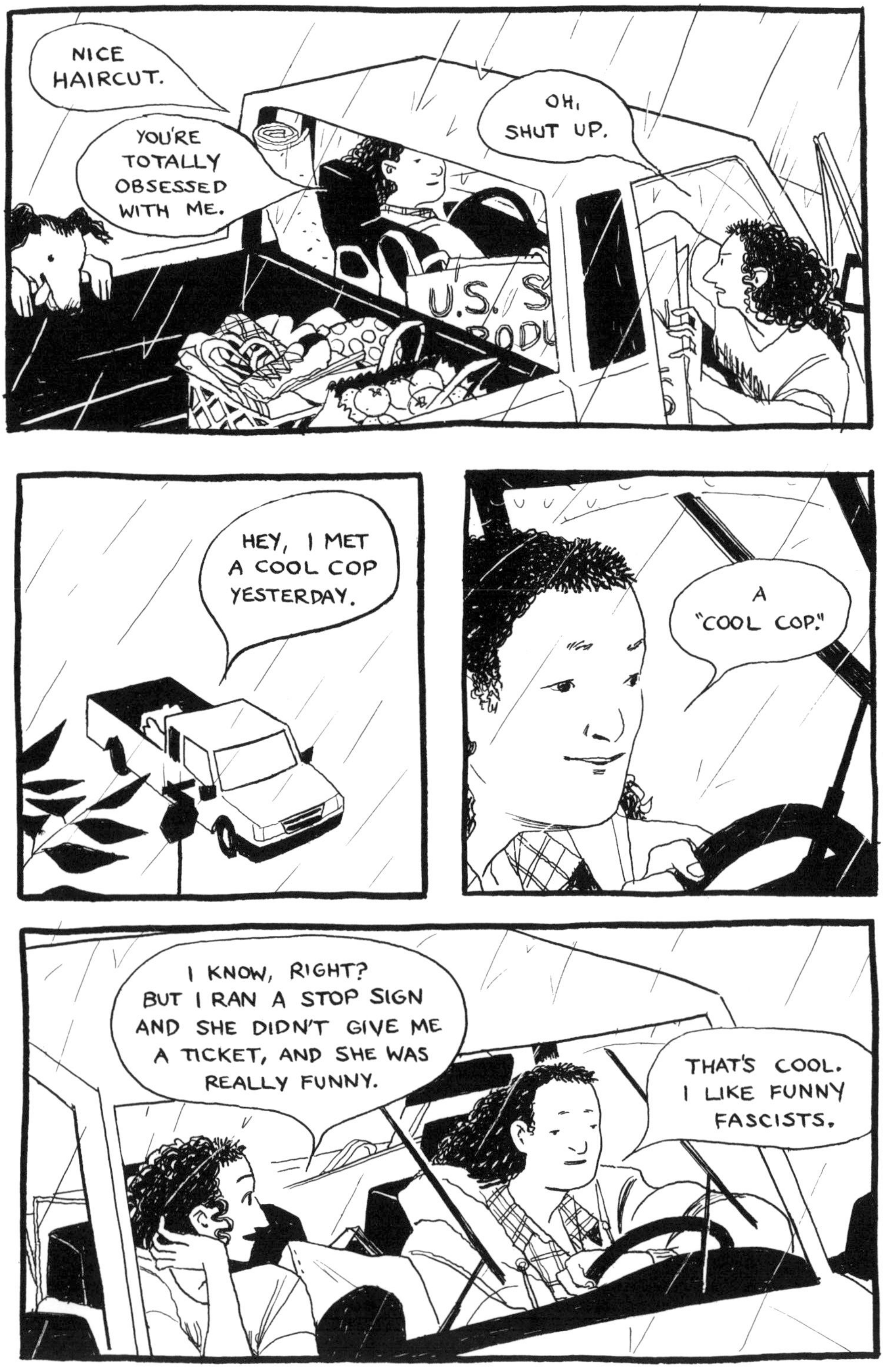
NICE HAIRCUT.
YOU'RE TOTALLY OBSESSED WITH ME.
OH, SHUT UP.
HEY, I MET A COOL COP YESTERDAY.
A "COOL COP."
I KNOW, RIGHT? BUT I RAN A STOP SIGN AND SHE DIDN'T GIVE ME A TICKET, AND SHE WAS REALLY FUNNY.
THAT'S COOL. I LIKE FUNNY FASCISTS.

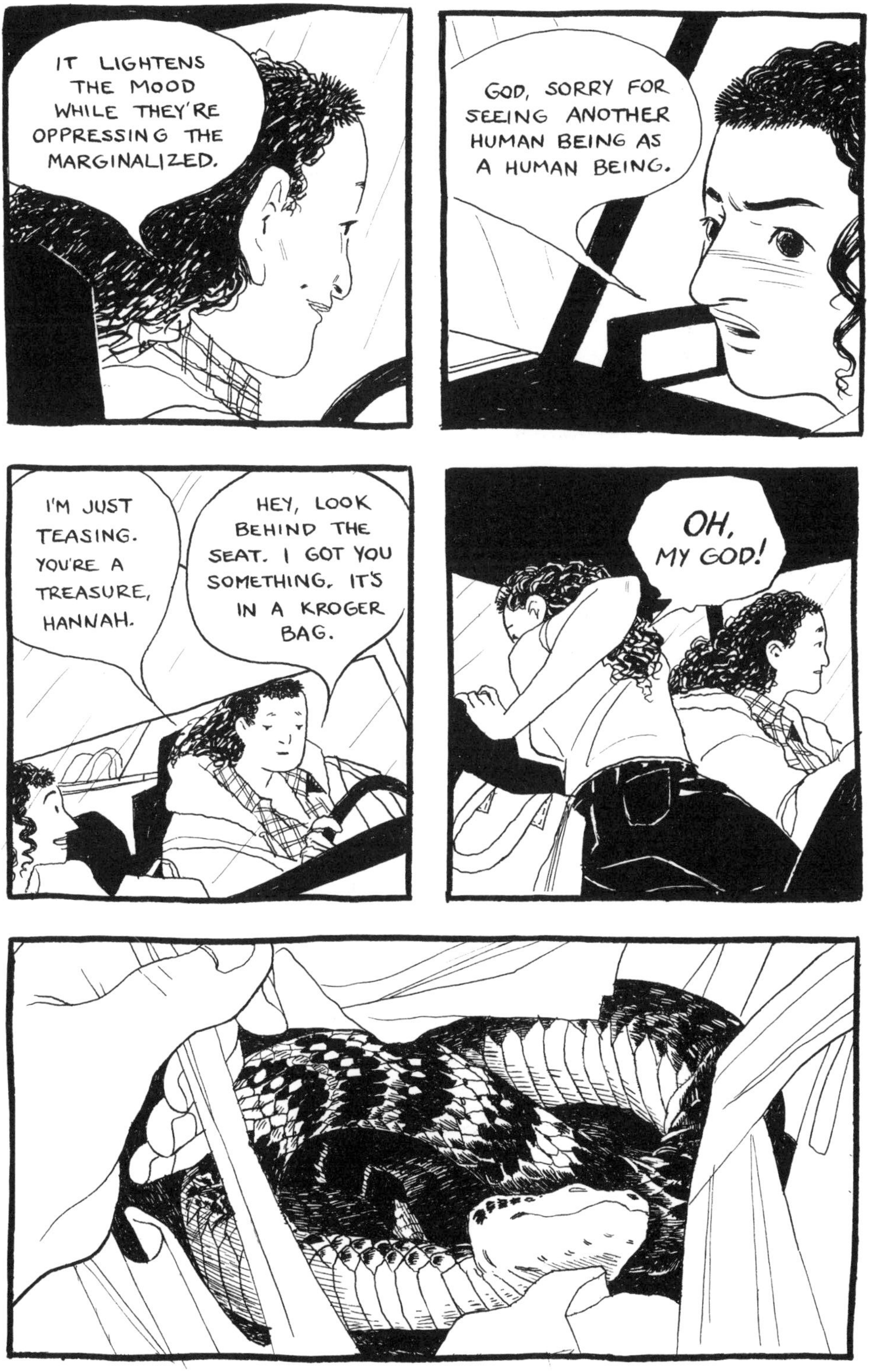
IT LIGHTENS THE MOOD WHILE THEY'RE OPPRESSING THE MARGINALIZED.
GOD, SORRY FOR SEEING ANOTHER HUMAN BEING AS A HUMAN BEING.
I'M JUST TEASING. YOU'RE A TREASURE, HANNAH.
HEY, LOOK BEHIND THE SEAT. I GOT YOU SOMETHING. IT'S IN A KROGER BAG.
OH, MY GOD!

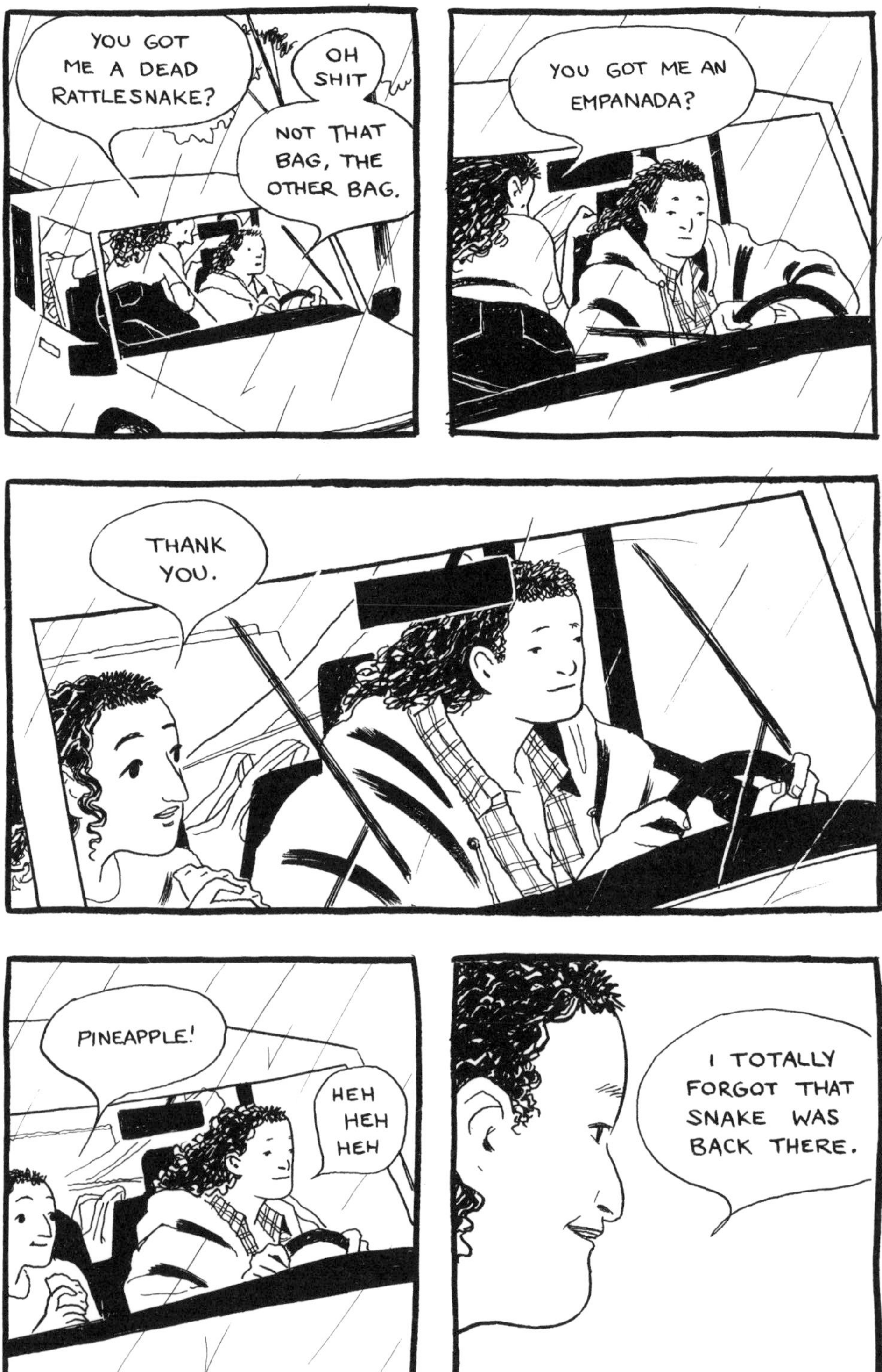
YOU GOT ME A DEAD RATTLESNAKE?
OH SHIT
NOT THAT BAG, THE OTHER BAG.
YOU GOT ME AN EMPANADA?
THANK YOU.
PINEAPPLE!
HEH HEH HEH
I TOTALLY FORGOT THAT SNAKE WAS BACK THERE.

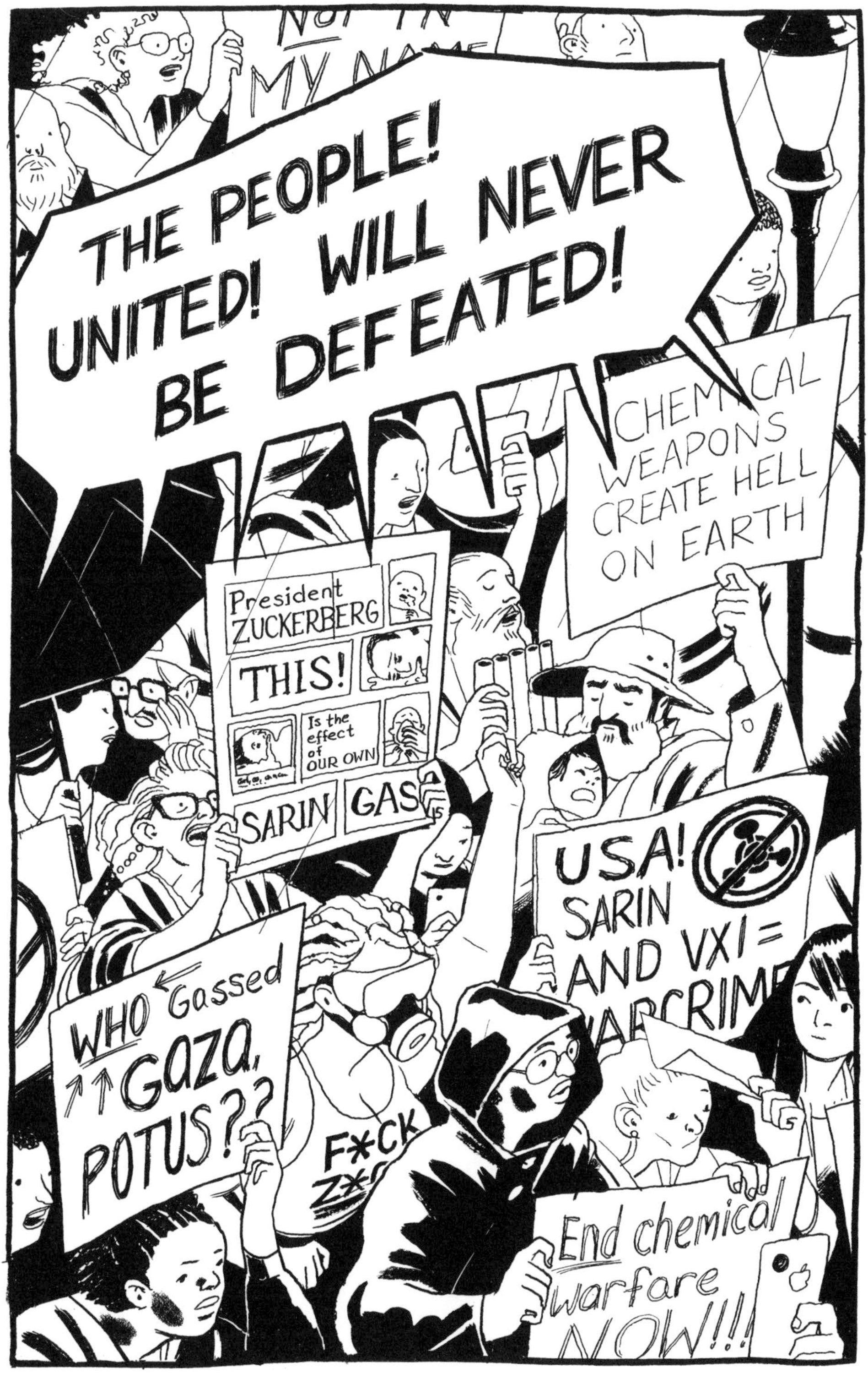
THE PEOPLE! UNITED! WILL NEVER BE DEFEATED!
CHEMICAL WEAPONS CREATE HELL ON EARTH
President ZUCKERBERG THIS! Is the effect of OUR OWN SARIN GAS
USA! SARIN AND VX =
WHO Gassed Gaza, POTUS??
End chemical warfare NOW!!!

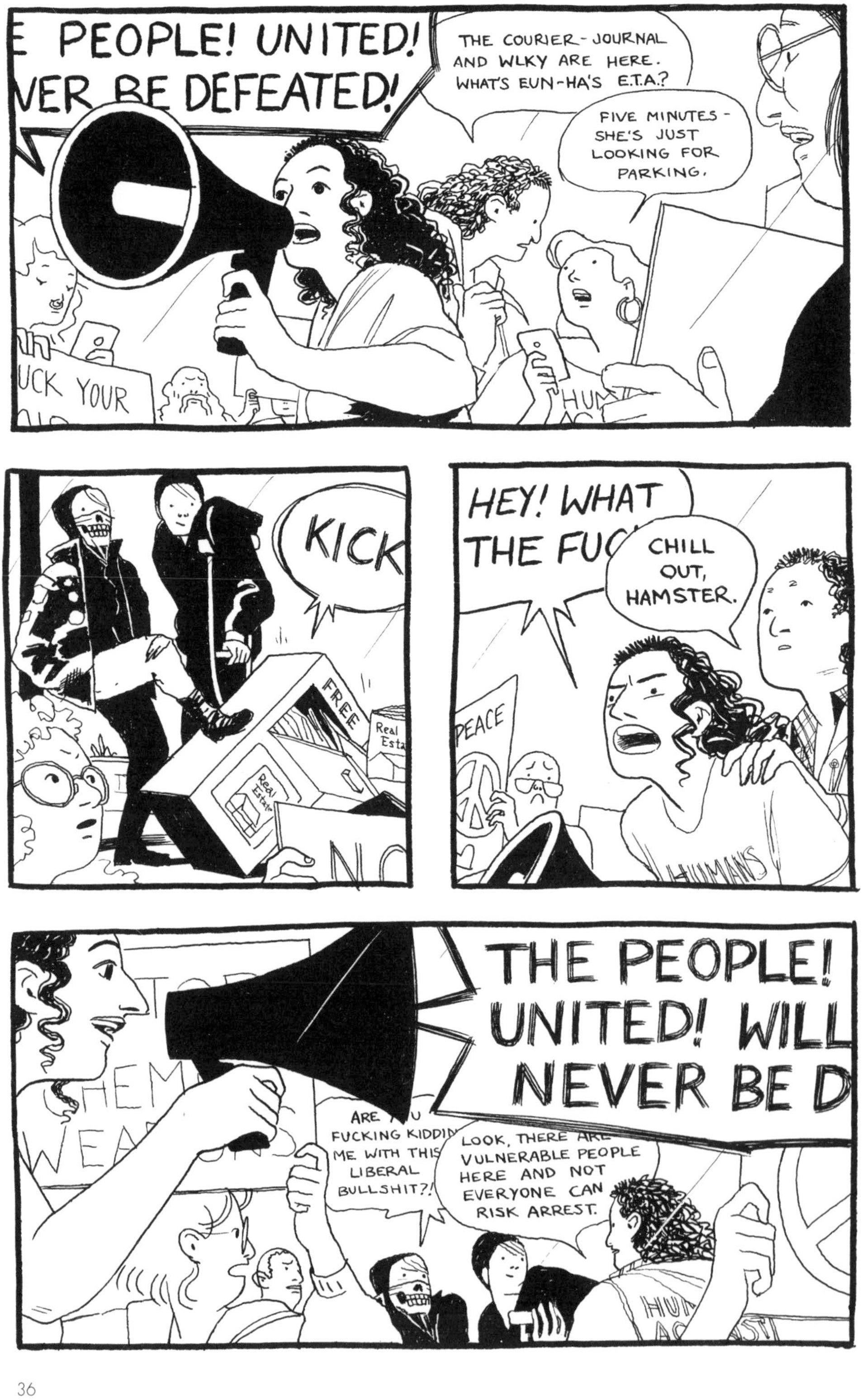
E PEOPLE! UNITED!
VER BE DEFEATED!
THE COURIER-JOURNAL AND WLKY ARE HERE. WHAT'S EUN-HA'S E.T.A.?
FIVE MINUTES - SHE'S JUST LOOKING FOR PARKING.
UCK YOUR
KICK
FREE
Real Esta
Real Estate
HEY! WHAT THE FUC
CHILL OUT, HAMSTER.
PEACE
HUMANS
THE PEOPLE! UNITED! WILL NEVER BE D
ARE U FUCKING KIDDIN ME WITH THIS LIBERAL BULLSHIT?!
LOOK, THERE ARE VULNERABLE PEOPLE HERE AND NOT EVERYONE CAN RISK ARREST.

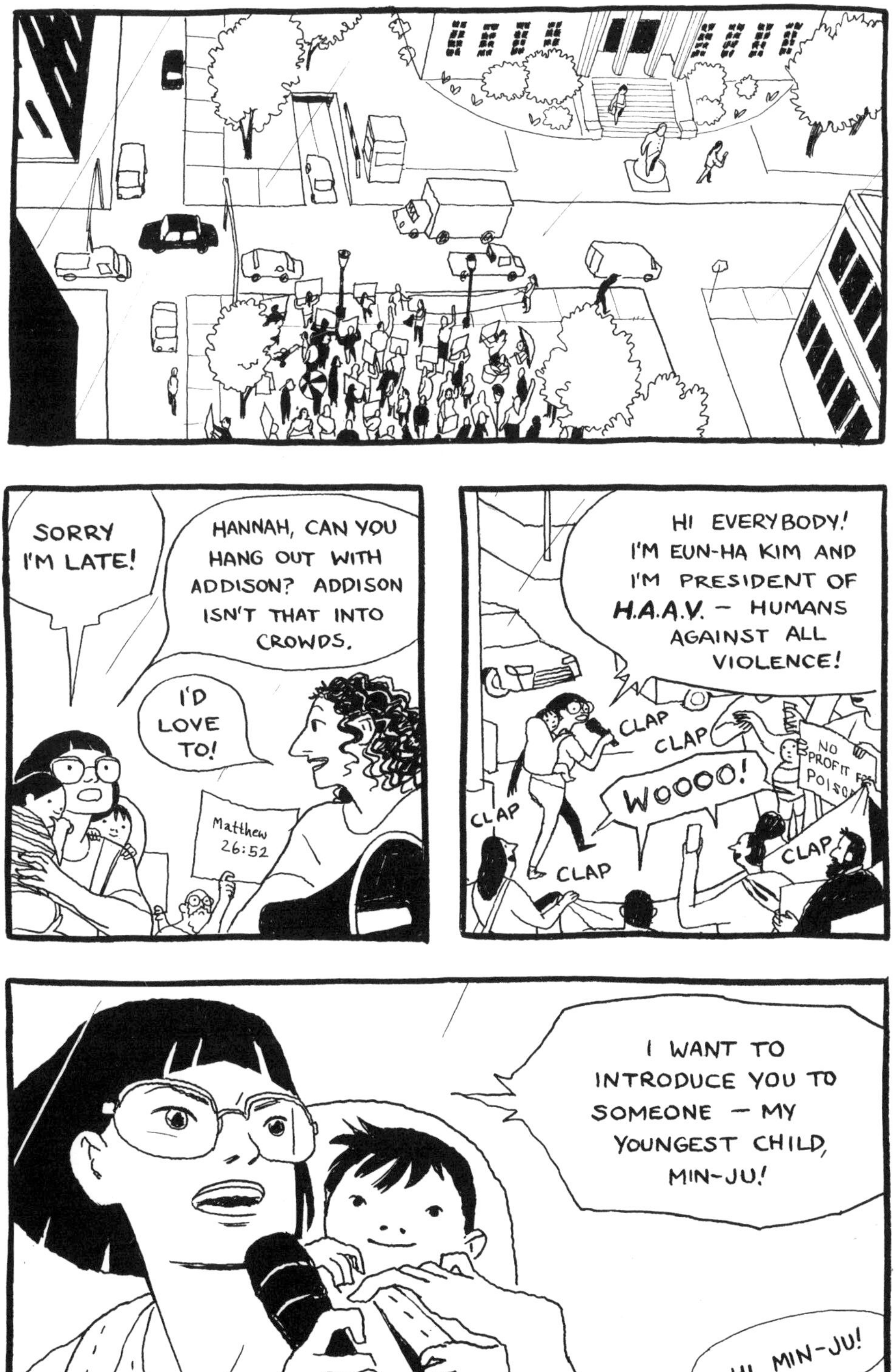
SORRY I'M LATE!
HANNAH, CAN YOU HANG OUT WITH ADDISON? ADDISON ISN'T THAT INTO CROWDS.
I'D LOVE TO!
Matthew 26:52
HI EVERYBODY! I'M EUN-HA KIM AND I'M PRESIDENT OF H.A.A.V. – HUMANS AGAINST ALL VIOLENCE!
CLAP
CLAP
NO PROFIT
WOOOO!
CLAP
CLAP
CLAP
I WANT TO INTRODUCE YOU TO SOMEONE – MY YOUNGEST CHILD, MIN-JU!
HI MIN-JU!

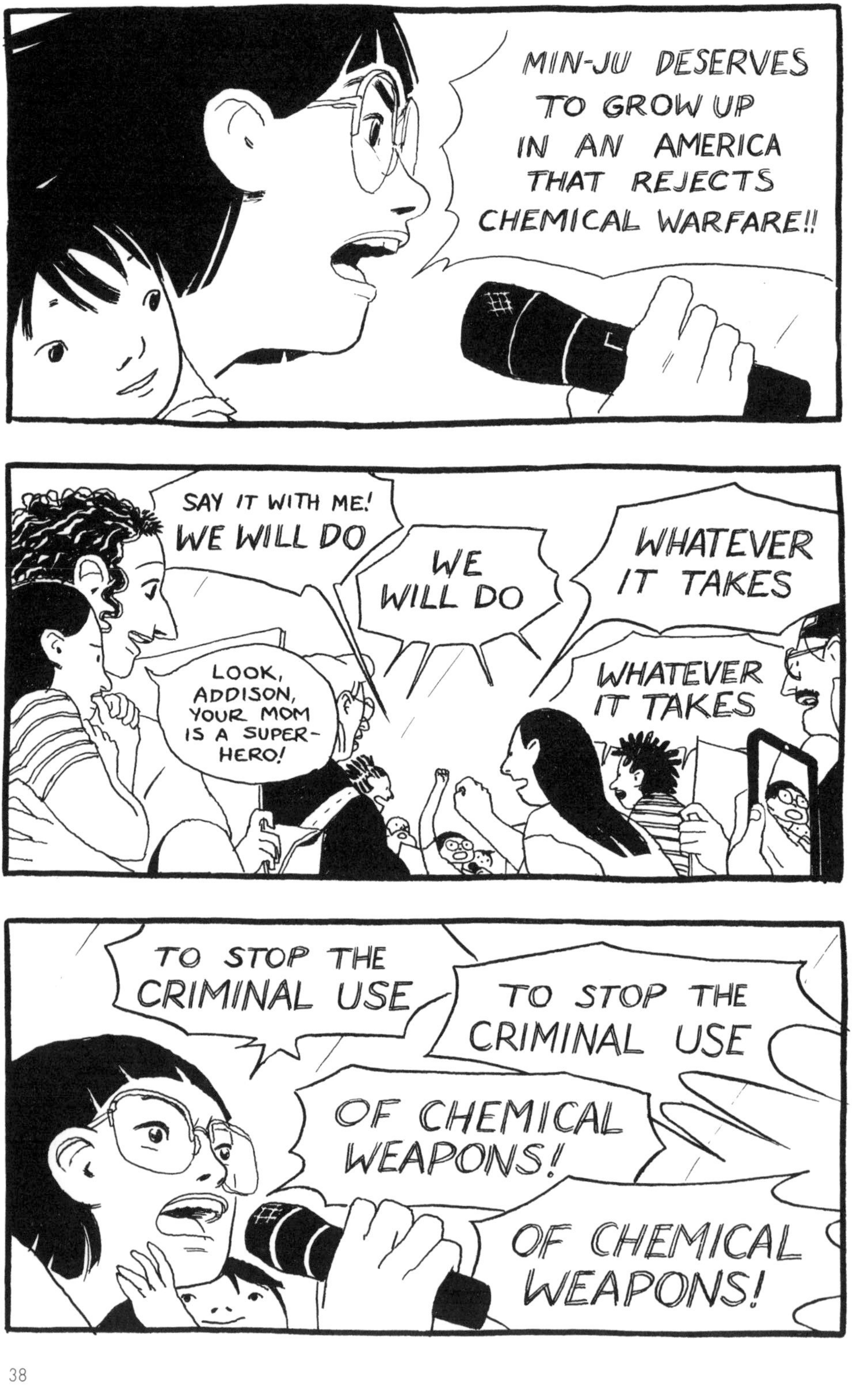
MIN-JU DESERVES TO GROW UP IN AN AMERICA THAT REJECTS CHEMICAL WARFARE!!
SAY IT WITH ME! WE WILL DO
WE WILL DO
WHATEVER IT TAKES
LOOK, ADDISON, YOUR MOM IS A SUPER-HERO!
WHATEVER IT TAKES
TO STOP THE CRIMINAL USE
TO STOP THE CRIMINAL USE
OF CHEMICAL WEAPONS!
OF CHEMICAL WEAPONS!

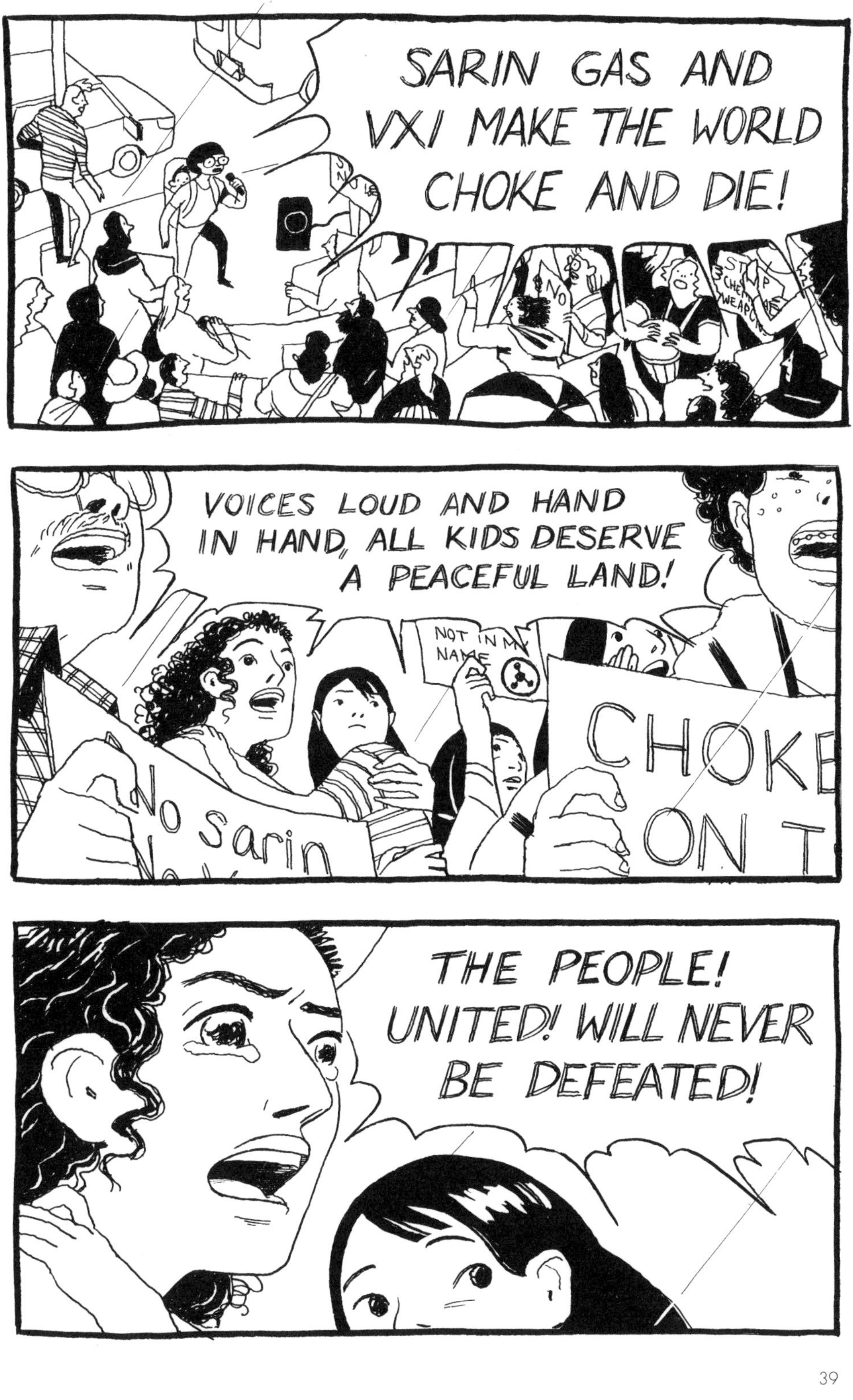
SARIN GAS AND VXI MAKE THE WORLD CHOKE AND DIE!
NO
VOICES LOUD AND HAND IN HAND, ALL KIDS DESERVE A PEACEFUL LAND!
NOT IN MY NAME
No Sarin
CHOKE ON T
THE PEOPLE! UNITED! WILL NEVER BE DEFEATED!

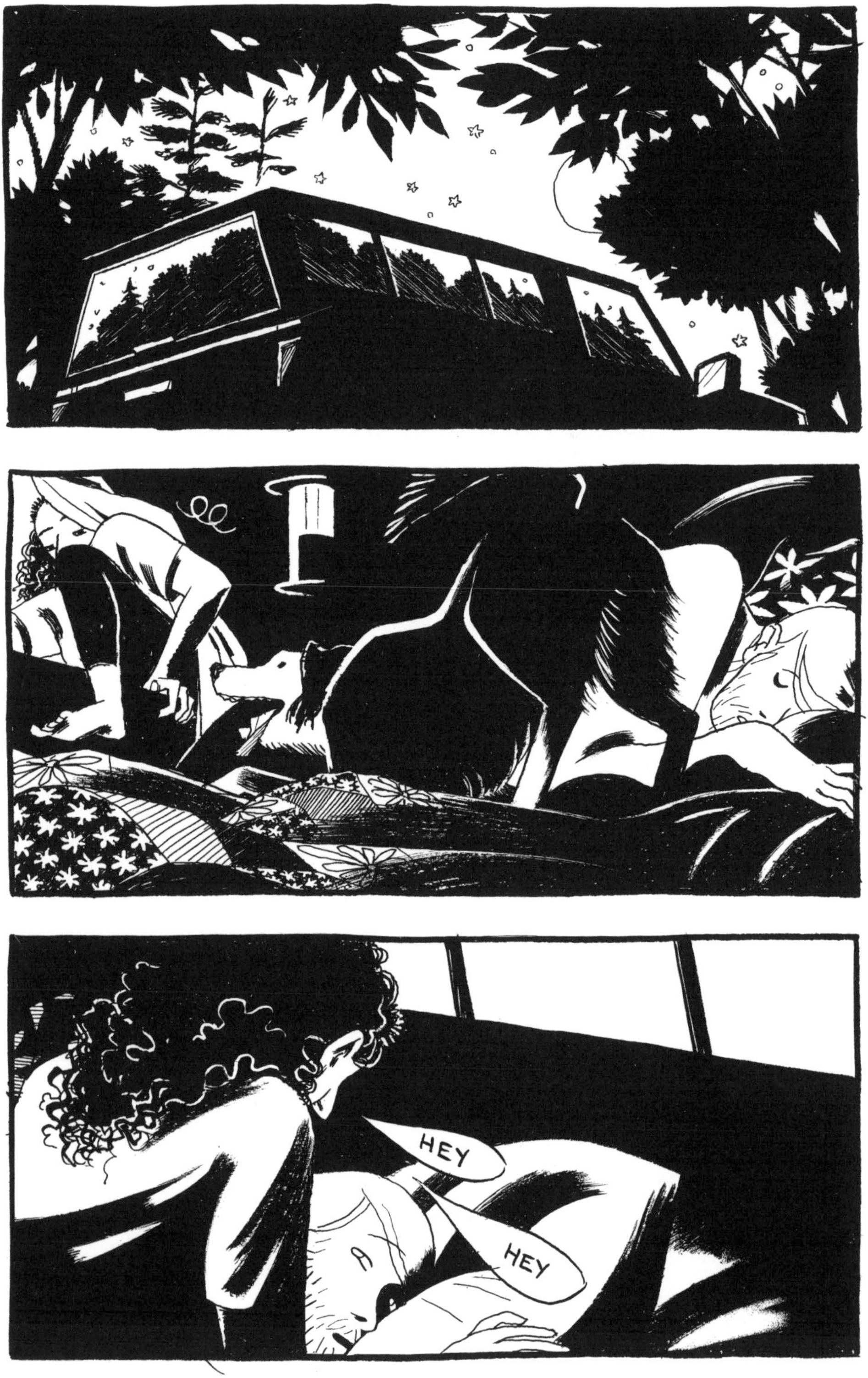
HEY
HEY

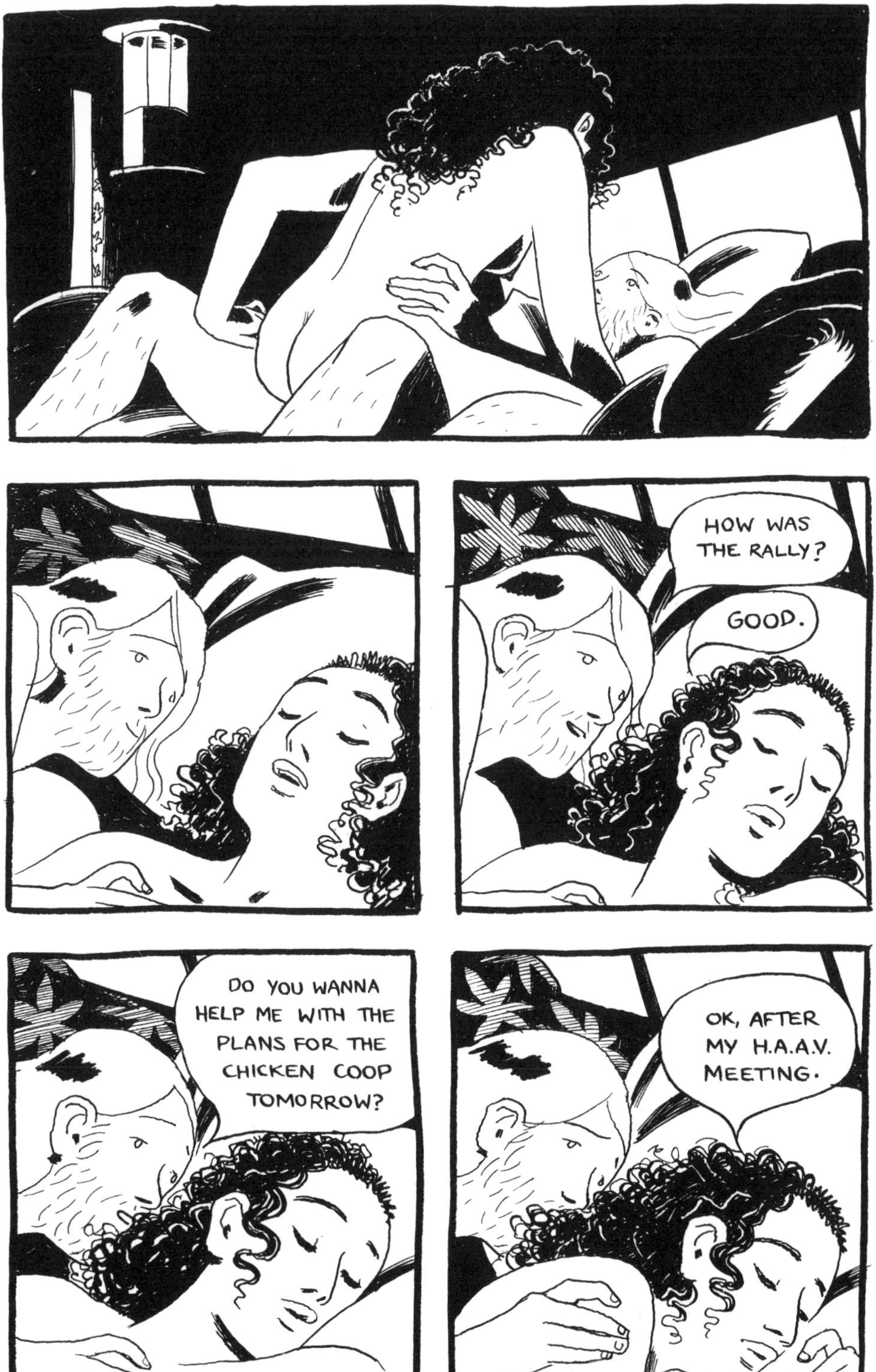
HOW WAS THE RALLY?
GOOD.
DO YOU WANNA HELP ME WITH THE PLANS FOR THE CHICKEN COOP TOMORROW?
OK, AFTER MY H.A.A.V. MEETING.

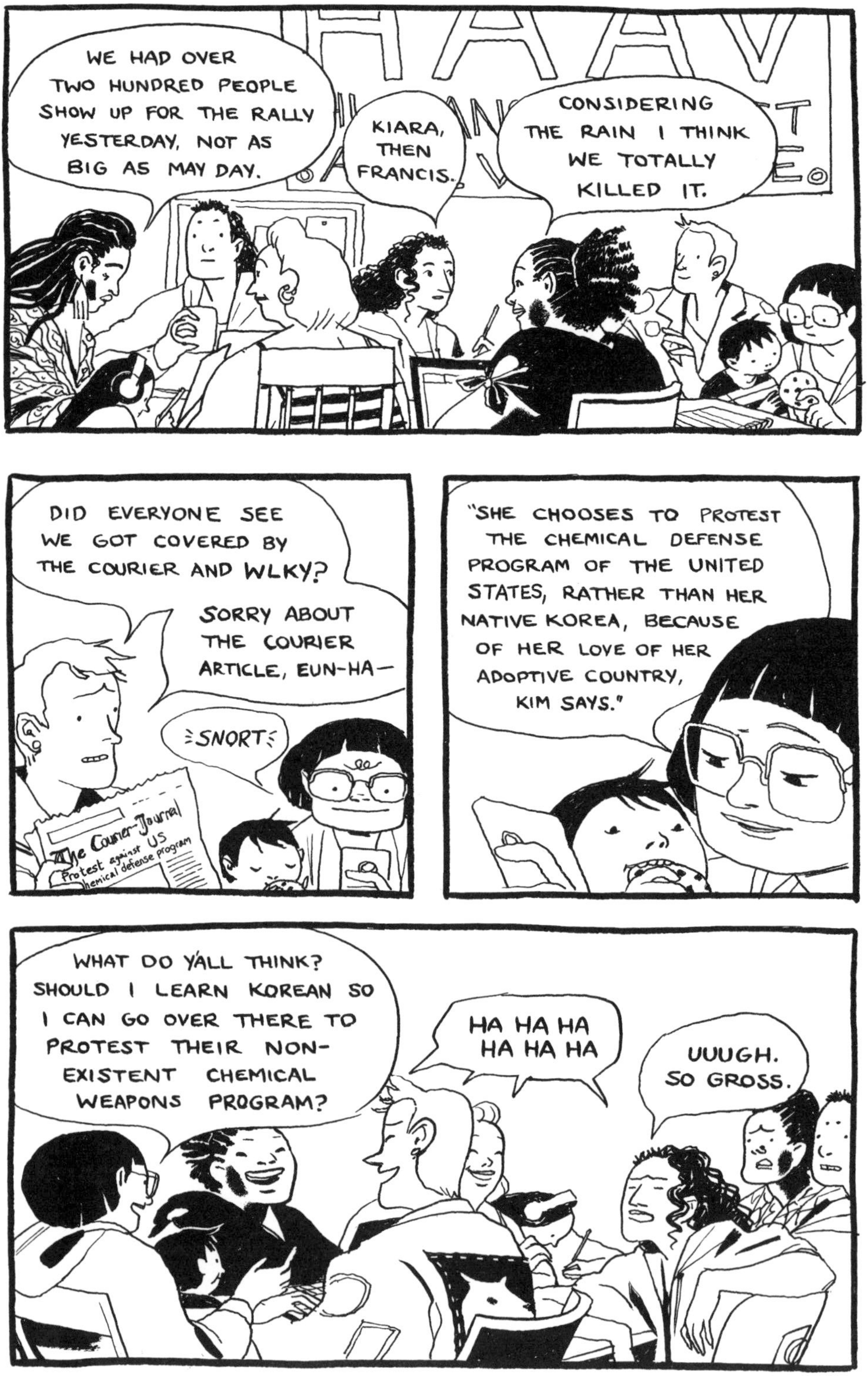
WE HAD OVER TWO HUNDRED PEOPLE SHOW UP FOR THE RALLY YESTERDAY, NOT AS BIG AS MAY DAY.
KIARA, THEN FRANCIS.
CONSIDERING THE RAIN I THINK WE TOTALLY KILLED IT.
DID EVERYONE SEE WE GOT COVERED BY THE COURIER AND WLKY?
SORRY ABOUT THE COURIER ARTICLE, EUN-HA—
SNORT
The Courier-Journal
Protest against US chemical defense program
"SHE CHOOSES TO PROTEST THE CHEMICAL DEFENSE PROGRAM OF THE UNITED STATES, RATHER THAN HER NATIVE KOREA, BECAUSE OF HER LOVE OF HER ADOPTIVE COUNTRY, KIM SAYS."
WHAT DO Y'ALL THINK? SHOULD I LEARN KOREAN SO I CAN GO OVER THERE TO PROTEST THEIR NON-EXISTENT CHEMICAL WEAPONS PROGRAM?
HA HA HA HA HA HA
UUUGH. SO GROSS.

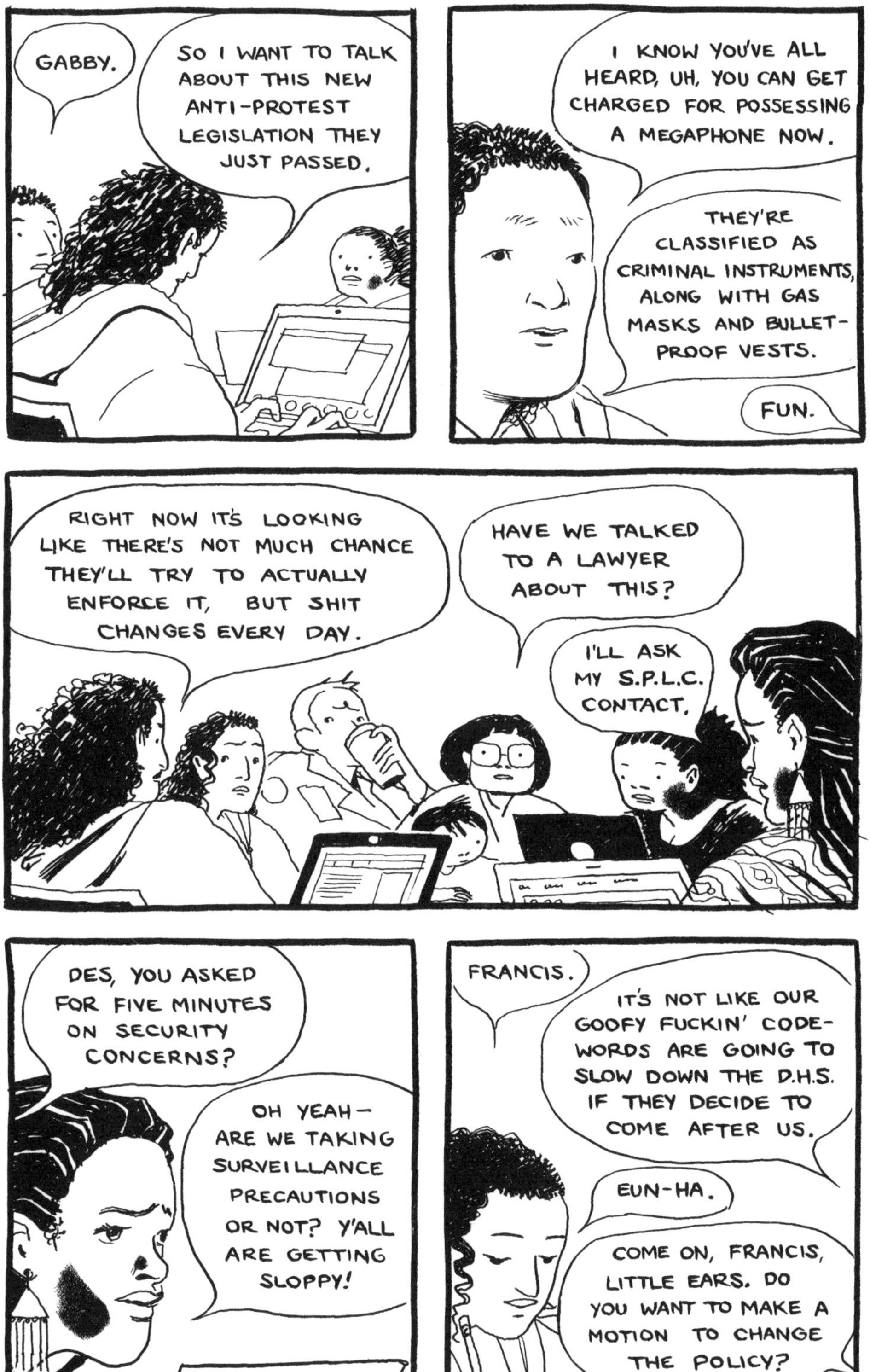
GABBY.
SO I WANT TO TALK ABOUT THIS NEW ANTI-PROTEST LEGISLATION THEY JUST PASSED.
I KNOW YOU'VE ALL HEARD, UH, YOU CAN GET CHARGED FOR POSSESSING A MEGAPHONE NOW.
THEY'RE CLASSIFIED AS CRIMINAL INSTRUMENTS, ALONG WITH GAS MASKS AND BULLET-PROOF VESTS.
FUN.
RIGHT NOW IT'S LOOKING LIKE THERE'S NOT MUCH CHANCE THEY'LL TRY TO ACTUALLY ENFORCE IT, BUT SHIT CHANGES EVERY DAY.
HAVE WE TALKED TO A LAWYER ABOUT THIS?
I'LL ASK MY S.P.L.C. CONTACT.
DES, YOU ASKED FOR FIVE MINUTES ON SECURITY CONCERNS?
OH YEAH— ARE WE TAKING SURVEILLANCE PRECAUTIONS OR NOT? Y'ALL ARE GETTING SLOPPY!
FRANCIS.
IT'S NOT LIKE OUR GOOFY FUCKIN' CODE-WORDS ARE GOING TO SLOW DOWN THE D.H.S. IF THEY DECIDE TO COME AFTER US.
EUN-HA.
COME ON, FRANCIS, LITTLE EARS. DO YOU WANT TO MAKE A MOTION TO CHANGE THE POLICY?

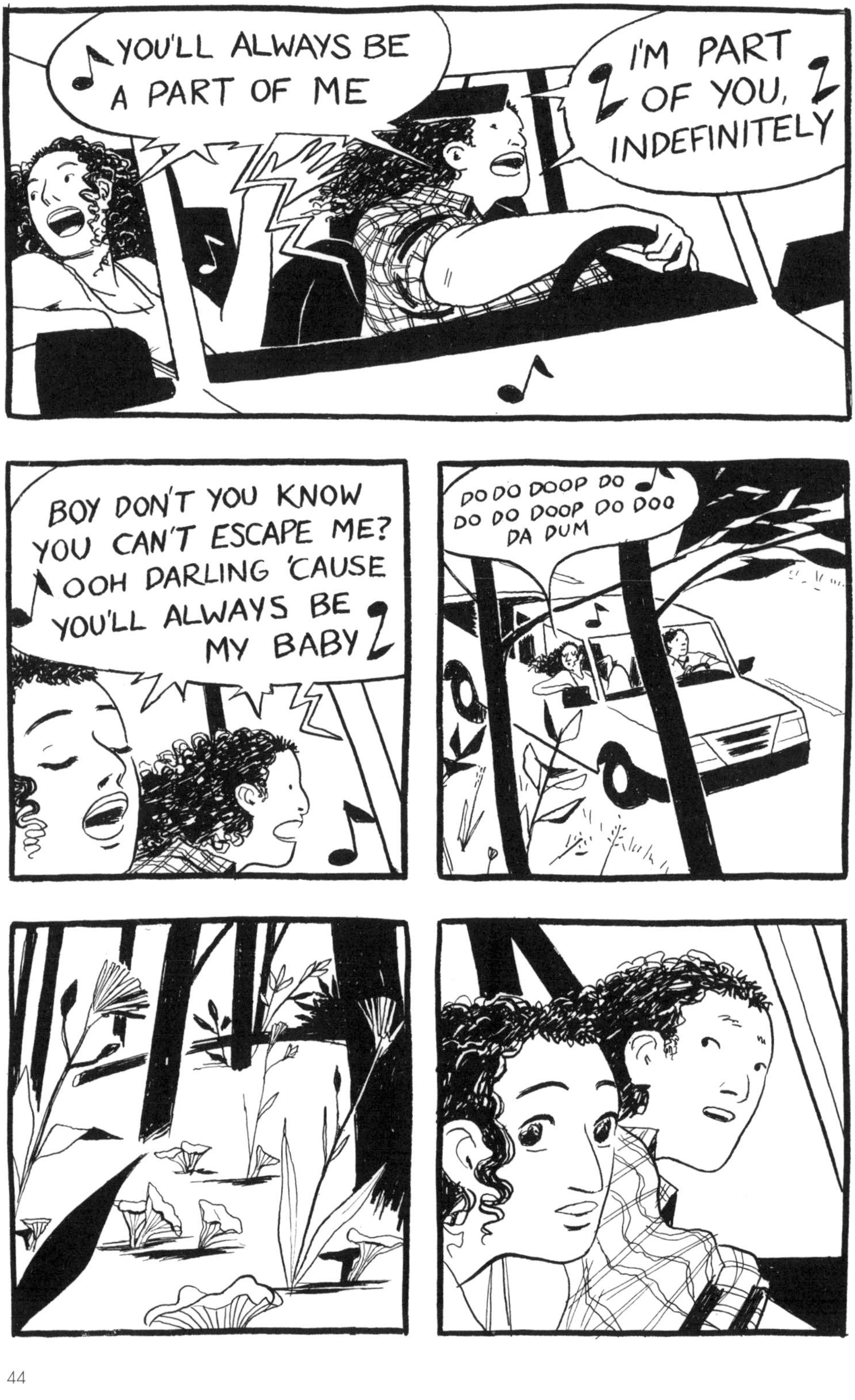
YOU'LL ALWAYS BE A PART OF ME
I'M PART OF YOU, INDEFINITELY
BOY DON'T YOU KNOW YOU CAN'T ESCAPE ME? OOH DARLING 'CAUSE YOU'LL ALWAYS BE MY BABY
DO DO DOOP DO DO DO DOOP DO DOO DA DUM

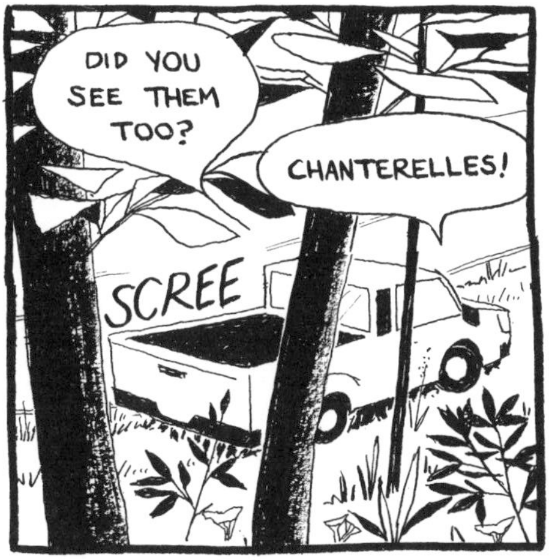
DID YOU SEE THEM TOO?
CHANTERELLES!
SCREE

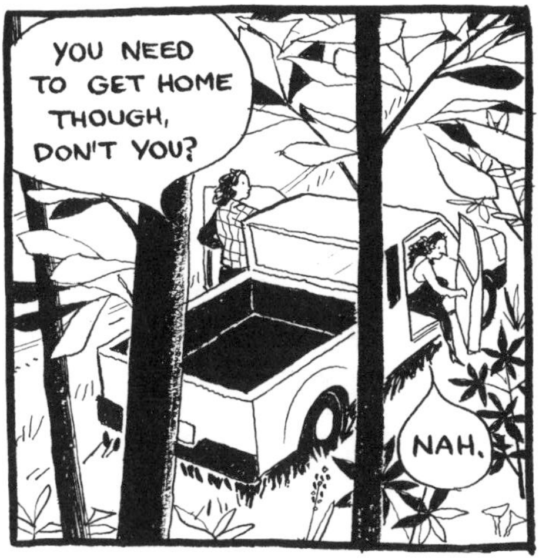
YOU NEED TO GET HOME THOUGH, DON'T YOU?
NAH.

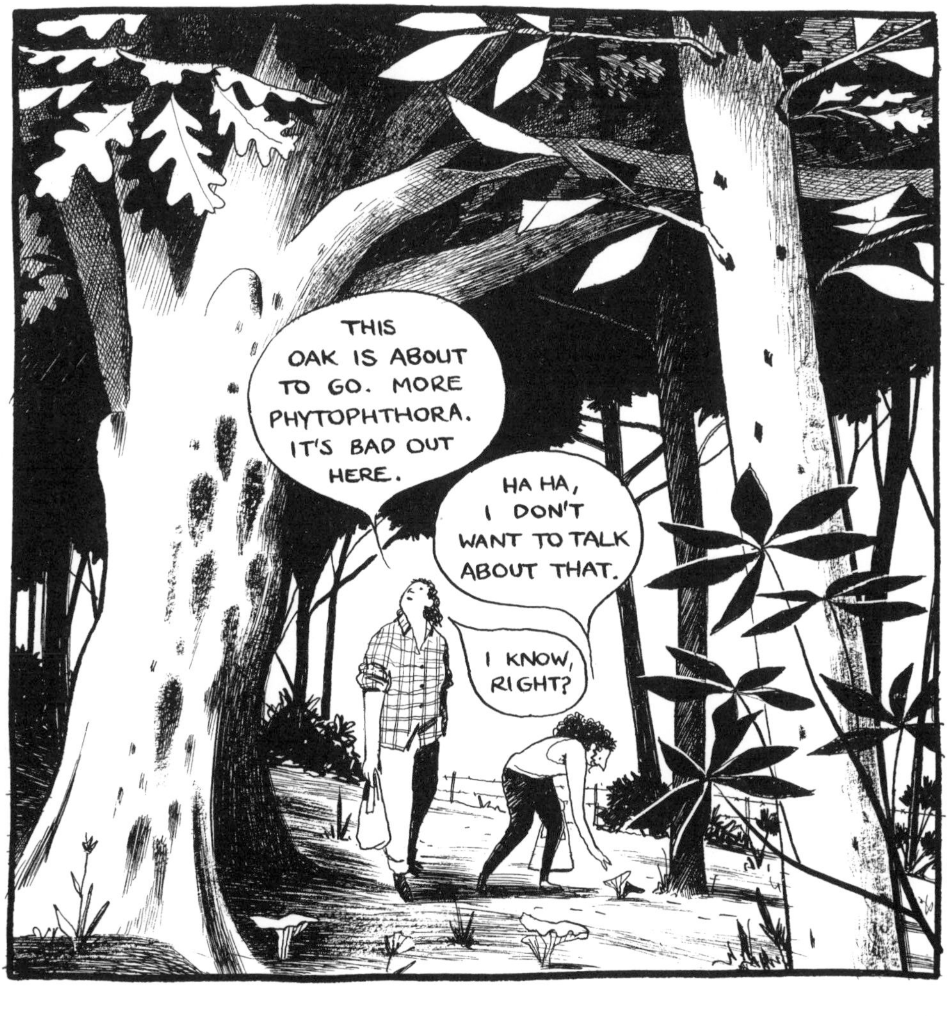
THIS OAK IS ABOUT TO GO. MORE PHYTOPHTHORA. IT'S BAD OUT HERE.
HA HA, I DON'T WANT TO TALK ABOUT THAT.
I KNOW, RIGHT?

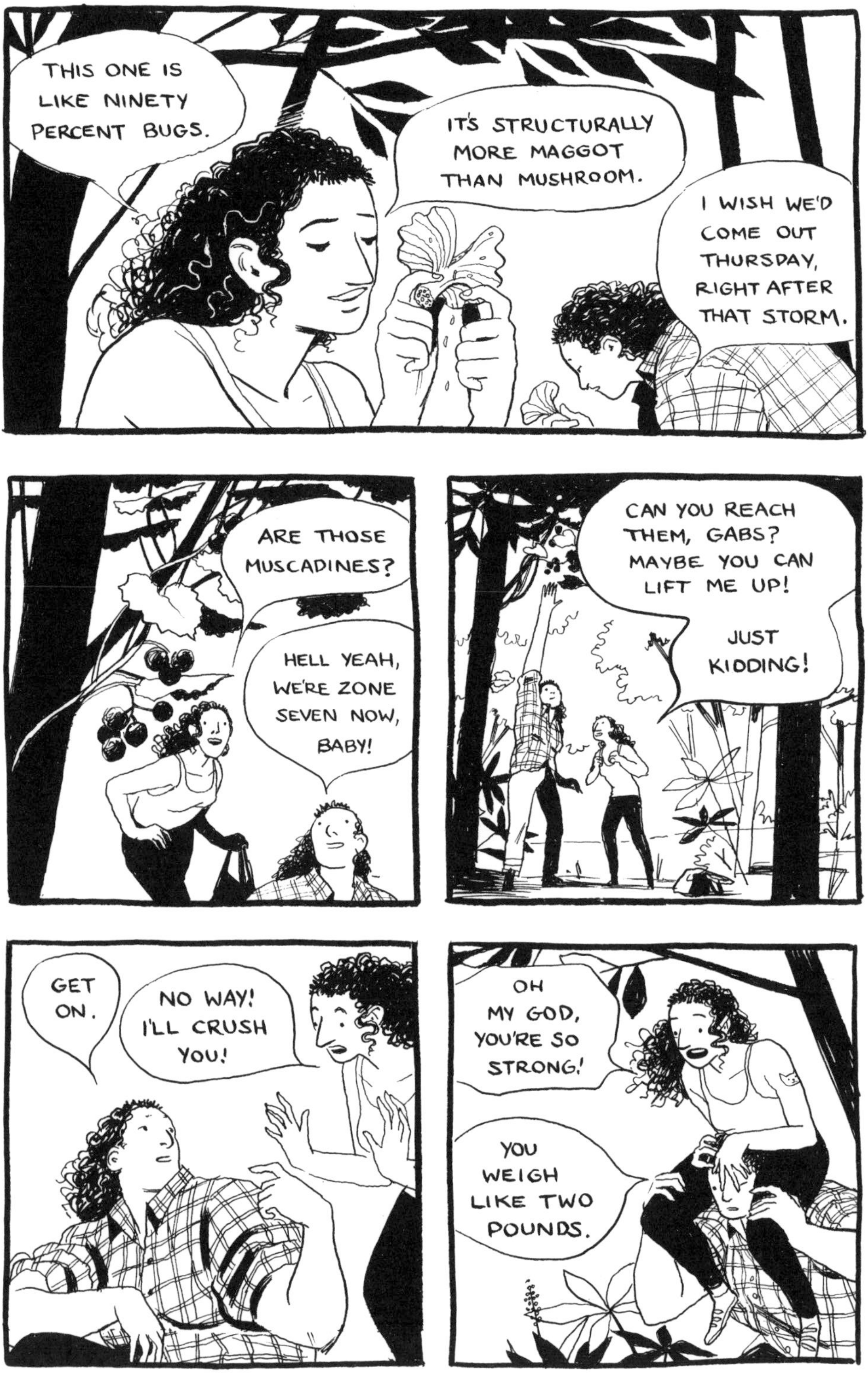
THIS ONE IS LIKE NINETY PERCENT BUGS.
IT'S STRUCTURALLY MORE MAGGOT THAN MUSHROOM.
I WISH WE'D COME OUT THURSDAY, RIGHT AFTER THAT STORM.
ARE THOSE MUSCADINES?
HELL YEAH, WE'RE ZONE SEVEN NOW, BABY!
CAN YOU REACH THEM, GABS? MAYBE YOU CAN LIFT ME UP!
JUST KIDDING!
GET ON.
NO WAY! I'LL CRUSH YOU!
OH MY GOD, YOU'RE SO STRONG!
YOU WEIGH LIKE TWO POUNDS.

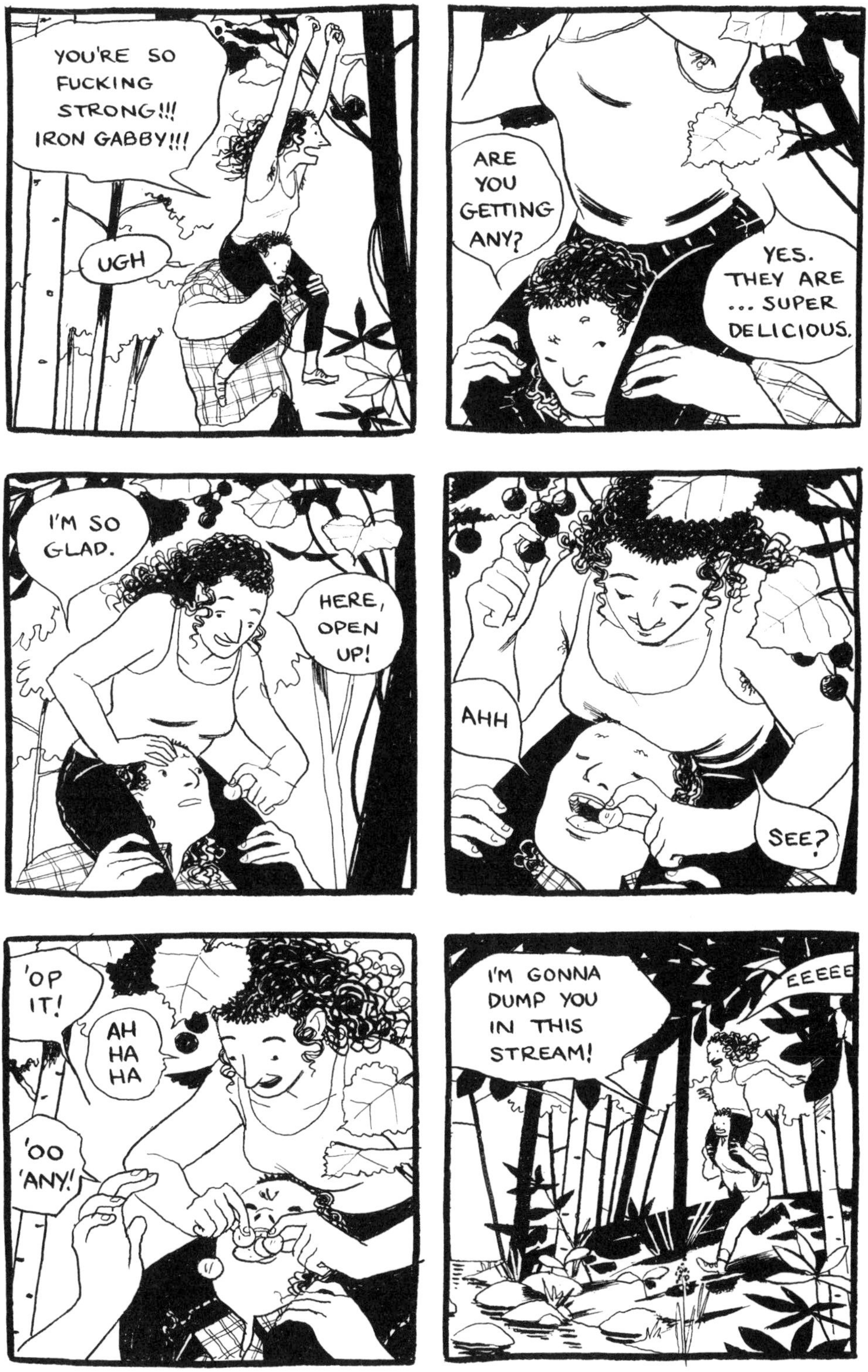
YOU'RE SO FUCKING STRONG!!! IRON GABBY!!!
UGH
ARE YOU GETTING ANY?
YES. THEY ARE ... SUPER DELICIOUS.
I'M SO GLAD.
HERE, OPEN UP!
AHH
SEE?
'OP IT!
AH HA HA
'OO 'ANY!
I'M GONNA DUMP YOU IN THIS STREAM!
EEEEE

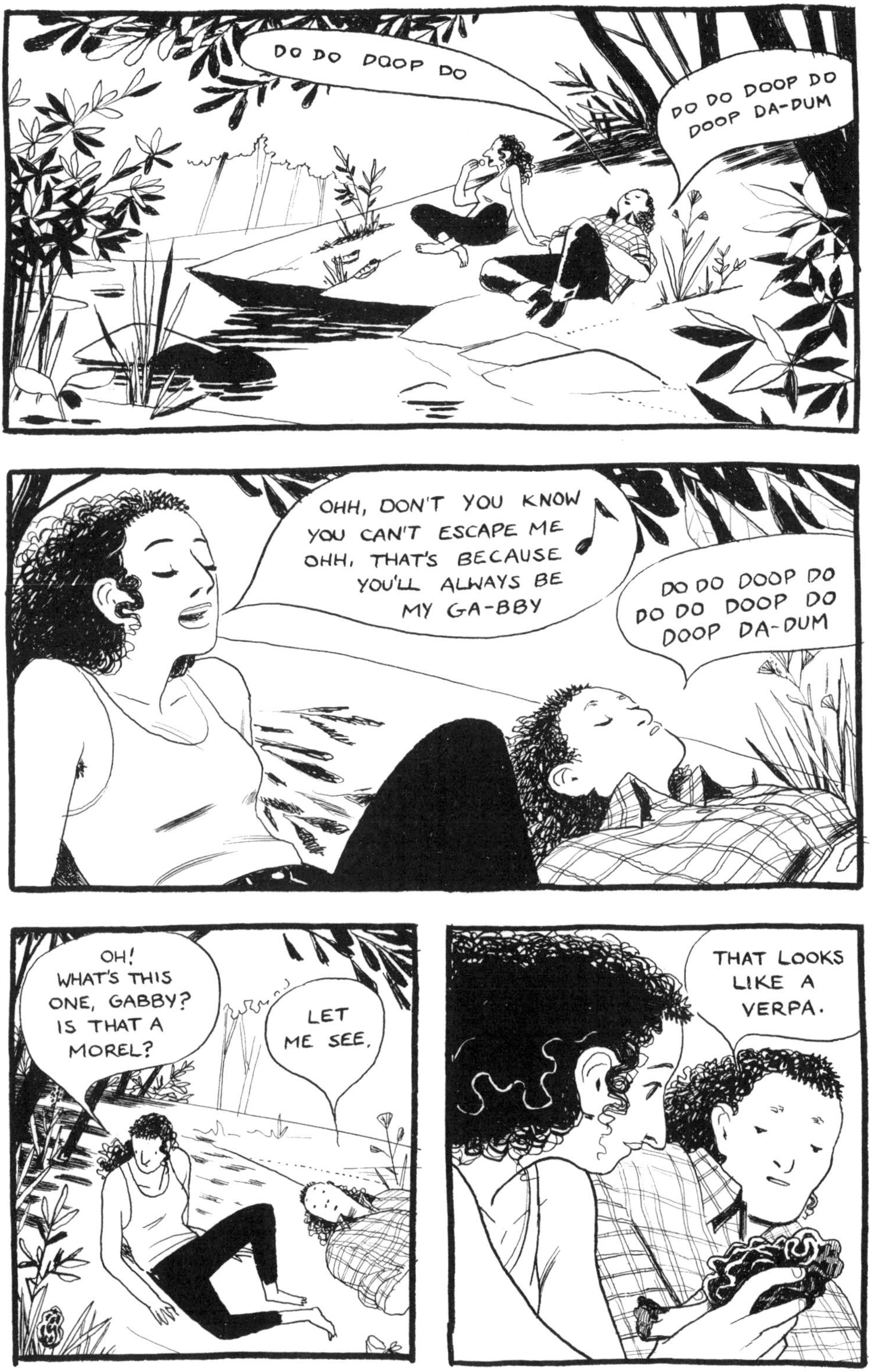
DO DO DOOP DO
DO DO DOOP DO DOOP DA-DUM
OHH, DON'T YOU KNOW YOU CAN'T ESCAPE ME OHH, THAT'S BECAUSE YOU'LL ALWAYS BE MY GA-BBY
DO DO DOOP DO DO DO DOOP DO DOOP DA-DUM
OH! WHAT'S THIS ONE, GABBY? IS THAT A MOREL?
LET ME SEE.
THAT LOOKS LIKE A VERPA.

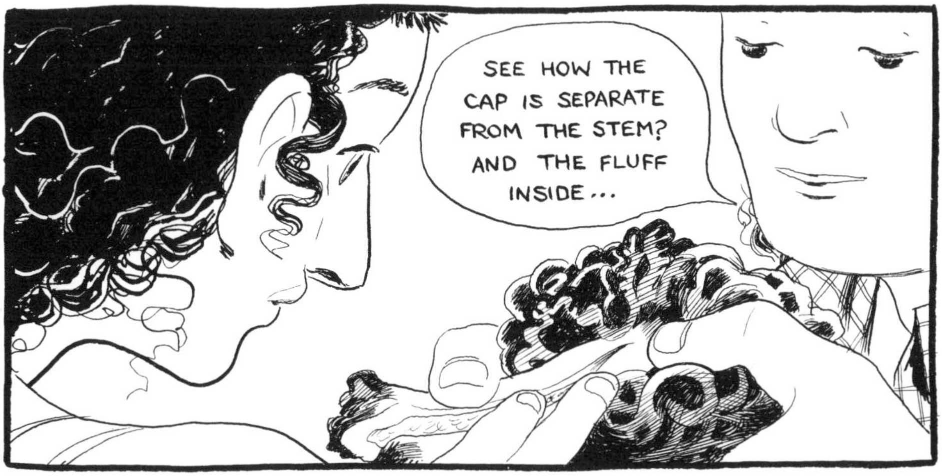
SEE HOW THE CAP IS SEPARATE FROM THE STEM? AND THE FLUFF INSIDE...

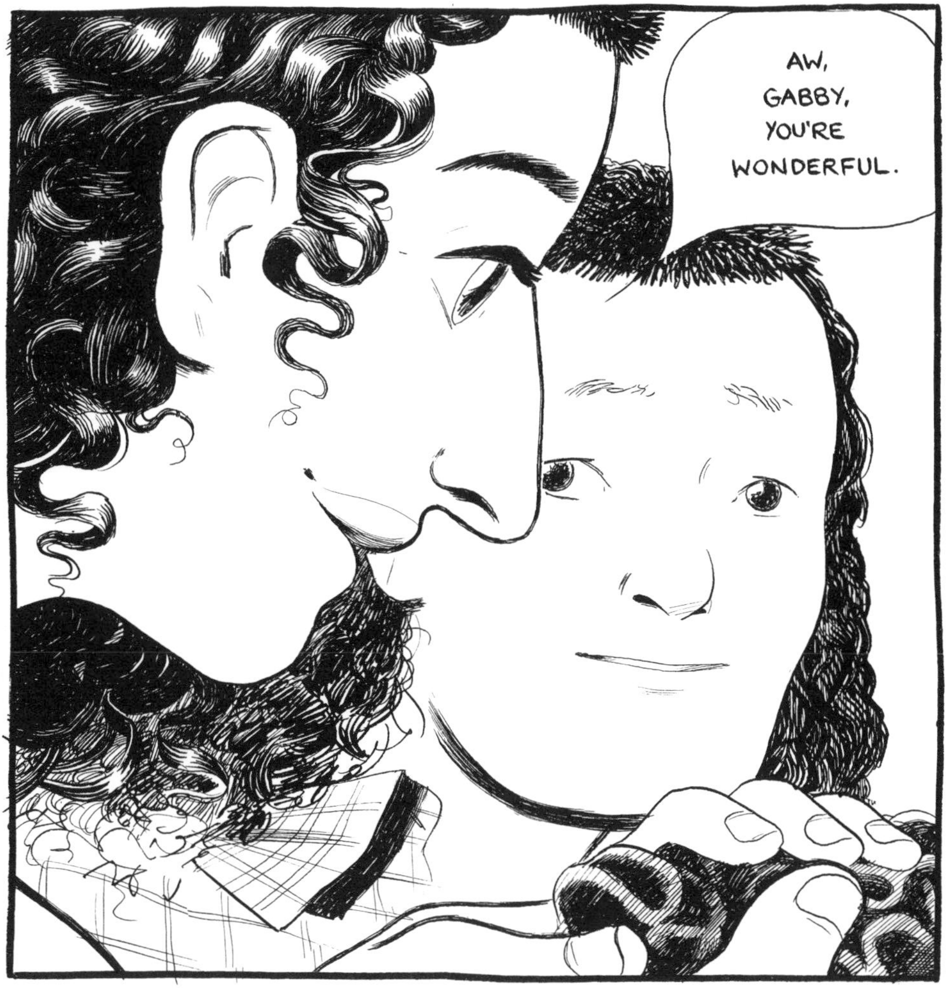
AW, GABBY, YOU'RE WONDERFUL.

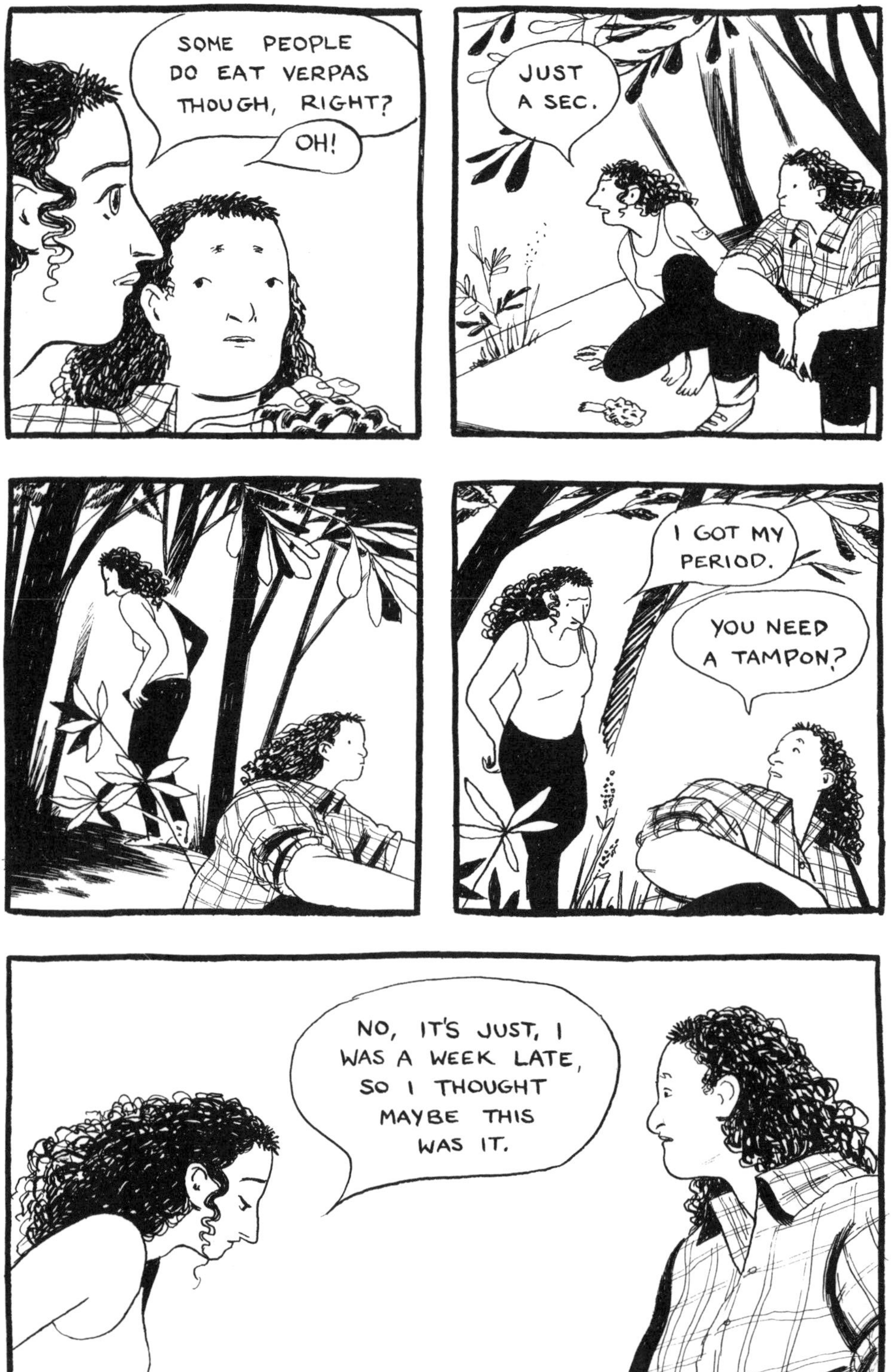
SOME PEOPLE DO EAT VERPAS THOUGH, RIGHT?
OH!
JUST A SEC.
I GOT MY PERIOD.
YOU NEED A TAMPON?
NO, IT'S JUST, I WAS A WEEK LATE, SO I THOUGHT MAYBE THIS WAS IT.

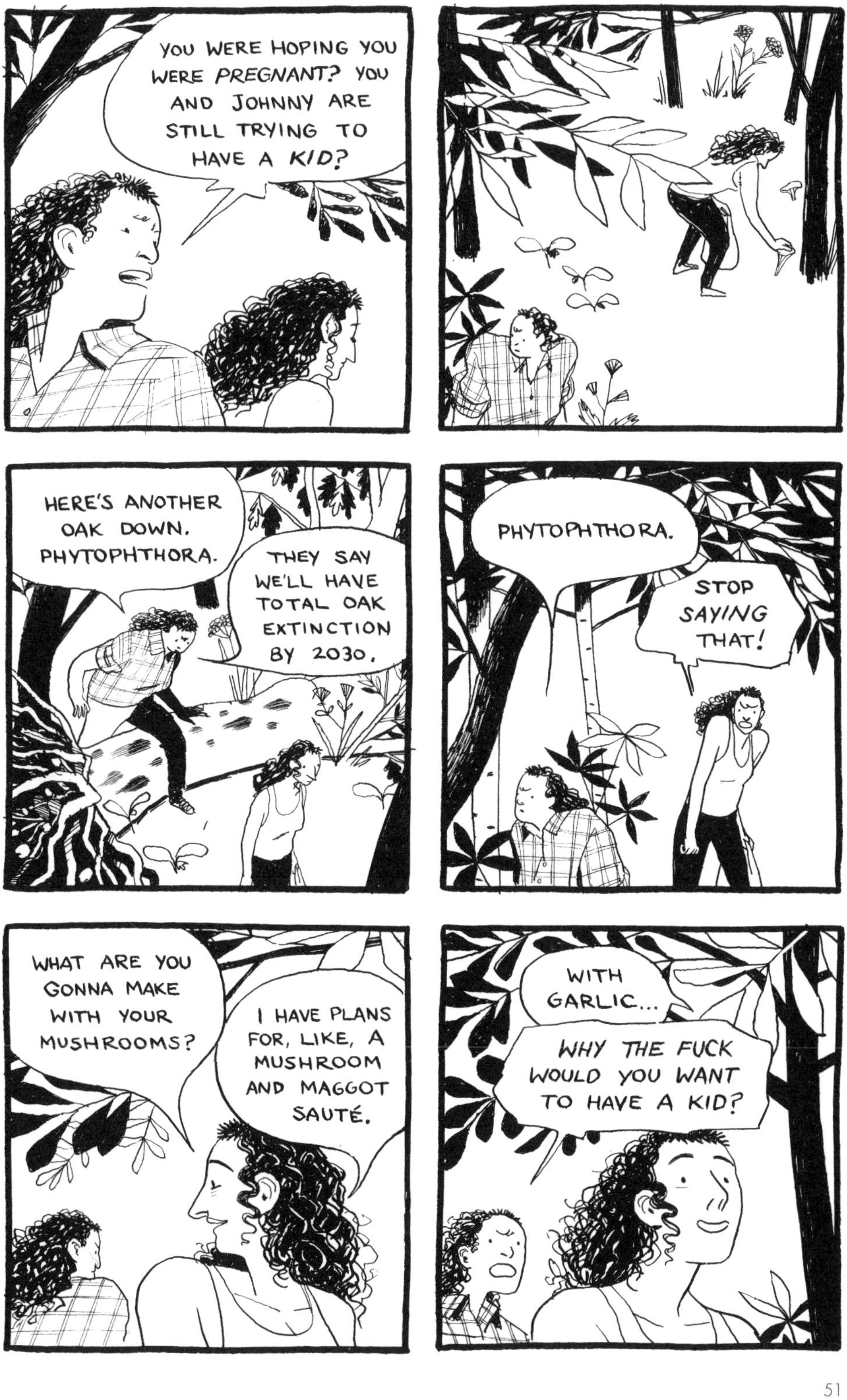
YOU WERE HOPING YOU WERE *PREGNANT*? YOU AND JOHNNY ARE STILL TRYING TO HAVE A *KID*?
HERE'S ANOTHER OAK DOWN. PHYTOPHTHORA.
THEY SAY WE'LL HAVE TOTAL OAK EXTINCTION BY 2030.
PHYTOPHTHORA.
STOP SAYING THAT!
WHAT ARE YOU GONNA MAKE WITH YOUR MUSHROOMS?
I HAVE PLANS FOR, LIKE, A MUSHROOM AND MAGGOT SAUTÉ.
WITH GARLIC...
WHY THE FUCK WOULD YOU WANT TO HAVE A KID?

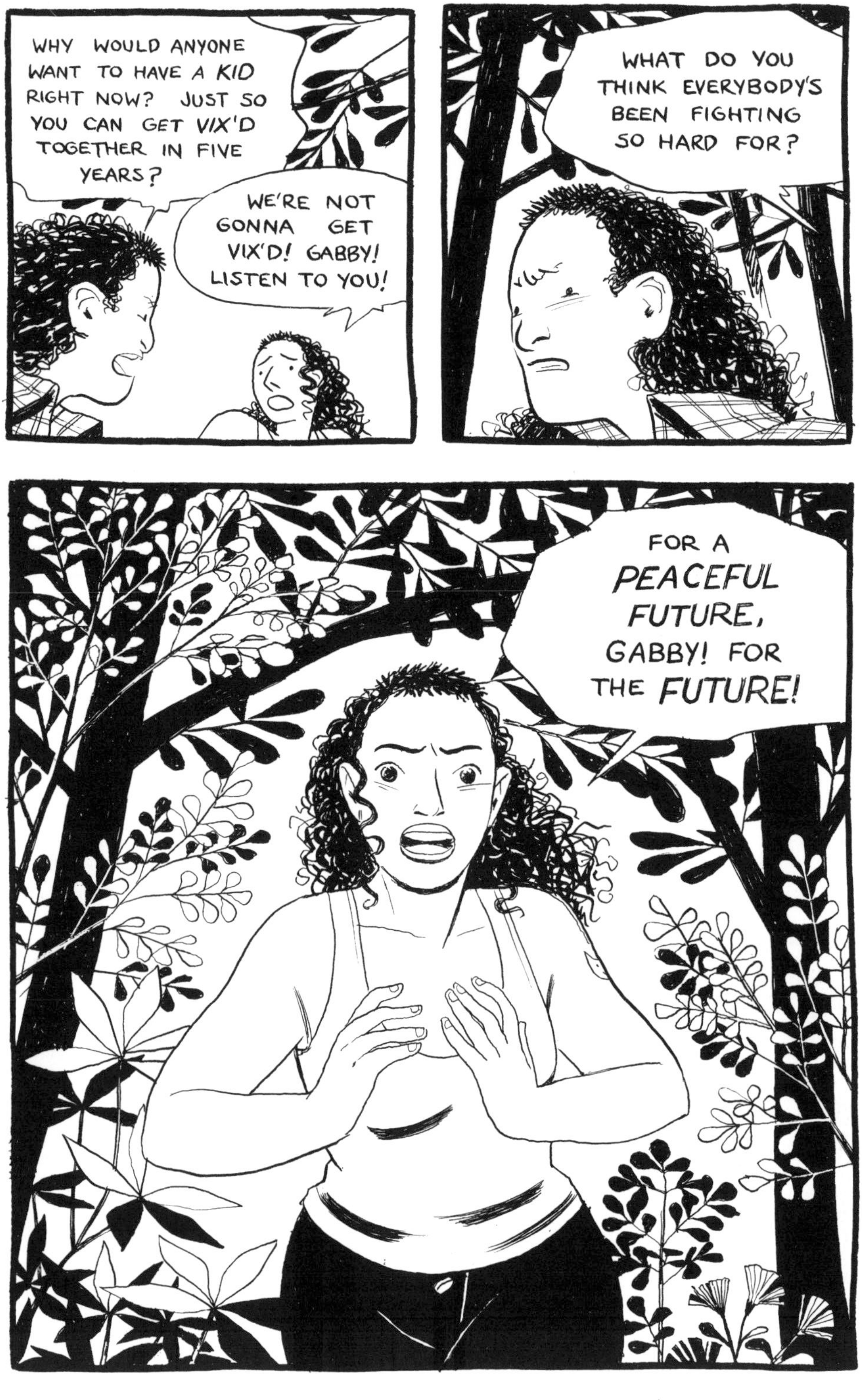
WHY WOULD ANYONE WANT TO HAVE A KID RIGHT NOW? JUST SO YOU CAN GET VIX'D TOGETHER IN FIVE YEARS?
WE'RE NOT GONNA GET VIX'D! GABBY! LISTEN TO YOU!
WHAT DO YOU THINK EVERYBODY'S BEEN FIGHTING SO HARD FOR?
FOR A PEACEFUL FUTURE, GABBY! FOR THE FUTURE!

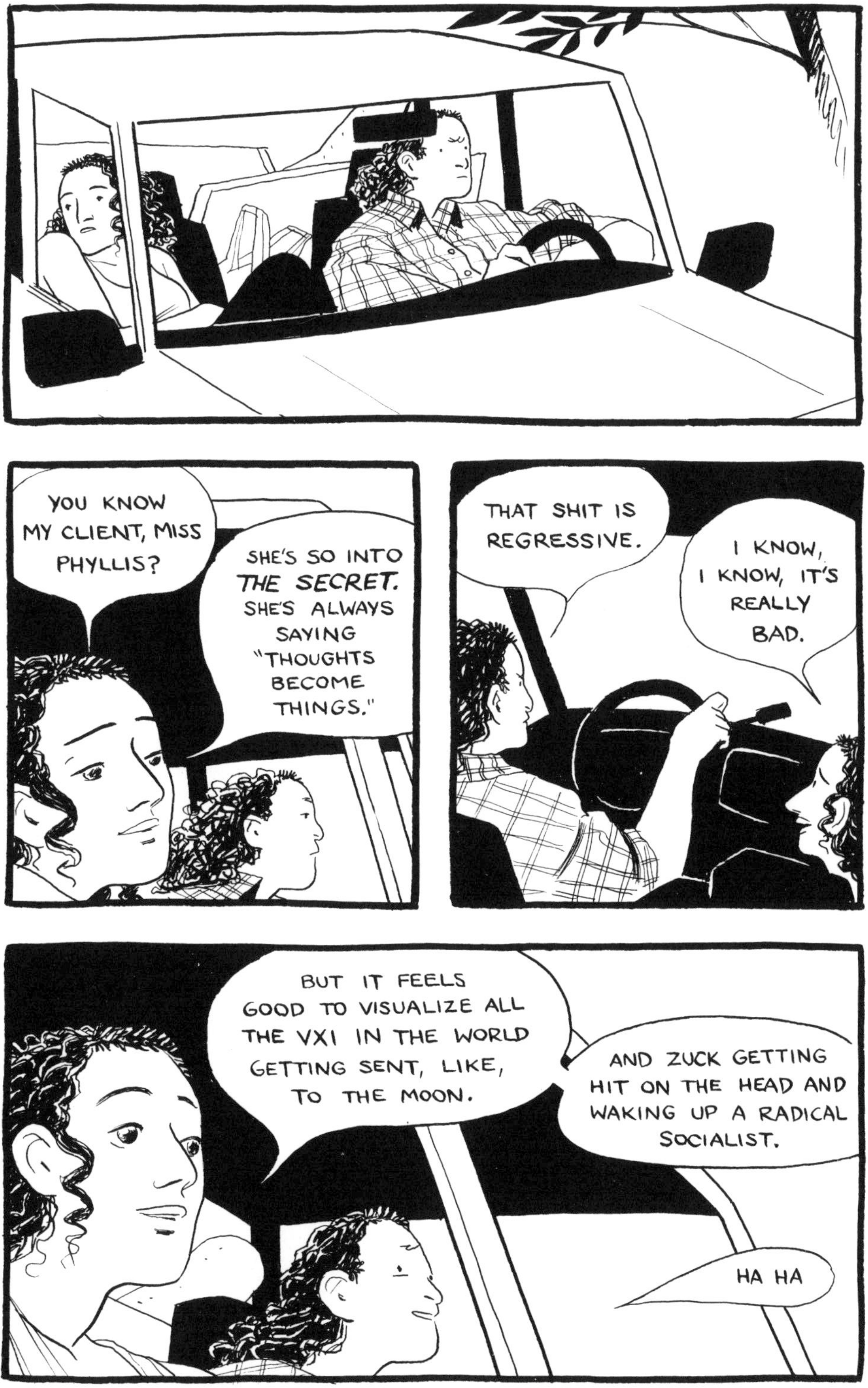
YOU KNOW MY CLIENT, MISS PHYLLIS?
SHE'S SO INTO THE SECRET. SHE'S ALWAYS SAYING "THOUGHTS BECOME THINGS."
THAT SHIT IS REGRESSIVE.
I KNOW, I KNOW, IT'S REALLY BAD.
BUT IT FEELS GOOD TO VISUALIZE ALL THE VXI IN THE WORLD GETTING SENT, LIKE, TO THE MOON.
AND ZUCK GETTING HIT ON THE HEAD AND WAKING UP A RADICAL SOCIALIST.
HA HA

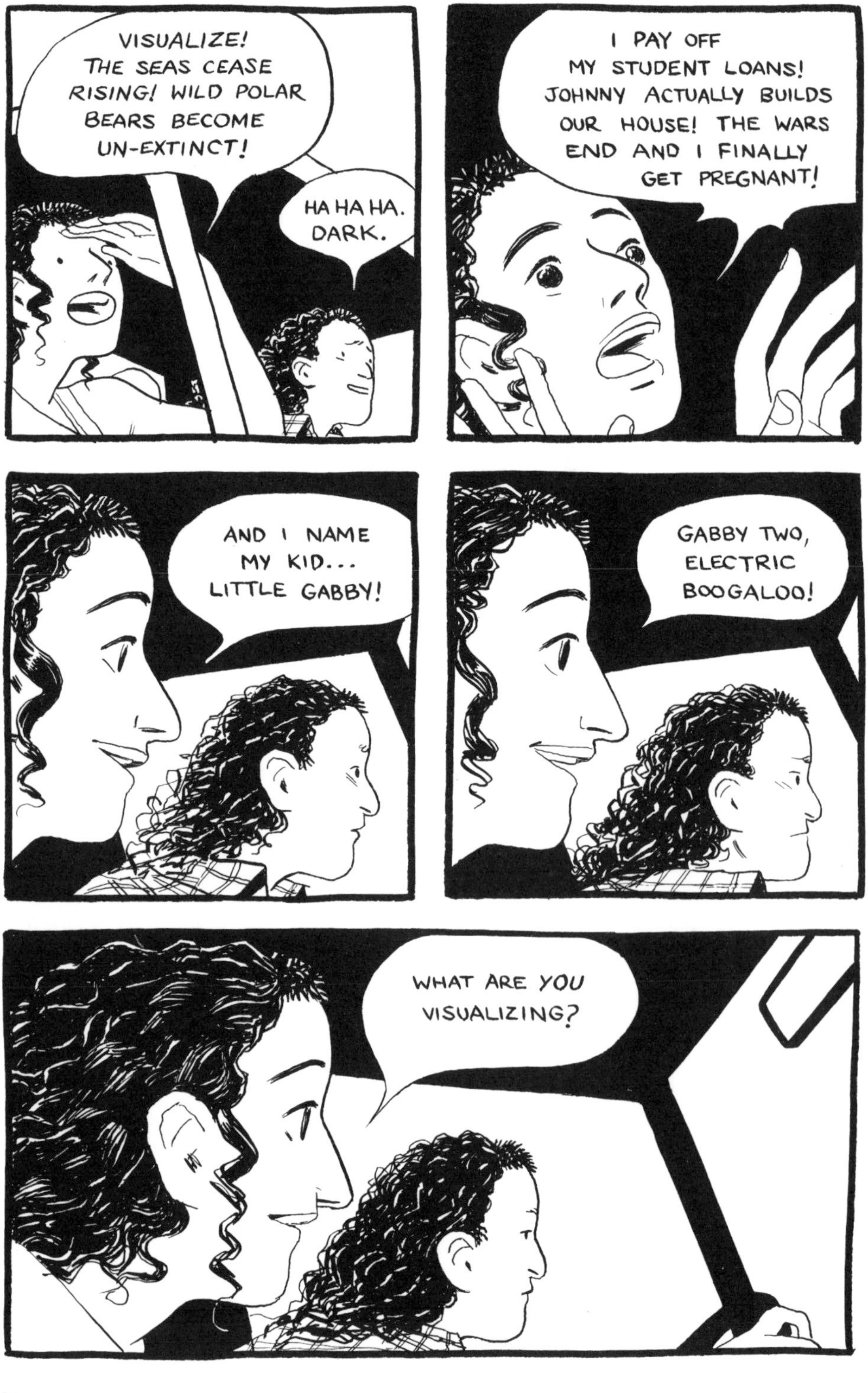
VISUALIZE! THE SEAS CEASE RISING! WILD POLAR BEARS BECOME UN-EXTINCT!
HA HA HA. DARK.
I PAY OFF MY STUDENT LOANS! JOHNNY ACTUALLY BUILDS OUR HOUSE! THE WARS END AND I FINALLY GET PREGNANT!
AND I NAME MY KID... LITTLE GABBY!
GABBY TWO, ELECTRIC BOOGALOO!
WHAT ARE *YOU* VISUALIZING?

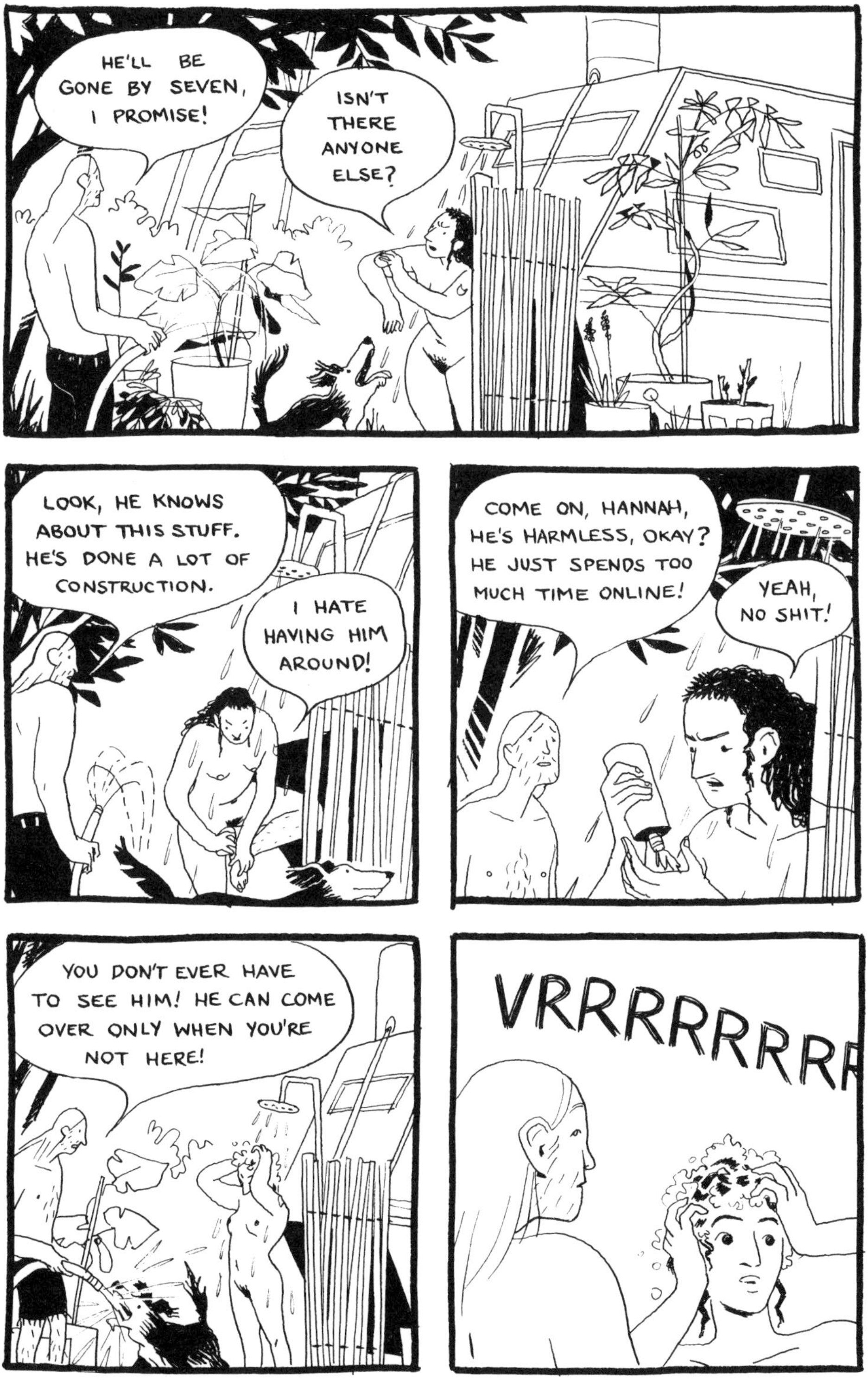
HE'LL BE GONE BY SEVEN, I PROMISE!
ISN'T THERE ANYONE ELSE?
LOOK, HE KNOWS ABOUT THIS STUFF. HE'S DONE A LOT OF CONSTRUCTION.
I HATE HAVING HIM AROUND!
COME ON, HANNAH, HE'S HARMLESS, OKAY? HE JUST SPENDS TOO MUCH TIME ONLINE!
YEAH, NO SHIT!
YOU DON'T EVER HAVE TO SEE HIM! HE CAN COME OVER ONLY WHEN YOU'RE NOT HERE!
VRRRRRRRR

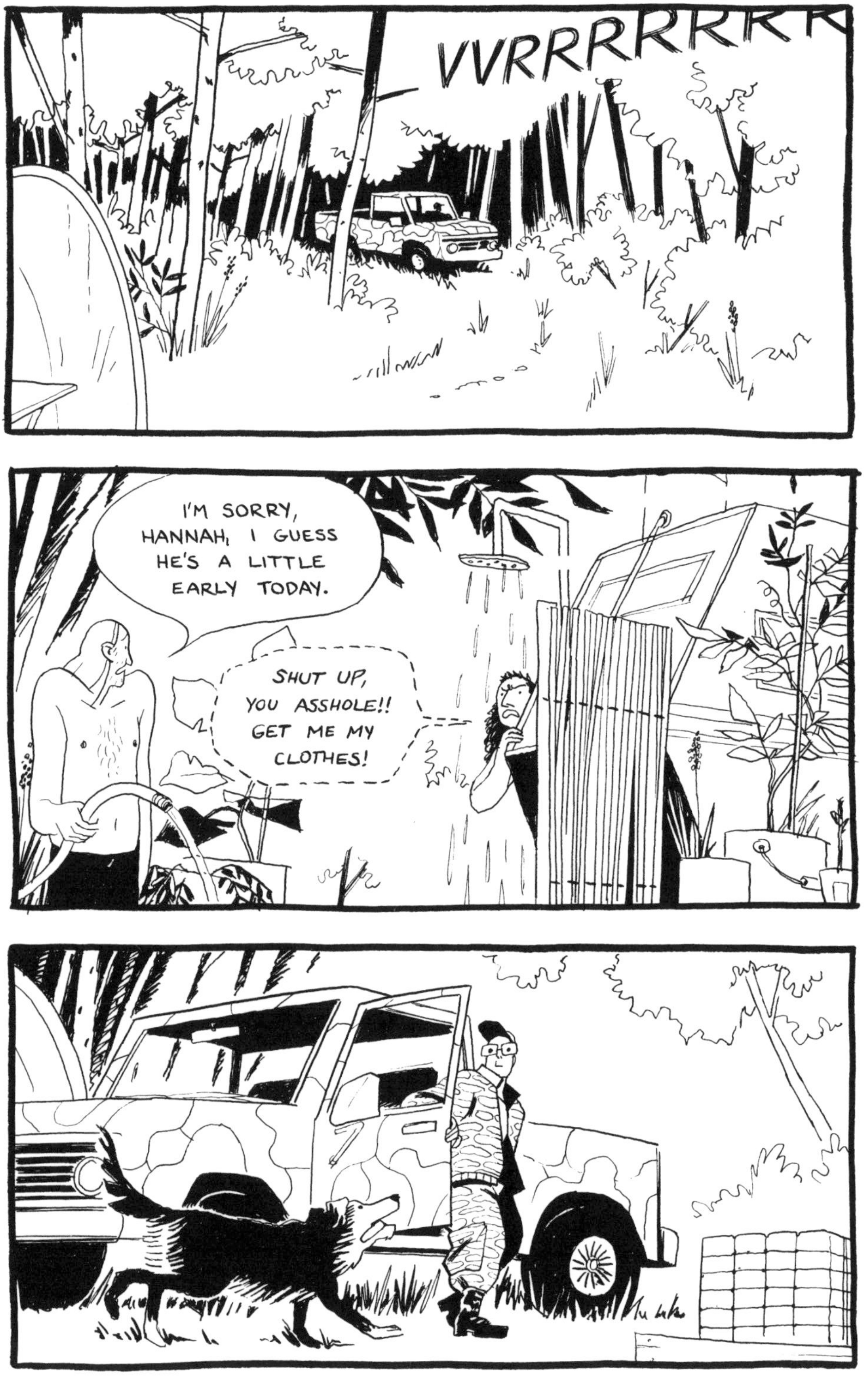
VVRRRRRRR
I'M SORRY, HANNAH, I GUESS HE'S A LITTLE EARLY TODAY.
SHUT UP, YOU ASSHOLE!! GET ME MY CLOTHES!

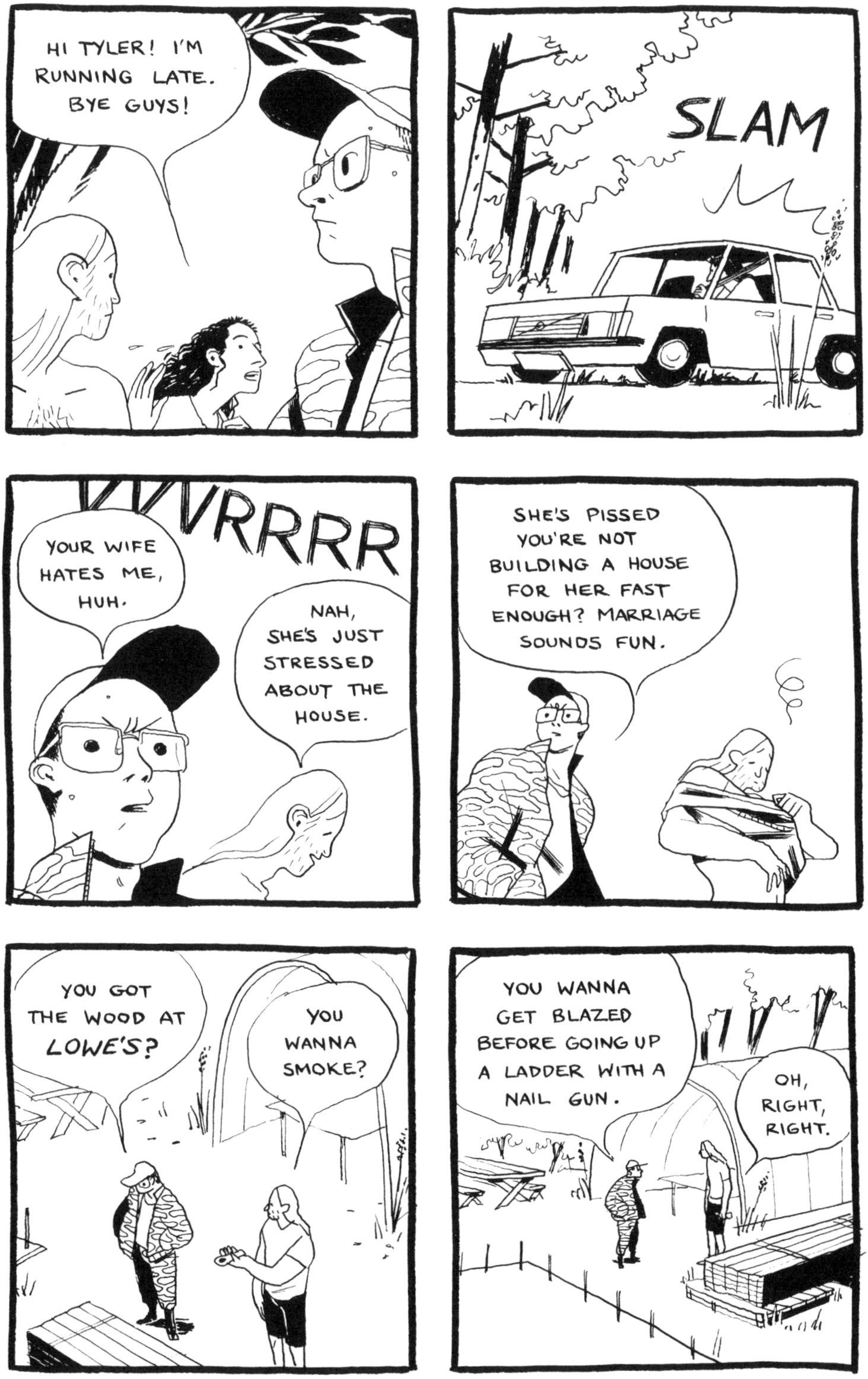
HI TYLER! I'M RUNNING LATE. BYE GUYS!
SLAM
RRRRR
YOUR WIFE HATES ME, HUH.
NAH, SHE'S JUST STRESSED ABOUT THE HOUSE.
SHE'S PISSED YOU'RE NOT BUILDING A HOUSE FOR HER FAST ENOUGH? MARRIAGE SOUNDS FUN.
YOU GOT THE WOOD AT LOWE'S?
YOU WANNA SMOKE?
YOU WANNA GET BLAZED BEFORE GOING UP A LADDER WITH A NAIL GUN.
OH, RIGHT, RIGHT.

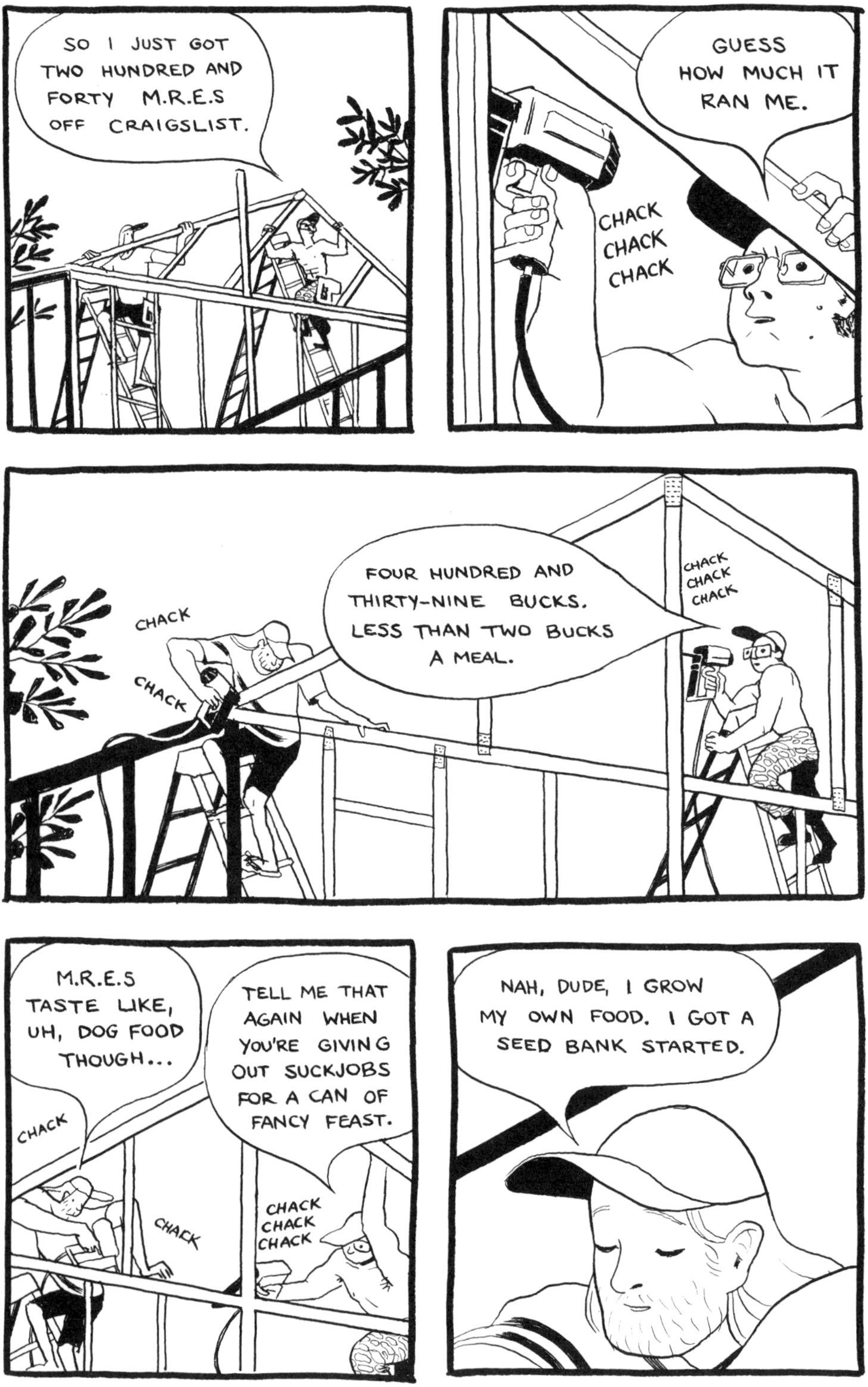
SO I JUST GOT TWO HUNDRED AND FORTY M.R.E.S OFF CRAIGSLIST.
GUESS HOW MUCH IT RAN ME.
CHACK CHACK CHACK
CHACK
CHACK
FOUR HUNDRED AND THIRTY-NINE BUCKS. LESS THAN TWO BUCKS A MEAL.
CHACK CHACK CHACK
M.R.E.S TASTE LIKE, UH, DOG FOOD THOUGH...
TELL ME THAT AGAIN WHEN YOU'RE GIVING OUT SUCKJOBS FOR A CAN OF FANCY FEAST.
CHACK
CHACK
CHACK CHACK CHACK
NAH, DUDE, I GROW MY OWN FOOD. I GOT A SEED BANK STARTED.

I'VE GOT TOMATOES, SWEET POTATOES, KALE...

AFTER I GET THE HOUSE DONE WE'RE BUYING CHICKENS. HANNAH RAISED CHICKENS WHEN SHE WAS IN MONTANA.

YEAH, YOU TOLD ME. GOOD LUCK WITH ALL THAT HIPPIE SHIT, FARMER JOHN.

DID YOU KNOW THAT WOMEN ARE SEVENTY-FIVE PERCENT LESS EFFICIENT AT BURNING ENERGY THAN MEN? IT'S THEIR BODY FAT.

THEY CONSUME ALL THOSE CALORIES AND THERE'S NO RETURN ON YOUR INVESTMENT.

HAHA. OKAY.

HANNAH DOESN'T EAT, LIKE, A TON.

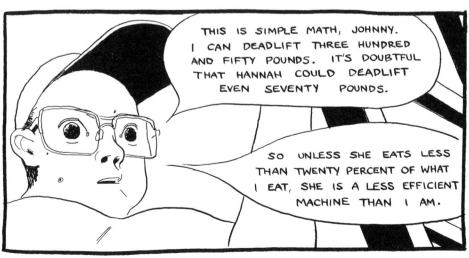

THIS IS SIMPLE MATH, JOHNNY. I CAN DEADLIFT THREE HUNDRED AND FIFTY POUNDS. IT'S DOUBTFUL THAT HANNAH COULD DEADLIFT EVEN SEVENTY POUNDS.

SO UNLESS SHE EATS LESS THAN TWENTY PERCENT OF WHAT I EAT, SHE IS A LESS EFFICIENT MACHINE THAN I AM.

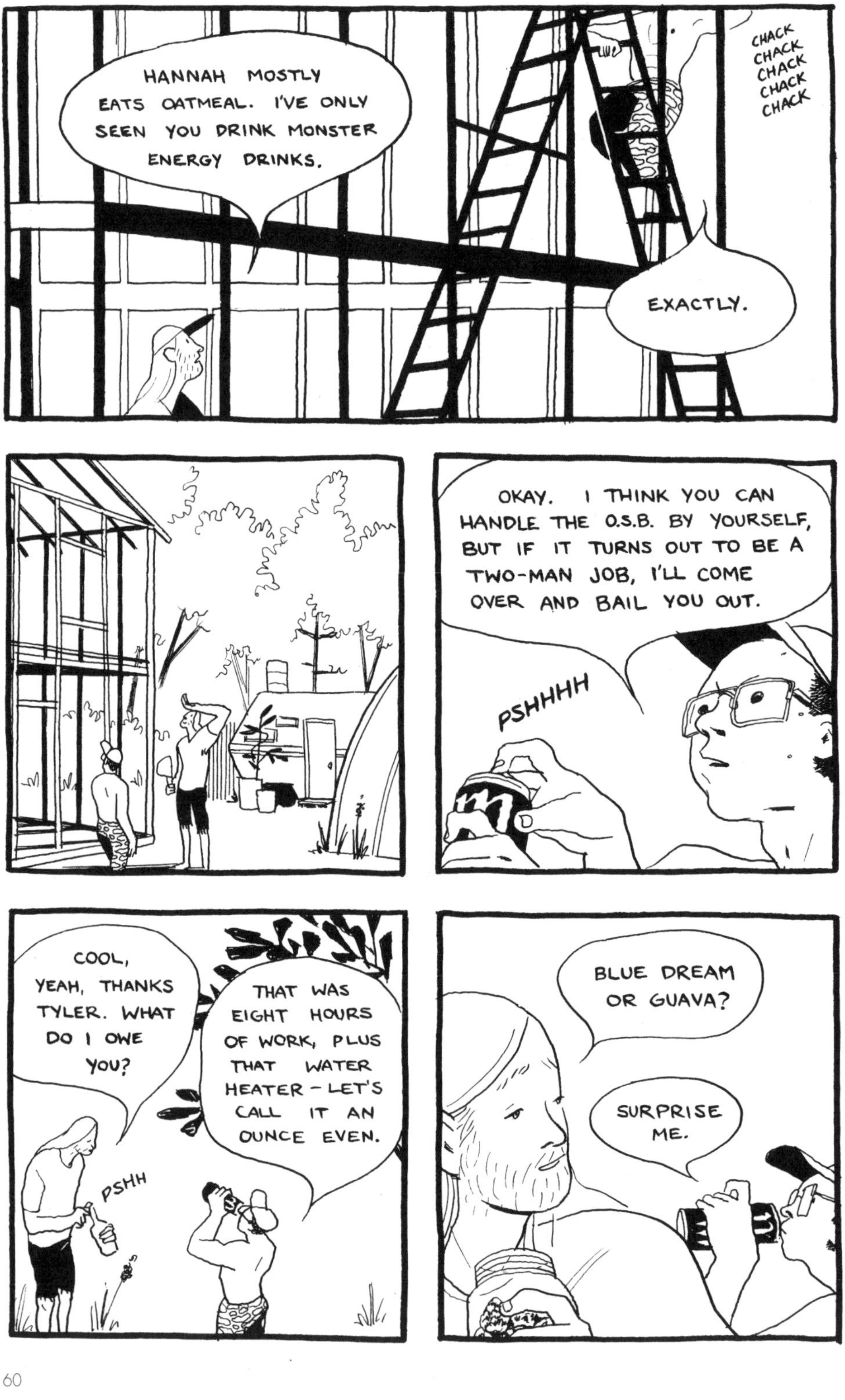
HANNAH MOSTLY EATS OATMEAL. I'VE ONLY SEEN YOU DRINK MONSTER ENERGY DRINKS.
CHACK CHACK CHACK CHACK CHACK
EXACTLY.
OKAY. I THINK YOU CAN HANDLE THE O.S.B. BY YOURSELF, BUT IF IT TURNS OUT TO BE A TWO-MAN JOB, I'LL COME OVER AND BAIL YOU OUT.
PSHHHH
COOL, YEAH, THANKS TYLER. WHAT DO I OWE YOU?
THAT WAS EIGHT HOURS OF WORK, PLUS THAT WATER HEATER - LET'S CALL IT AN OUNCE EVEN.
PSHH
BLUE DREAM OR GUAVA?
SURPRISE ME.

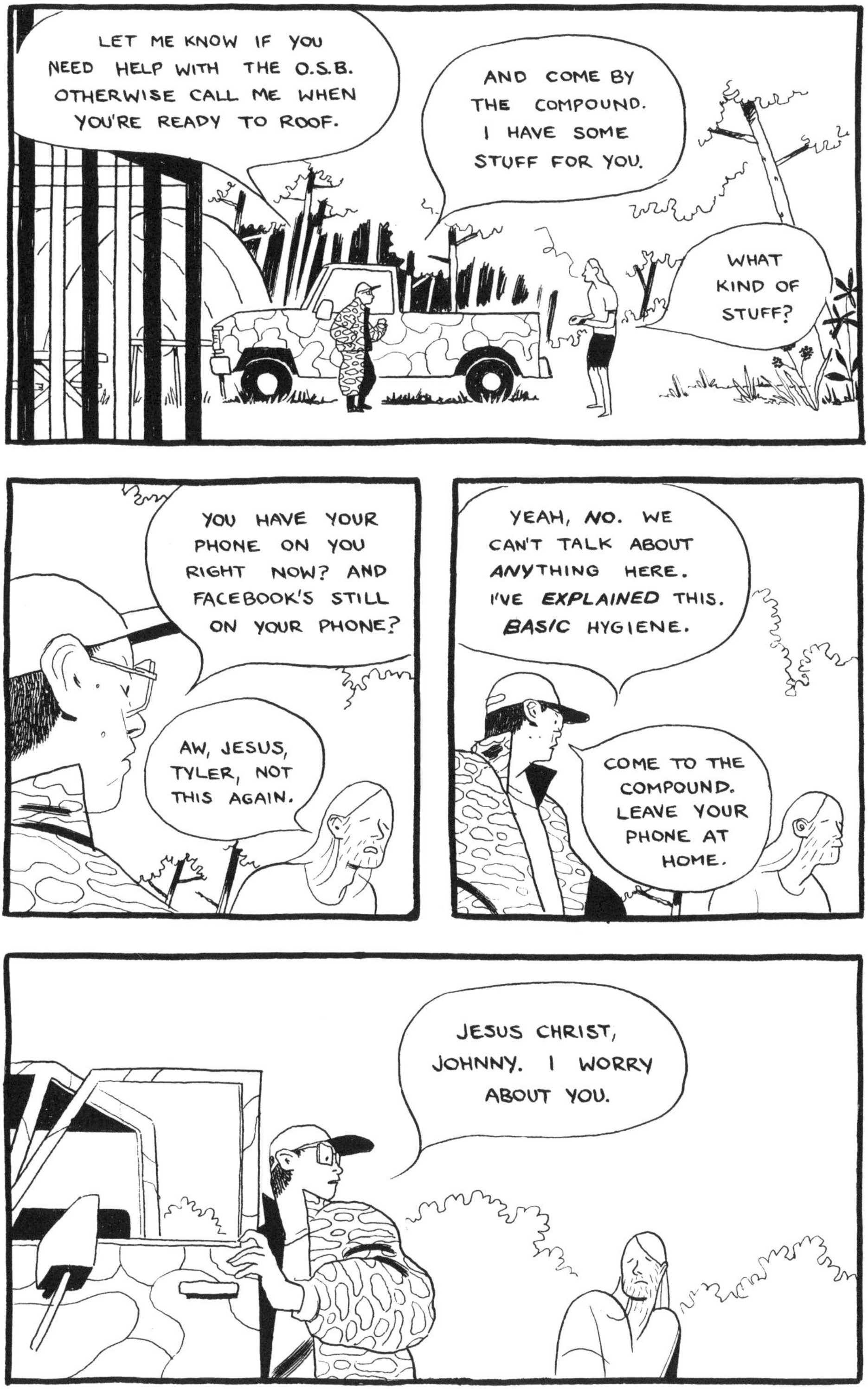
LET ME KNOW IF YOU NEED HELP WITH THE O.S.B. OTHERWISE CALL ME WHEN YOU'RE READY TO ROOF.
AND COME BY THE COMPOUND. I HAVE SOME STUFF FOR YOU.
WHAT KIND OF STUFF?
YOU HAVE YOUR PHONE ON YOU RIGHT NOW? AND FACEBOOK'S STILL ON YOUR PHONE?
AW, JESUS, TYLER, NOT THIS AGAIN.
YEAH, NO. WE CAN'T TALK ABOUT ANYTHING HERE. I'VE EXPLAINED THIS. BASIC HYGIENE.
COME TO THE COMPOUND. LEAVE YOUR PHONE AT HOME.
JESUS CHRIST, JOHNNY. I WORRY ABOUT YOU.

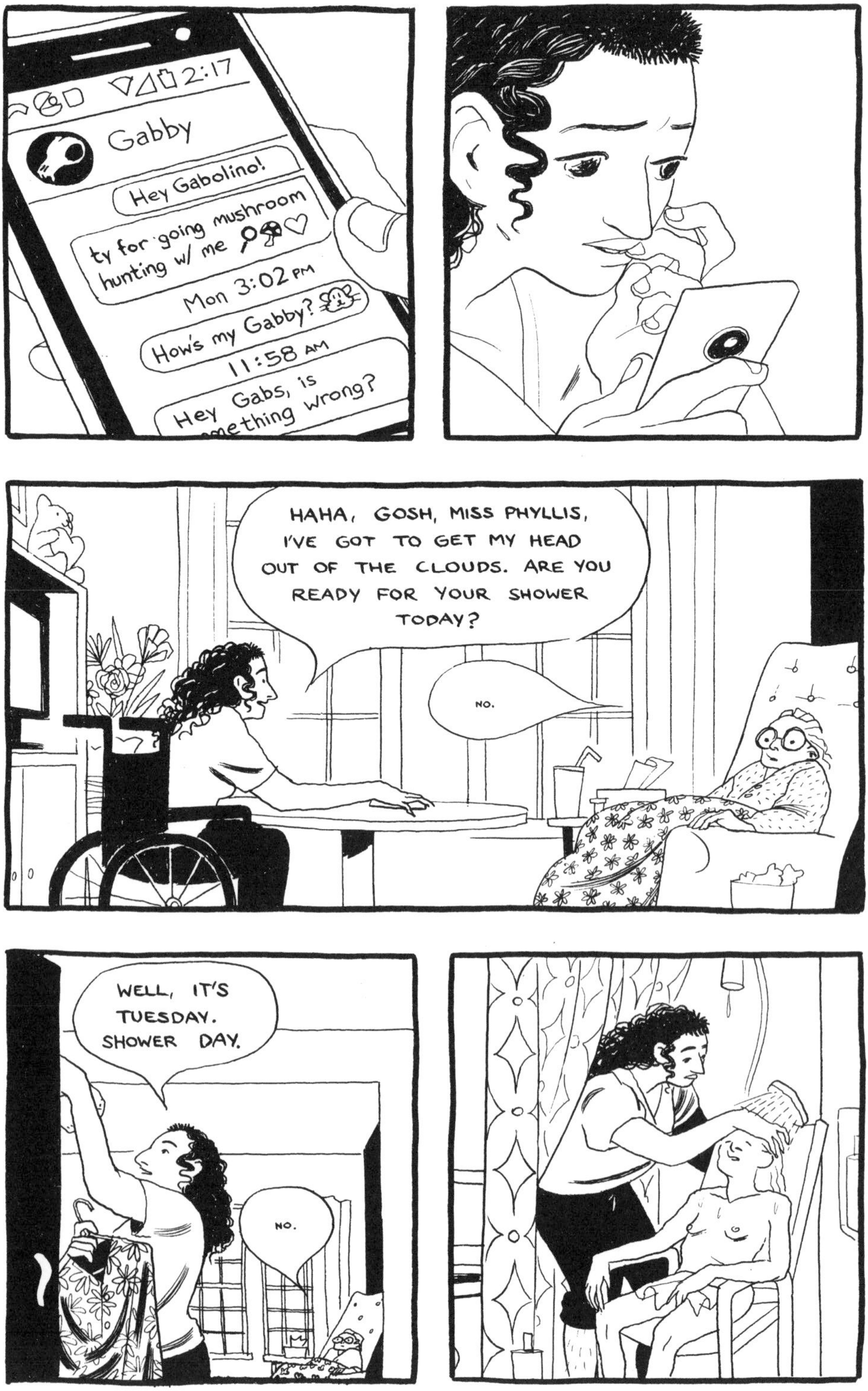
2:17
Gabby
Hey Gabolino!
ty for going mushroom hunting w/ me
Mon 3:02 PM
How's my Gabby?
11:58 AM
Hey Gabs, is something wrong?
HAHA, GOSH, MISS PHYLLIS, I'VE GOT TO GET MY HEAD OUT OF THE CLOUDS. ARE YOU READY FOR YOUR SHOWER TODAY?
NO.
WELL, IT'S TUESDAY. SHOWER DAY.
NO.

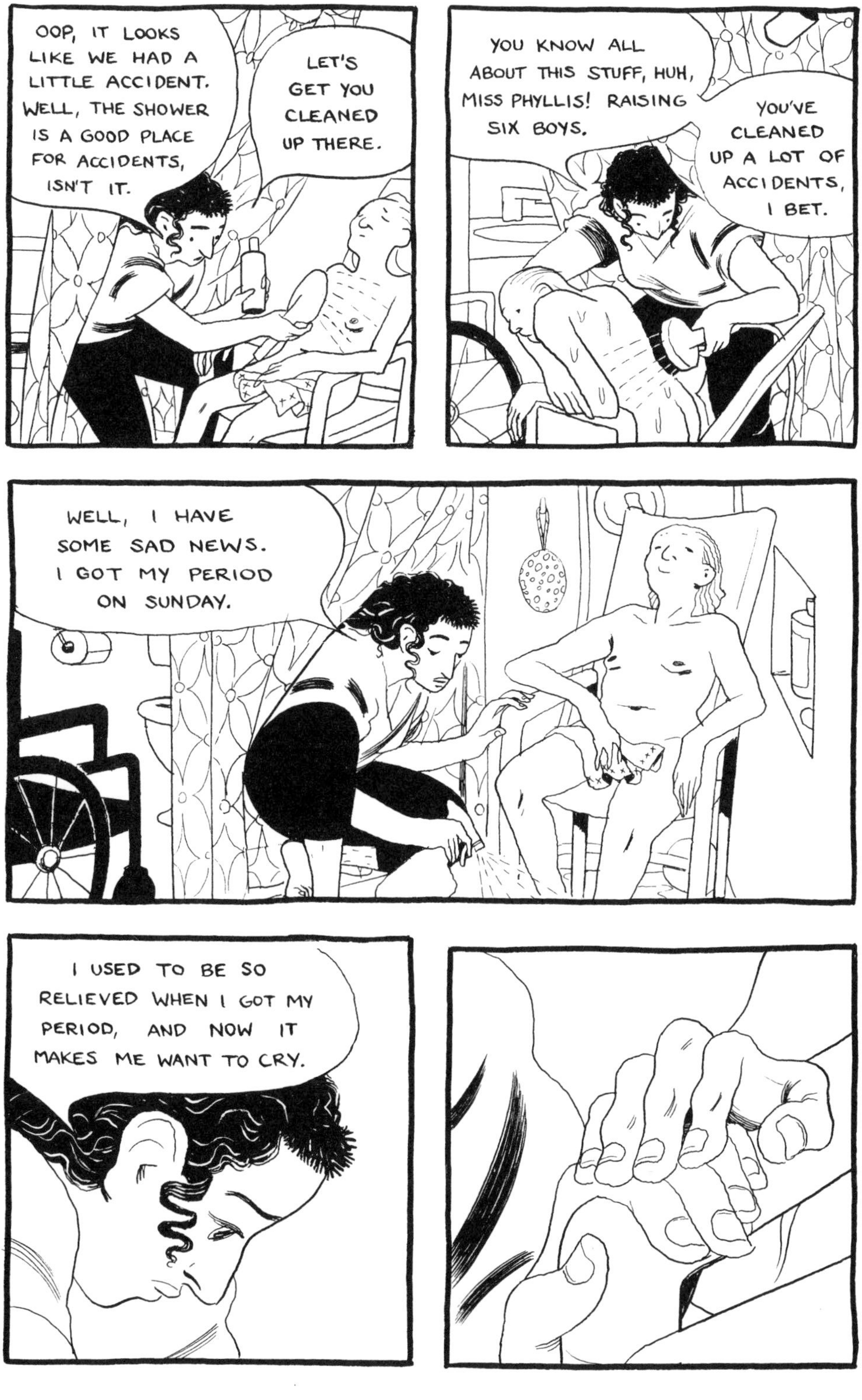
OOP, IT LOOKS LIKE WE HAD A LITTLE ACCIDENT. WELL, THE SHOWER IS A GOOD PLACE FOR ACCIDENTS, ISN'T IT.
LET'S GET YOU CLEANED UP THERE.
YOU KNOW ALL ABOUT THIS STUFF, HUH, MISS PHYLLIS! RAISING SIX BOYS.
YOU'VE CLEANED UP A LOT OF ACCIDENTS, I BET.
WELL, I HAVE SOME SAD NEWS. I GOT MY PERIOD ON SUNDAY.
I USED TO BE SO RELIEVED WHEN I GOT MY PERIOD, AND NOW IT MAKES ME WANT TO CRY.

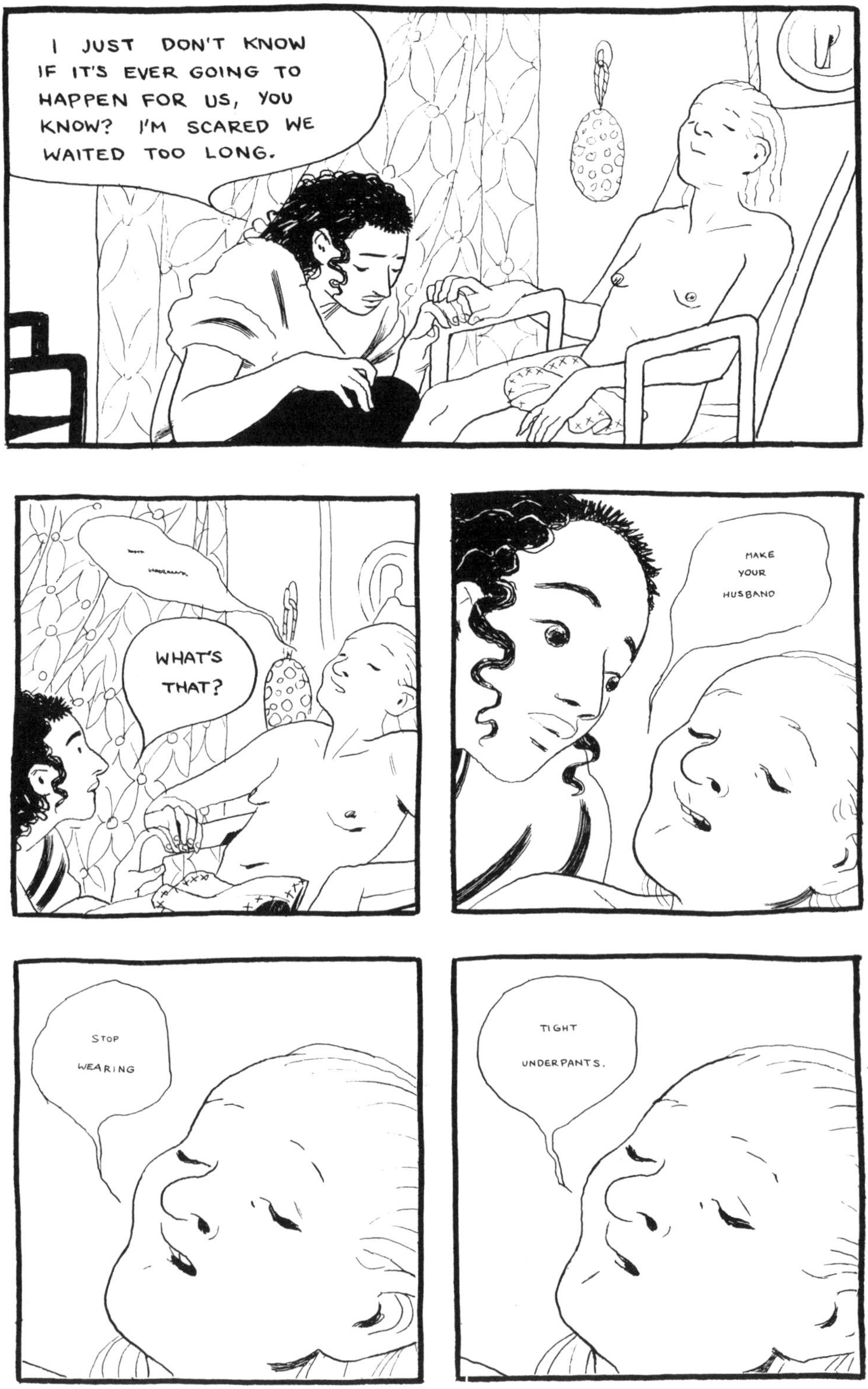
I JUST DON'T KNOW IF IT'S EVER GOING TO HAPPEN FOR US, YOU KNOW? I'M SCARED WE WAITED TOO LONG.
WHAT'S THAT?
MAKE YOUR HUSBAND
STOP WEARING
TIGHT UNDERPANTS.

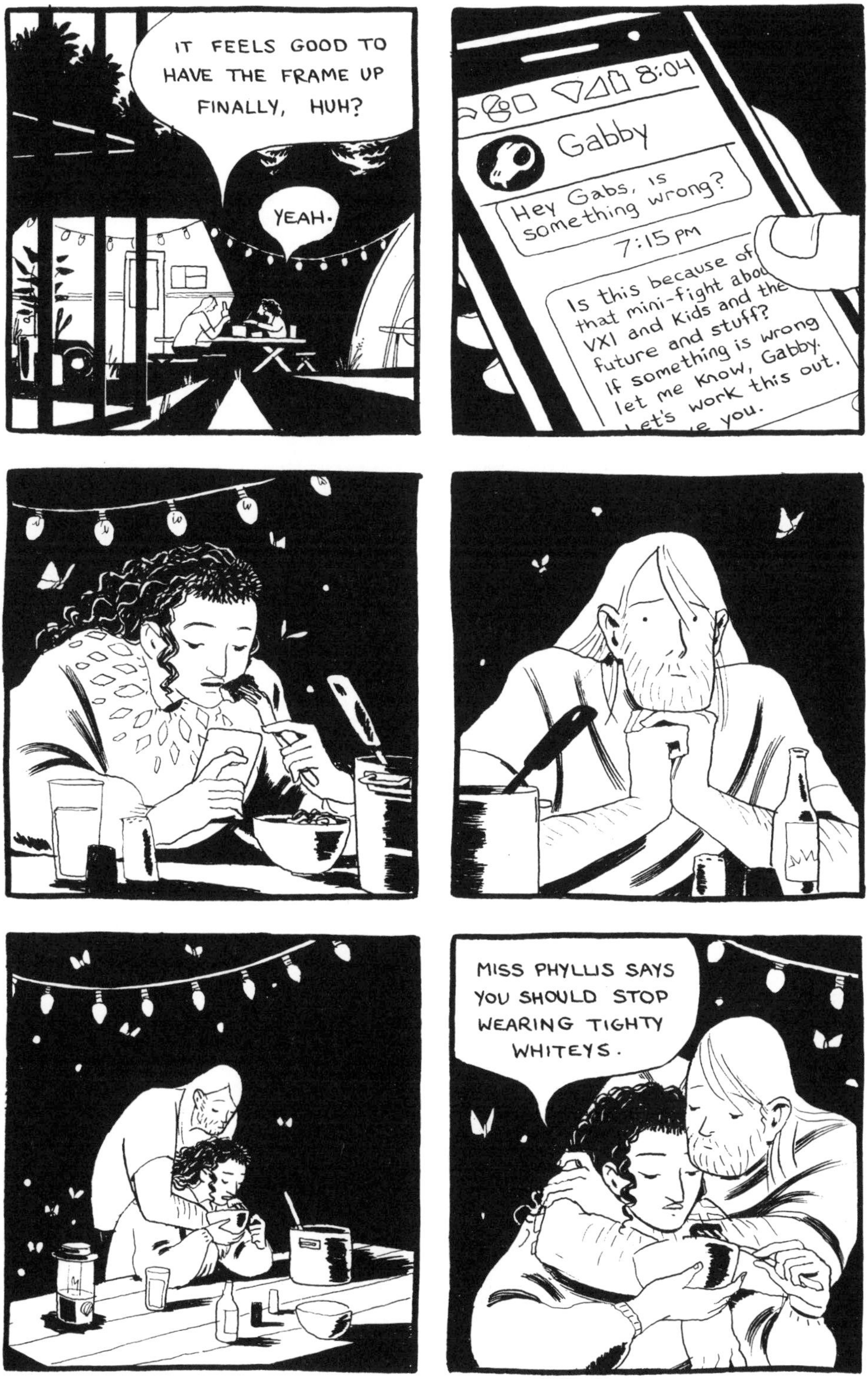
IT FEELS GOOD TO HAVE THE FRAME UP FINALLY, HUH?
YEAH.
8:04
Gabby
Hey Gabs, is something wrong?
7:15 PM
Is this because of that mini-fight abou[t] VXI and Kids and the future and stuff? If something is wrong let me know, Gabby. Let's work this out.
MISS PHYLLIS SAYS YOU SHOULD STOP WEARING TIGHTY WHITEYS.

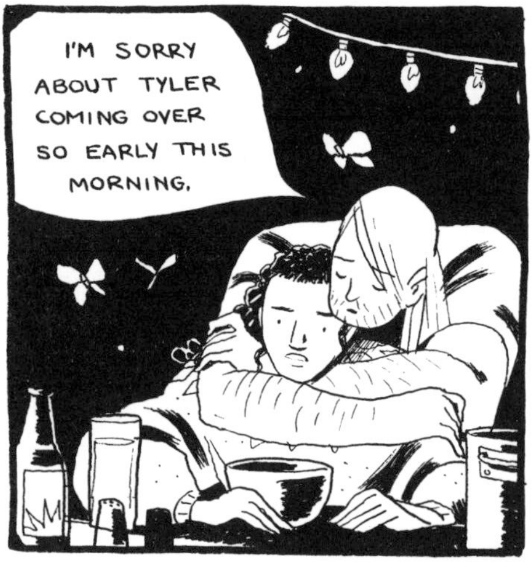
I'M SORRY ABOUT TYLER COMING OVER SO EARLY THIS MORNING.

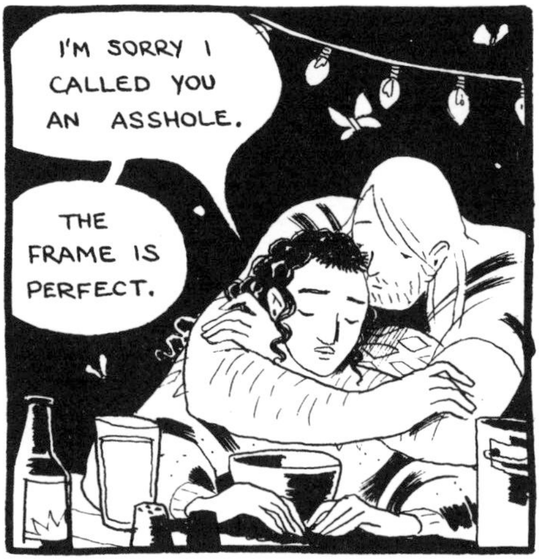
I'M SORRY I CALLED YOU AN ASSHOLE.
THE FRAME IS PERFECT.

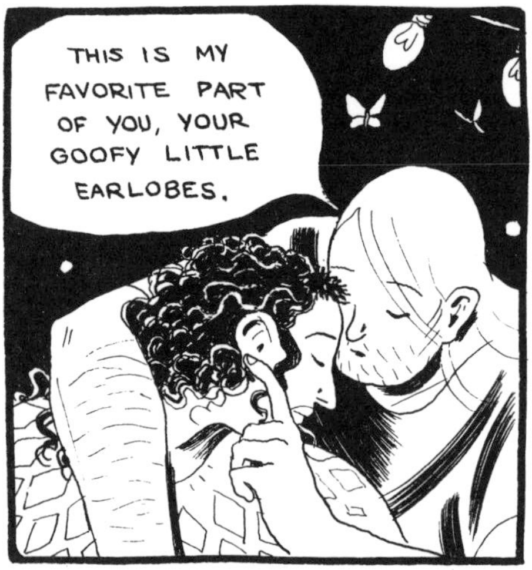
THIS IS MY FAVORITE PART OF YOU, YOUR GOOFY LITTLE EARLOBES.

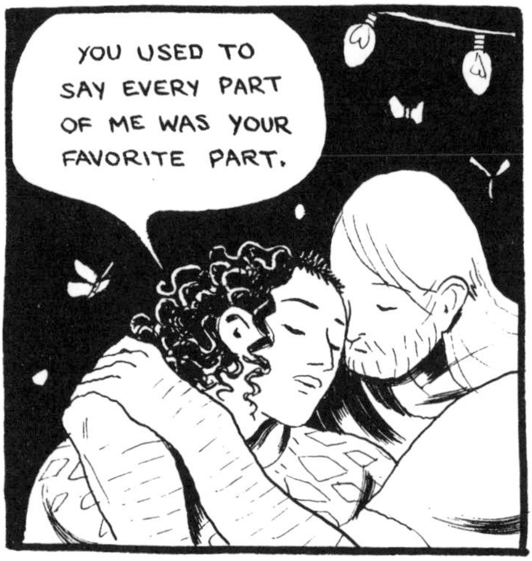
YOU USED TO SAY EVERY PART OF ME WAS YOUR FAVORITE PART.

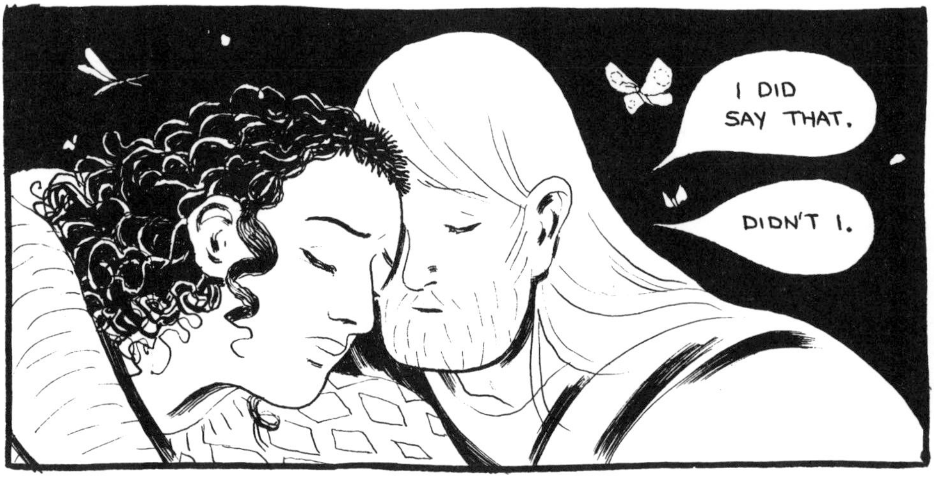
I DID SAY THAT.
DIDN'T I.

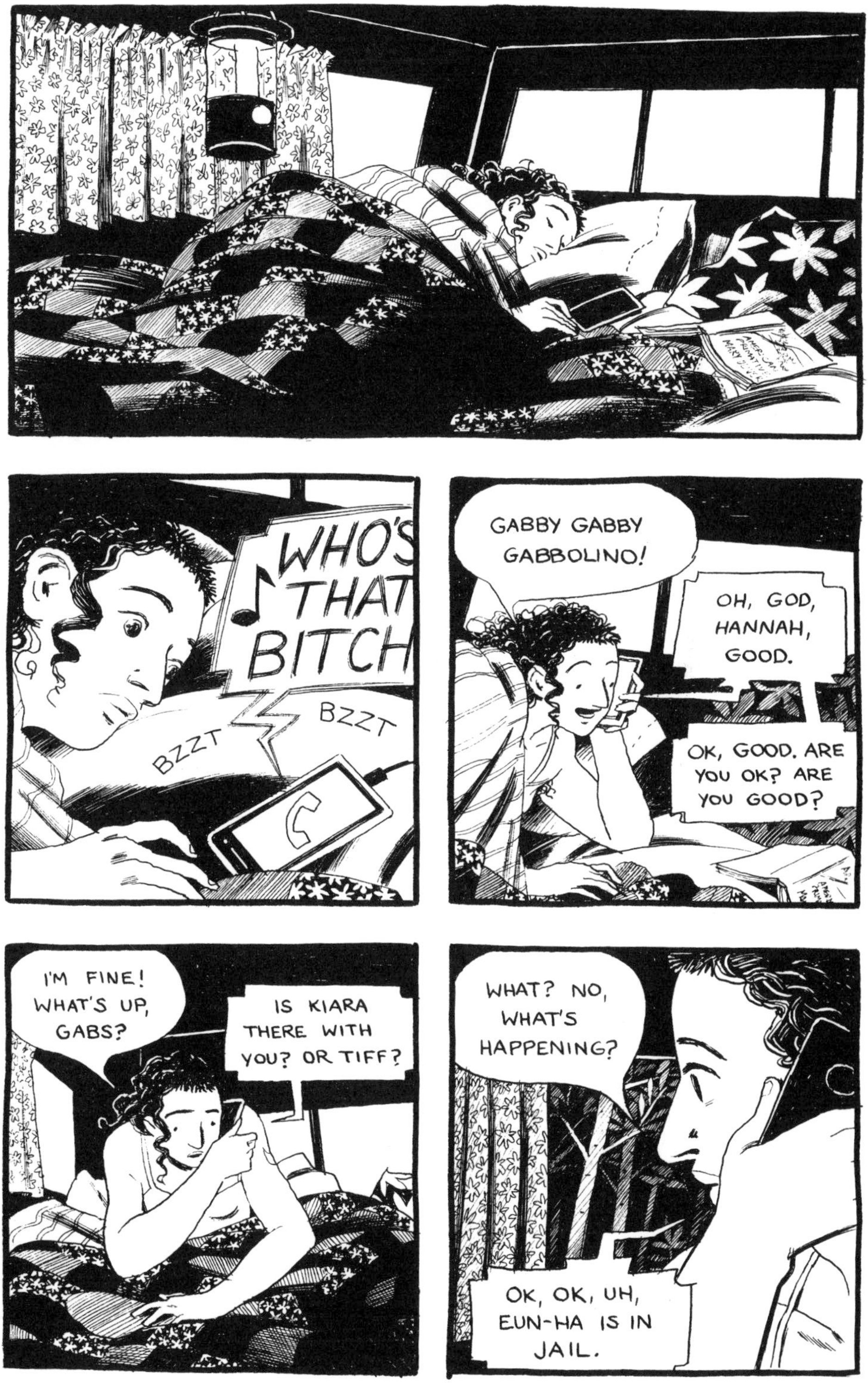
WHO'S THAT BITCH
BZZT
BZZT
GABBY GABBY GABBOLINO!
OH, GOD, HANNAH, GOOD.
OK, GOOD. ARE YOU OK? ARE YOU GOOD?
I'M FINE! WHAT'S UP, GABS?
IS KIARA THERE WITH YOU? OR TIFF?
WHAT? NO, WHAT'S HAPPENING?
OK, OK, UH, EUN-HA IS IN JAIL.

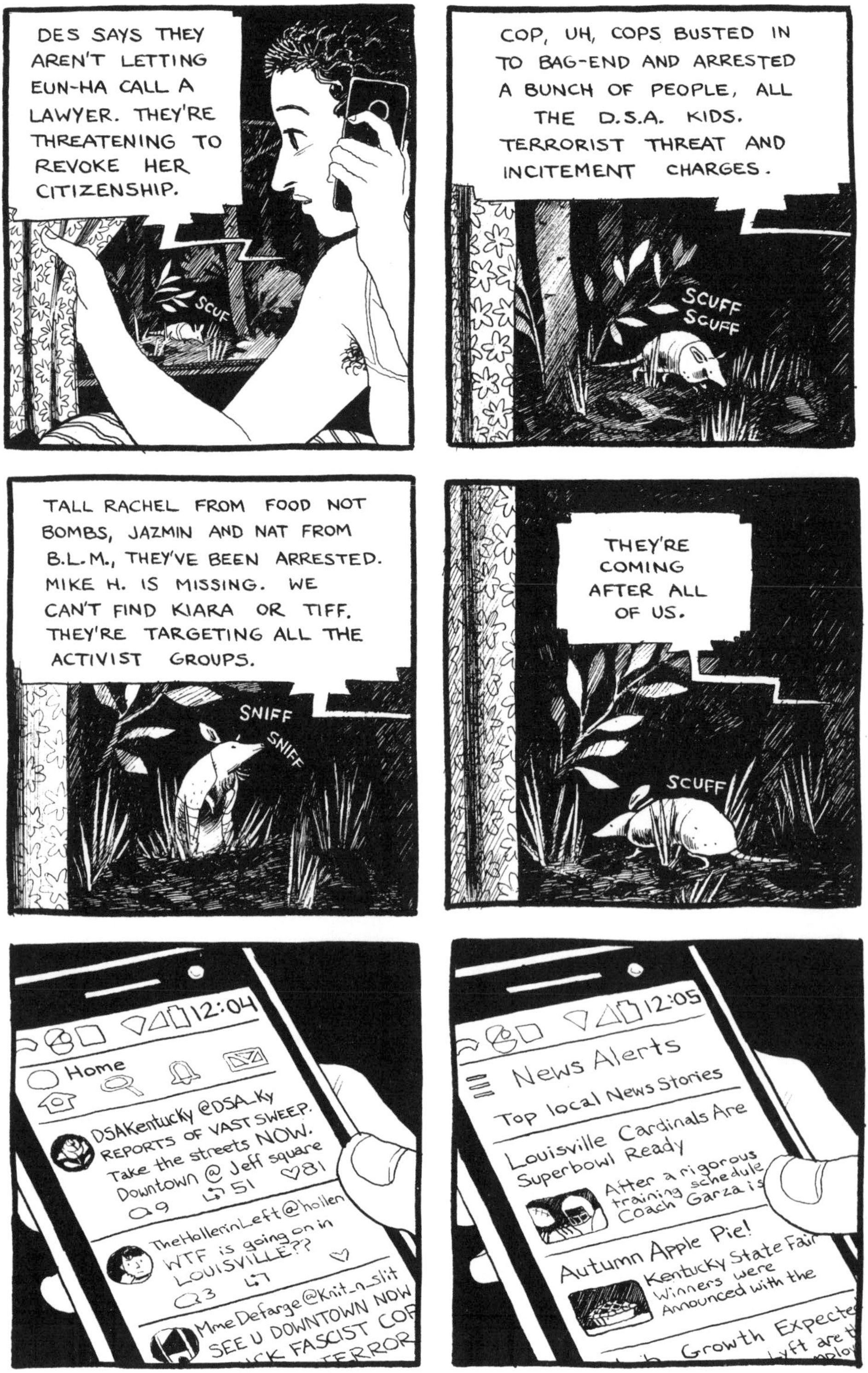
DES SAYS THEY AREN'T LETTING EUN-HA CALL A LAWYER. THEY'RE THREATENING TO REVOKE HER CITIZENSHIP.
SCUF
COP, UH, COPS BUSTED IN TO BAG-END AND ARRESTED A BUNCH OF PEOPLE, ALL THE D.S.A. KIDS. TERRORIST THREAT AND INCITEMENT CHARGES.
SCUFF SCUFF
TALL RACHEL FROM FOOD NOT BOMBS, JAZMIN AND NAT FROM B.L.M., THEY'VE BEEN ARRESTED. MIKE H. IS MISSING. WE CAN'T FIND KIARA OR TIFF. THEY'RE TARGETING ALL THE ACTIVIST GROUPS.
SNIFF SNIFF
THEY'RE COMING AFTER ALL OF US.
SCUFF
12:04
Home
DSAKentucky @DSA_Ky
REPORTS OF VAST SWEEP.
Take the streets NOW.
Downtown @ Jeff square
9 51 81
TheHollerinLeft @hollen
WTF is going on in LOUISVILLE??
3 7
Mme Defarge @Knit_n_slit
SEE U DOWNTOWN NOW
FASCIST
12:05
News Alerts
Top local News Stories
Louisville Cardinals Are Superbowl Ready
After a rigorous training schedule Coach Garza
Autumn Apple Pie!
Kentucky State Fair Winners were Announced with the
Growth

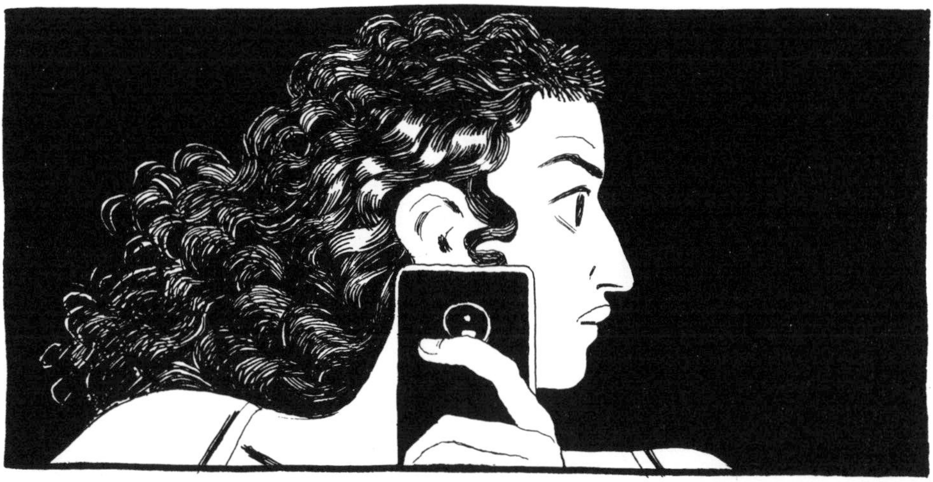

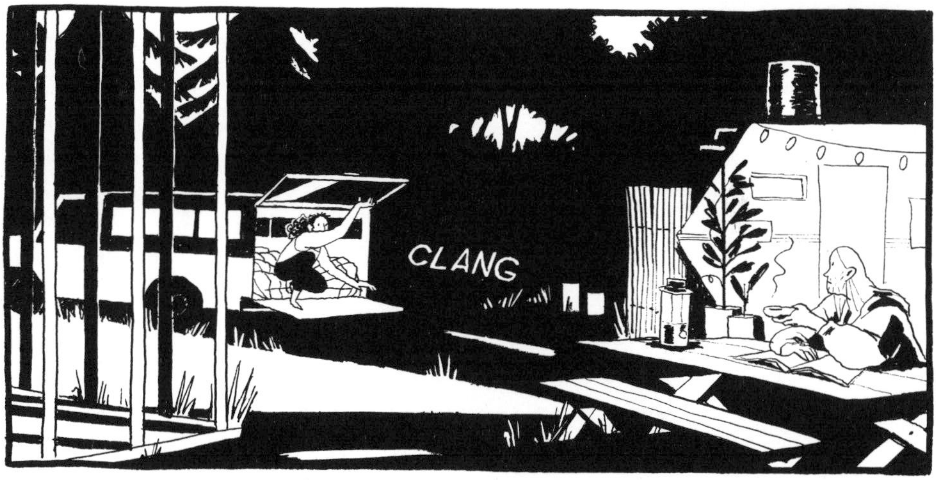
CLANG

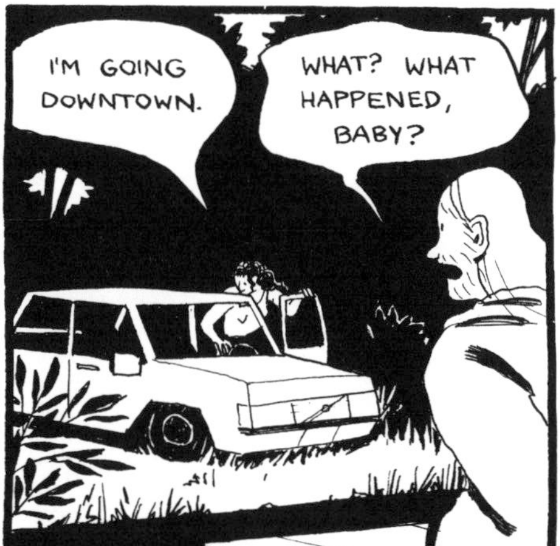
I'M GOING DOWNTOWN.
WHAT? WHAT HAPPENED, BABY?

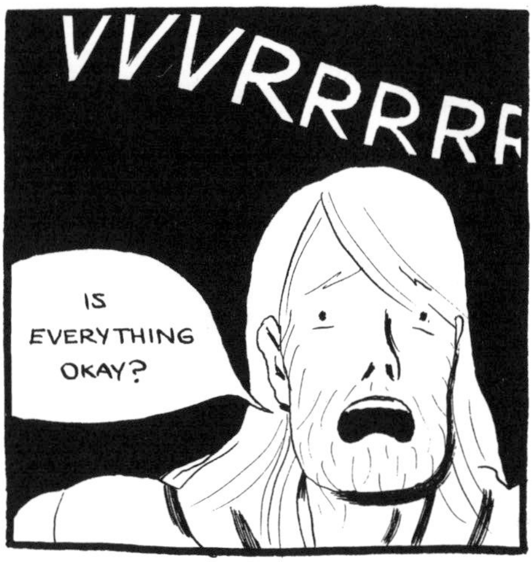
VVVRRRRRR
IS EVERYTHING OKAY?

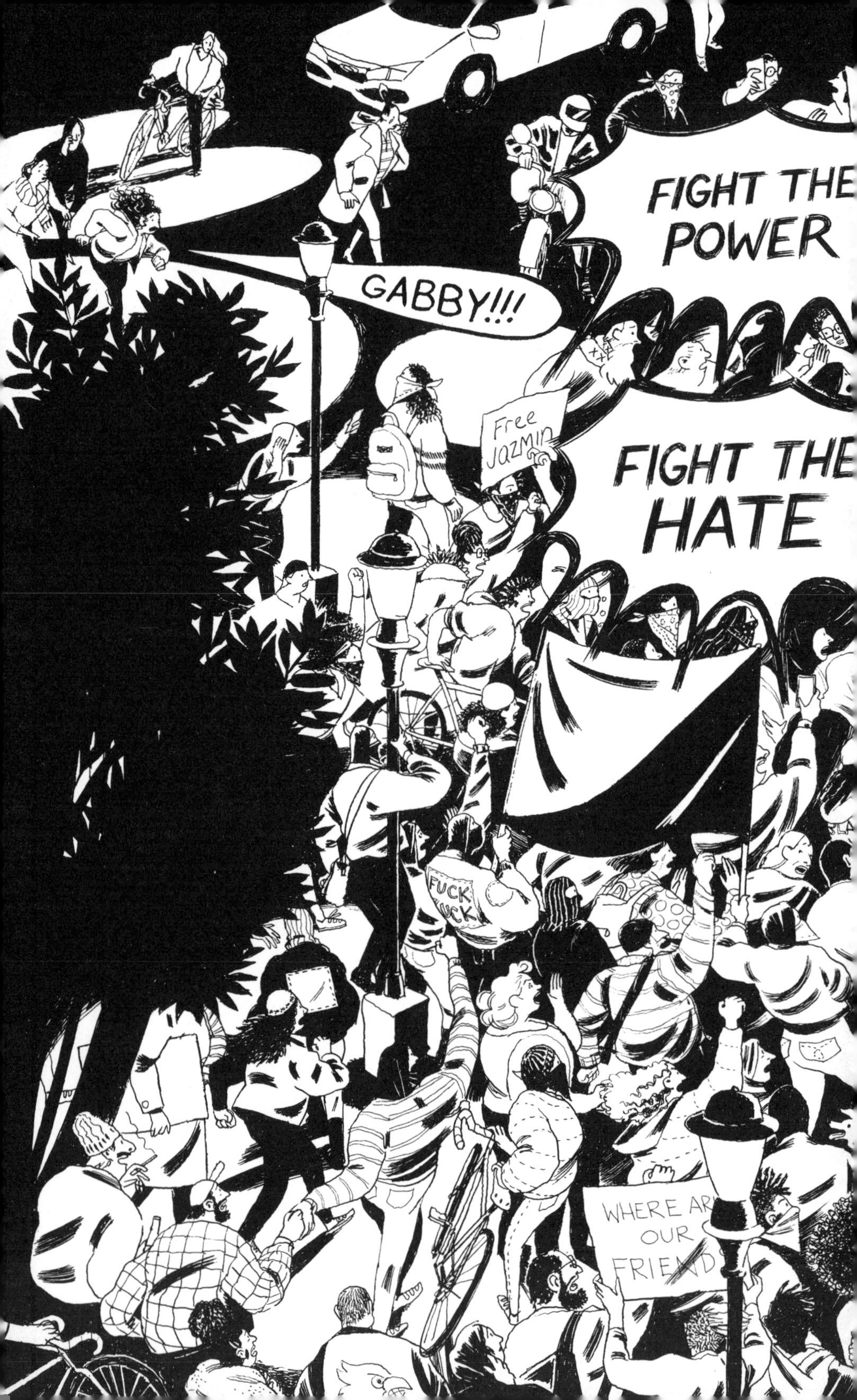
GABBY!!!
FIGHT THE POWER
Free JAZMIN
FIGHT THE HATE
FUCK
FUCK
WHERE AR OUR FRIENDS

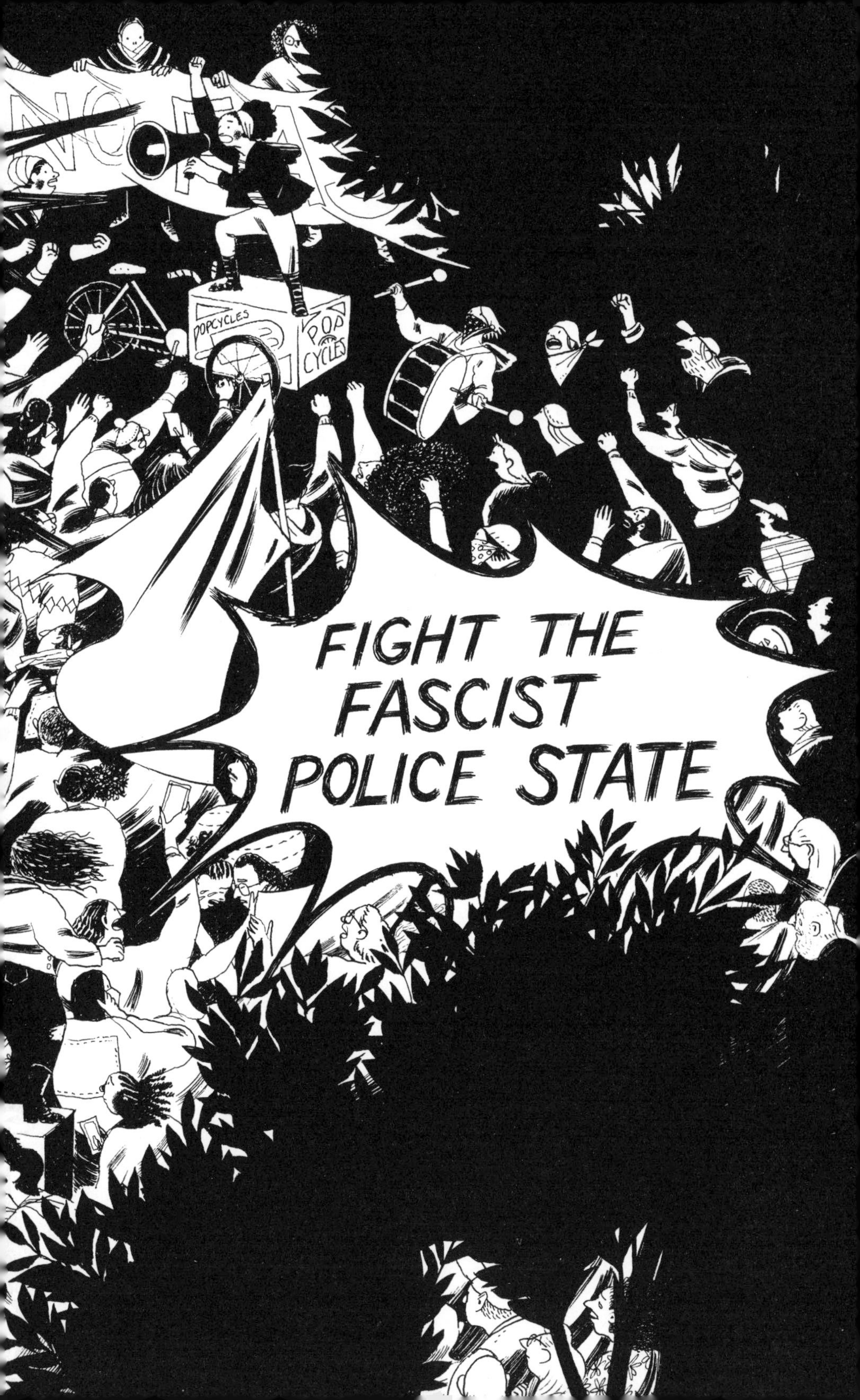
FIGHT THE FASCIST POLICE STATE
POPCYCLES
POP CYCLES

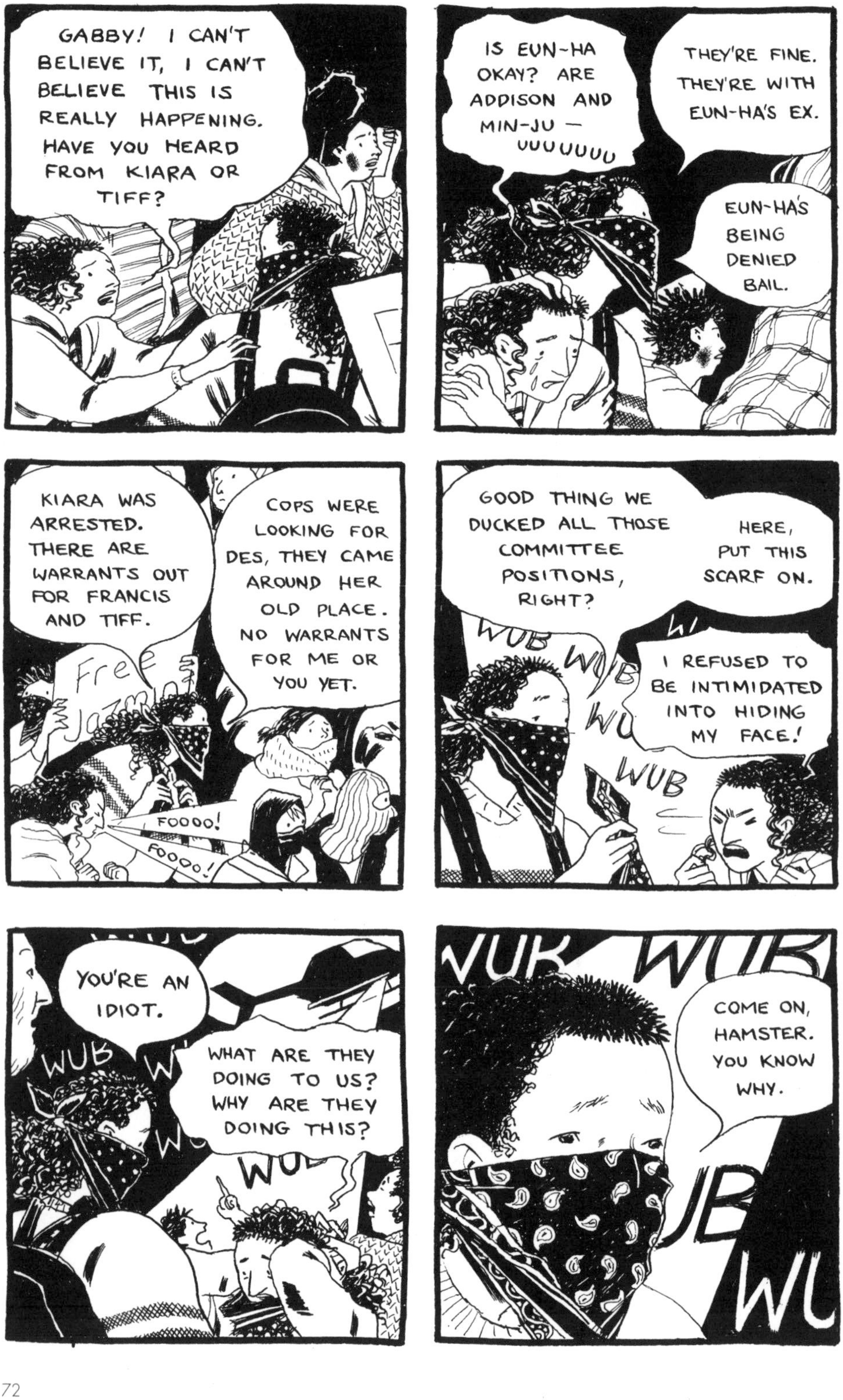
GABBY! I CAN'T BELIEVE IT, I CAN'T BELIEVE THIS IS REALLY HAPPENING. HAVE YOU HEARD FROM KIARA OR TIFF?
IS EUN-HA OKAY? ARE ADDISON AND MIN-JU — UUUUUUU
THEY'RE FINE. THEY'RE WITH EUN-HA'S EX.
EUN-HA'S BEING DENIED BAIL.
KIARA WAS ARRESTED. THERE ARE WARRANTS OUT FOR FRANCIS AND TIFF.
COPS WERE LOOKING FOR DES, THEY CAME AROUND HER OLD PLACE. NO WARRANTS FOR ME OR YOU YET.
Free
FOOOO!
FOOOO!
GOOD THING WE DUCKED ALL THOSE COMMITTEE POSITIONS, RIGHT?
HERE, PUT THIS SCARF ON.
WUB
WUB
I REFUSED TO BE INTIMIDATED INTO HIDING MY FACE!
WUB
YOU'RE AN IDIOT.
WUB
WHAT ARE THEY DOING TO US? WHY ARE THEY DOING THIS?
WUB
COME ON, HAMSTER. YOU KNOW WHY.

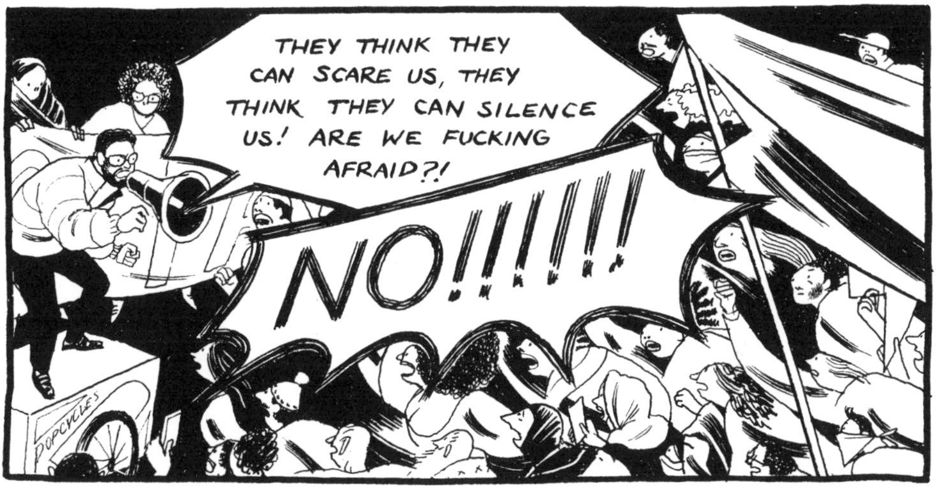
THEY THINK THEY CAN SCARE US, THEY THINK THEY CAN SILENCE US! ARE WE FUCKING AFRAID?!
NO!!!!!!!
POPCYCLES

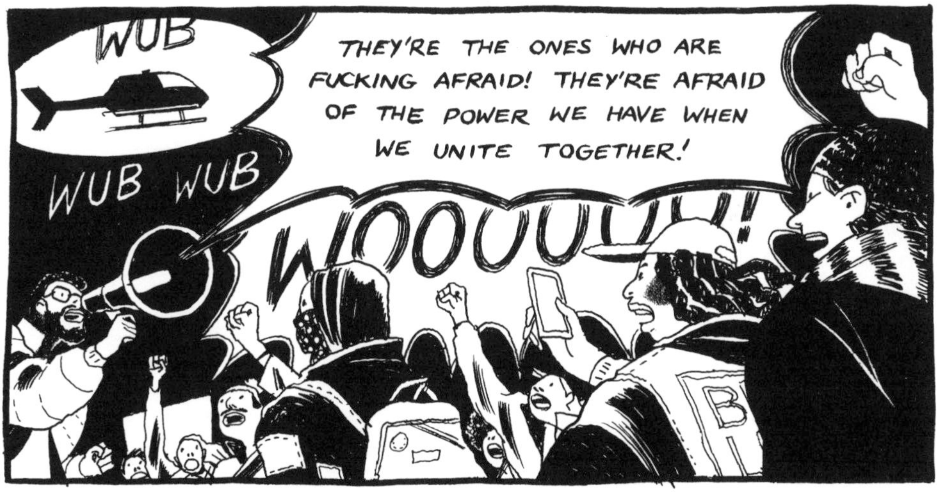
WUB
WUB WUB
THEY'RE THE ONES WHO ARE FUCKING AFRAID! THEY'RE AFRAID OF THE POWER WE HAVE WHEN WE UNITE TOGETHER!

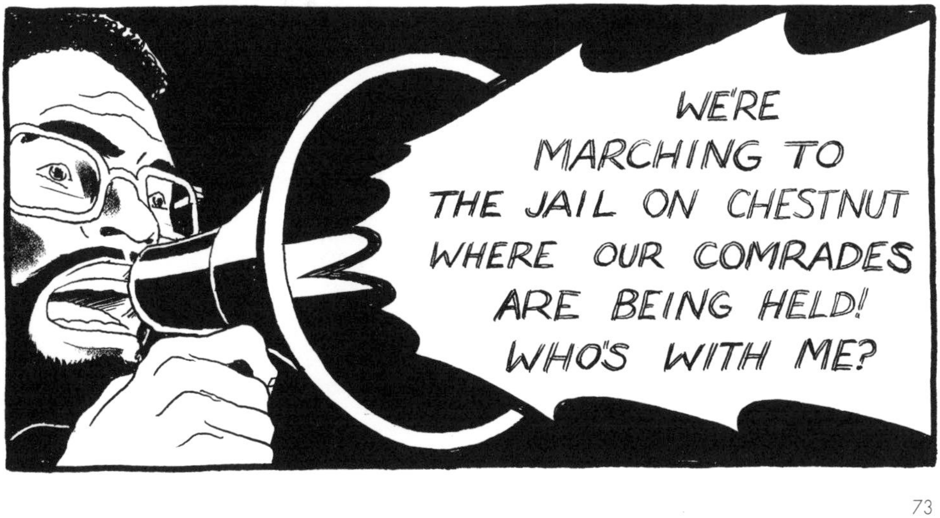
WE'RE MARCHING TO THE JAIL ON CHESTNUT WHERE OUR COMRADES ARE BEING HELD! WHO'S WITH ME?

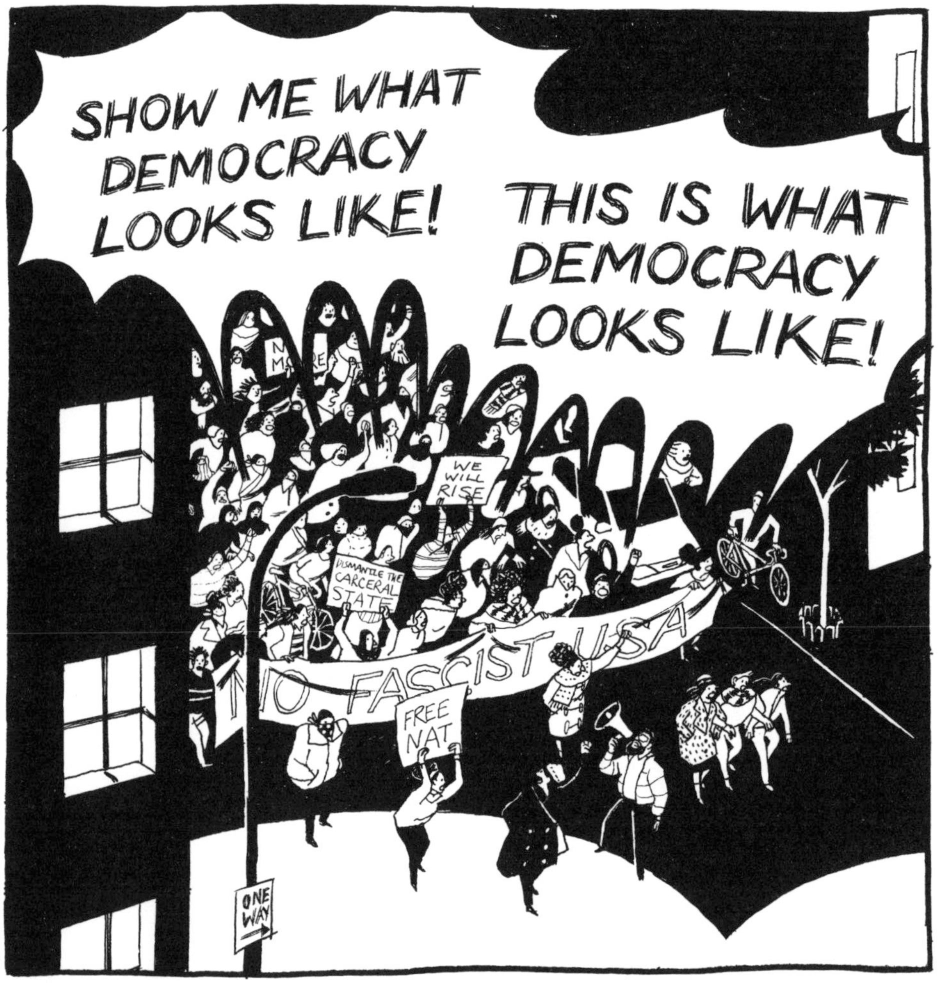
SHOW ME WHAT DEMOCRACY LOOKS LIKE!
THIS IS WHAT DEMOCRACY LOOKS LIKE!
WE WILL RISE
DISMANTLE THE CARCERAL STATE
NO FASCIST USA
FREE NAT
ONE WAY

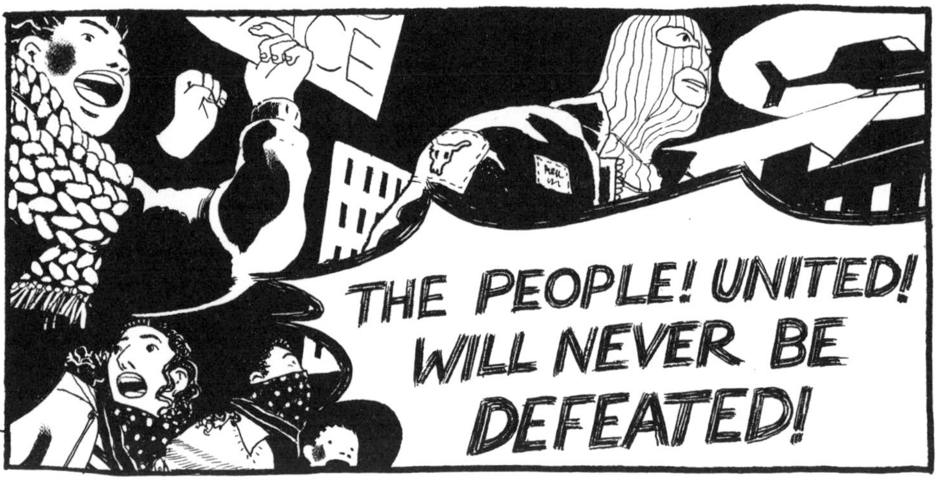
THE PEOPLE! UNITED! WILL NEVER BE DEFEATED!

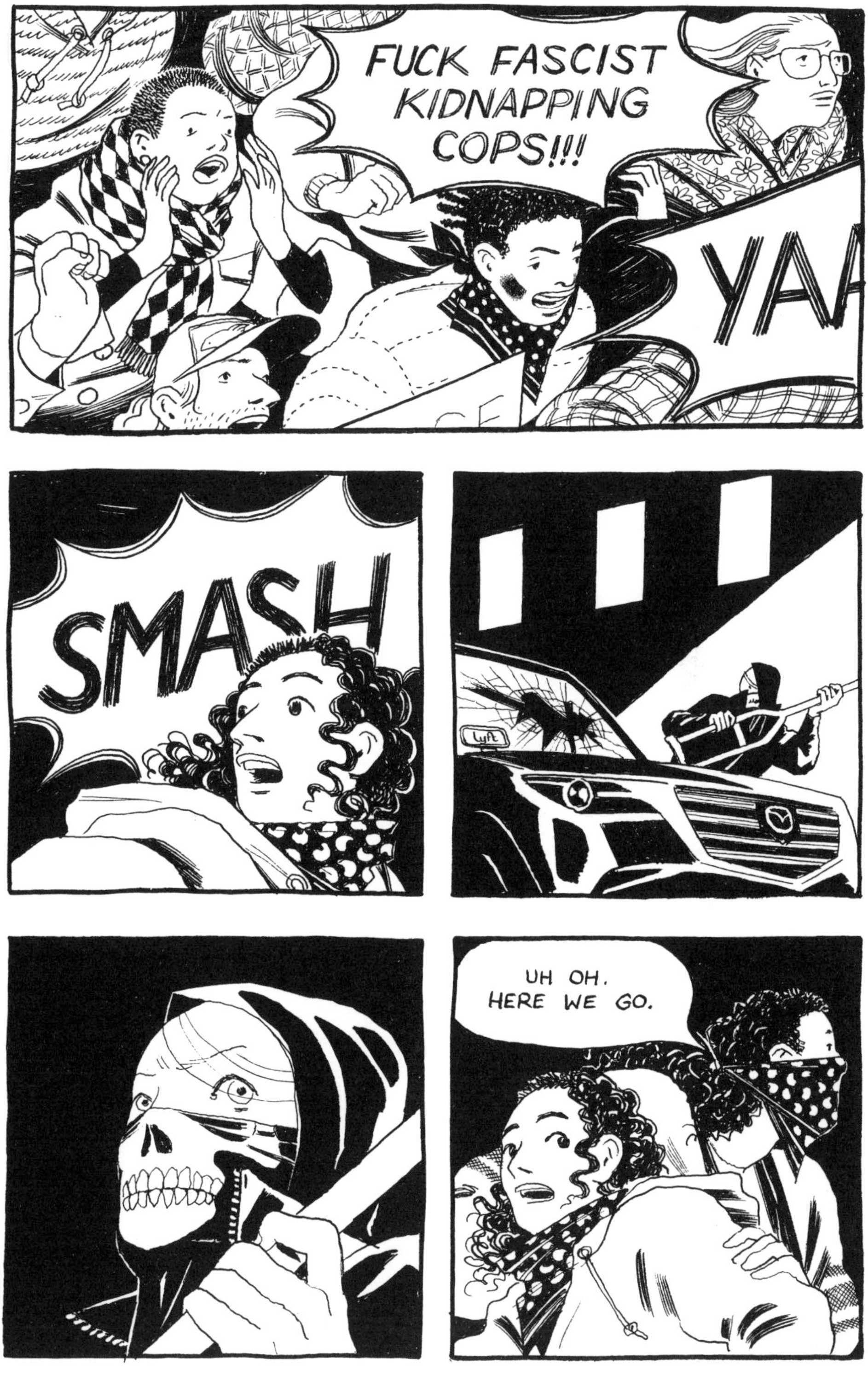
FUCK FASCIST KIDNAPPING COPS!!!
YAA
SMASH
Lyft
UH OH. HERE WE GO.

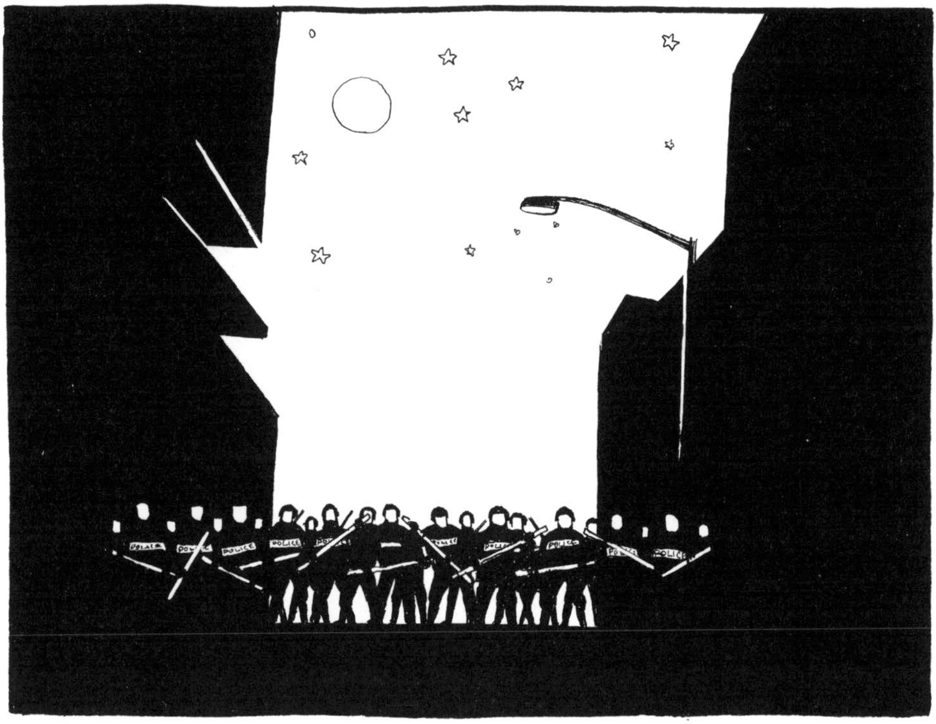
POLICE

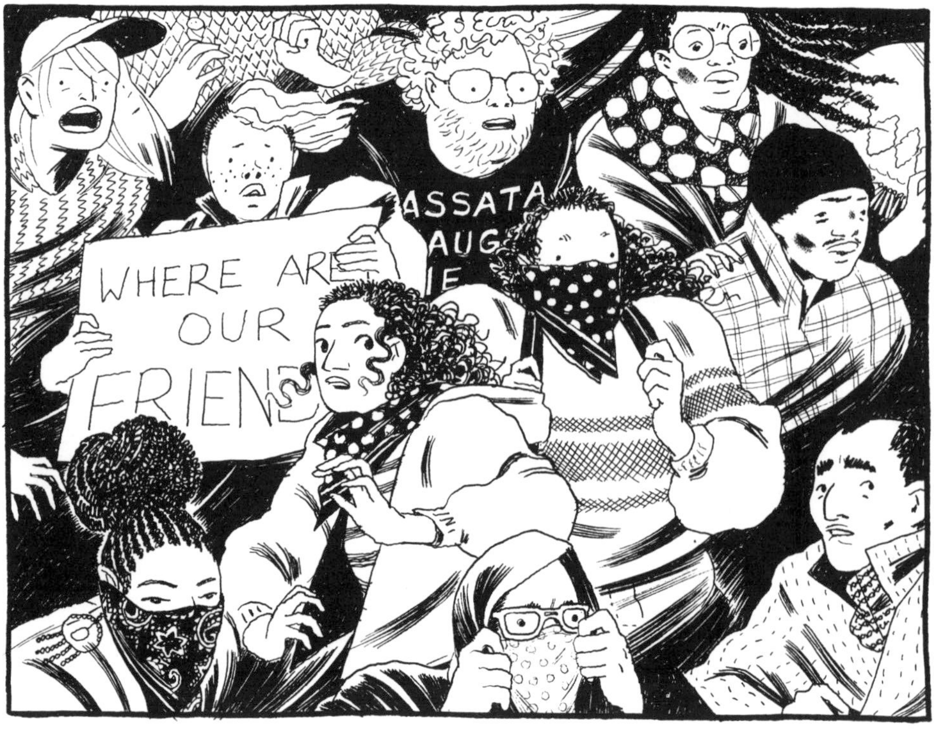
WHERE ARE
OUR
FRIEN
ASSATA
AUG

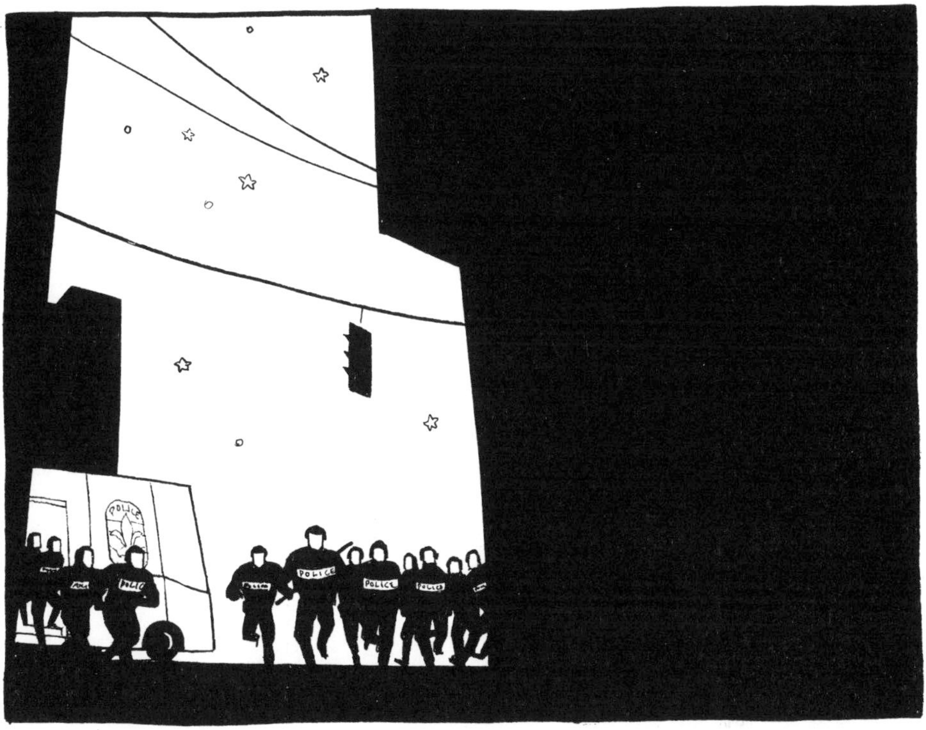
POLICE
POLICE
POLICE
POLICE

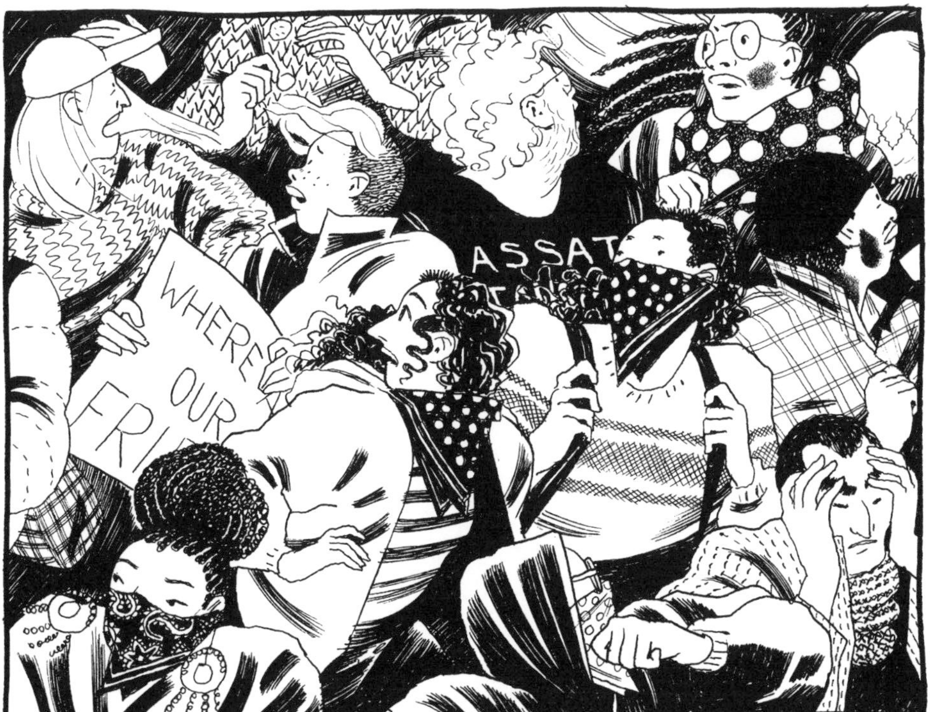
WHERE
OUR
FRI
ASSAT

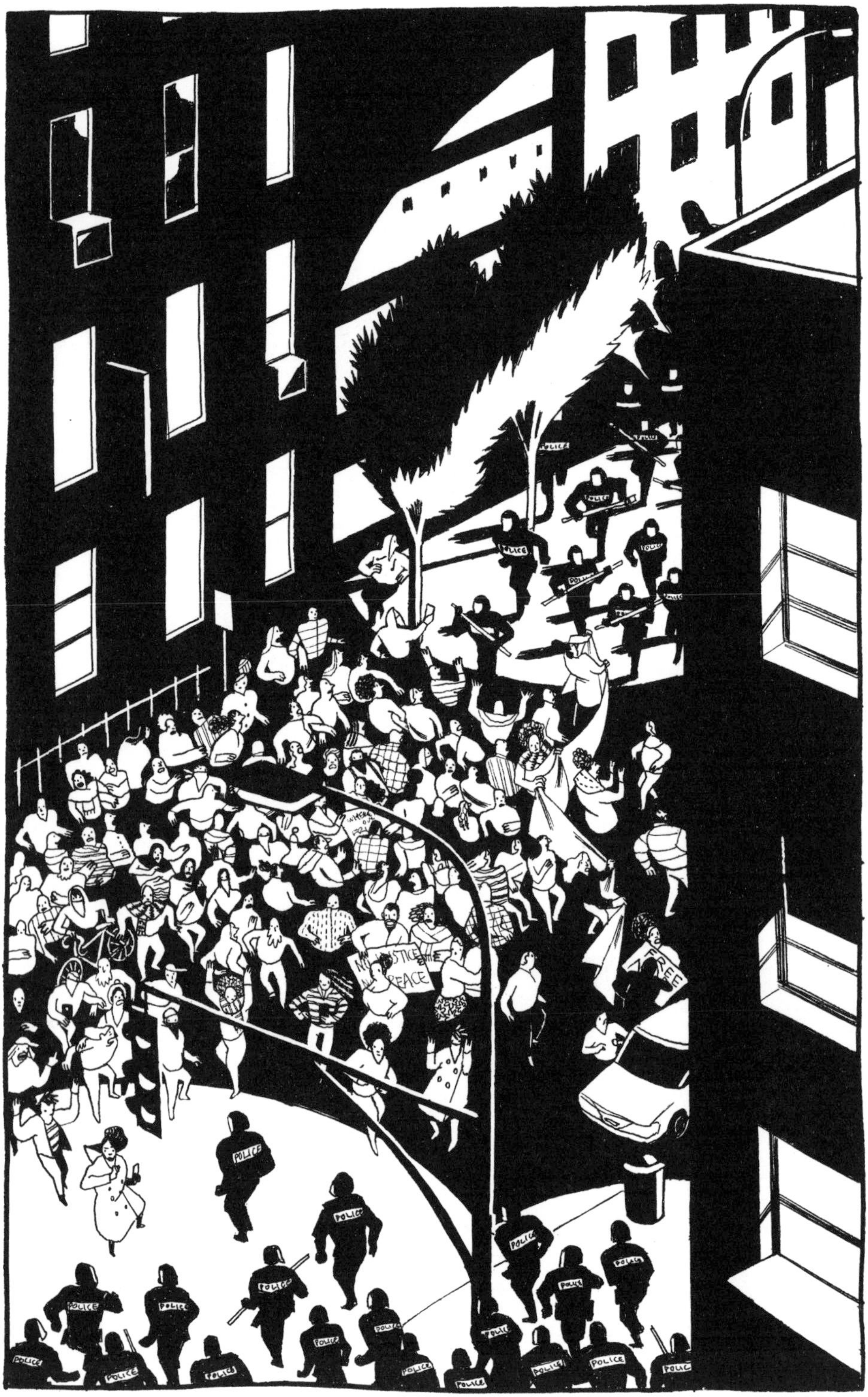
POLICE
STICE
PEACE
FREE

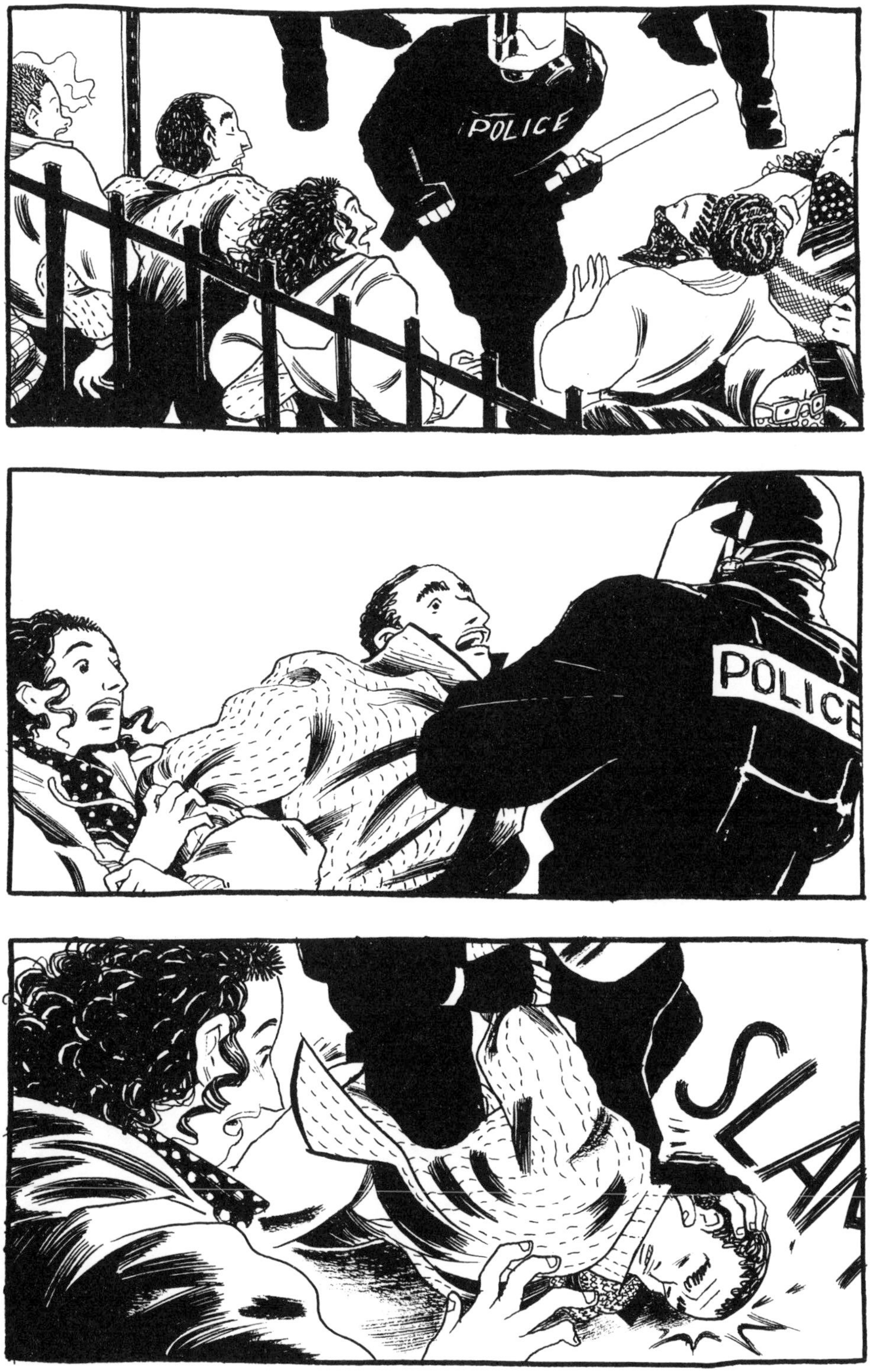
POLICE
POLICE
SLA

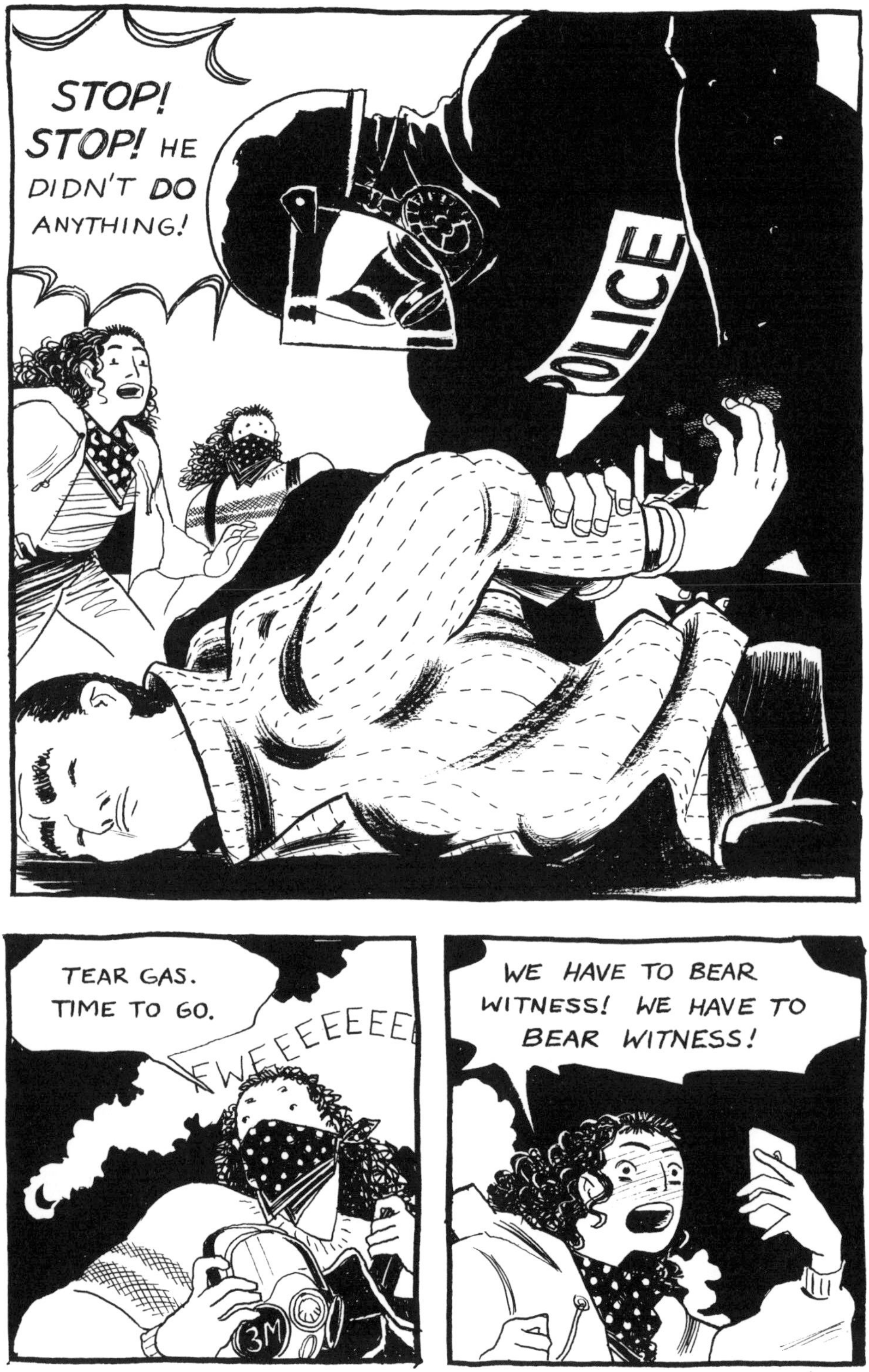
STOP! STOP! HE DIDN'T DO ANYTHING!
TEAR GAS. TIME TO GO.
FWEEEEEEEE
3M
WE HAVE TO BEAR WITNESS! WE HAVE TO BEAR WITNESS!

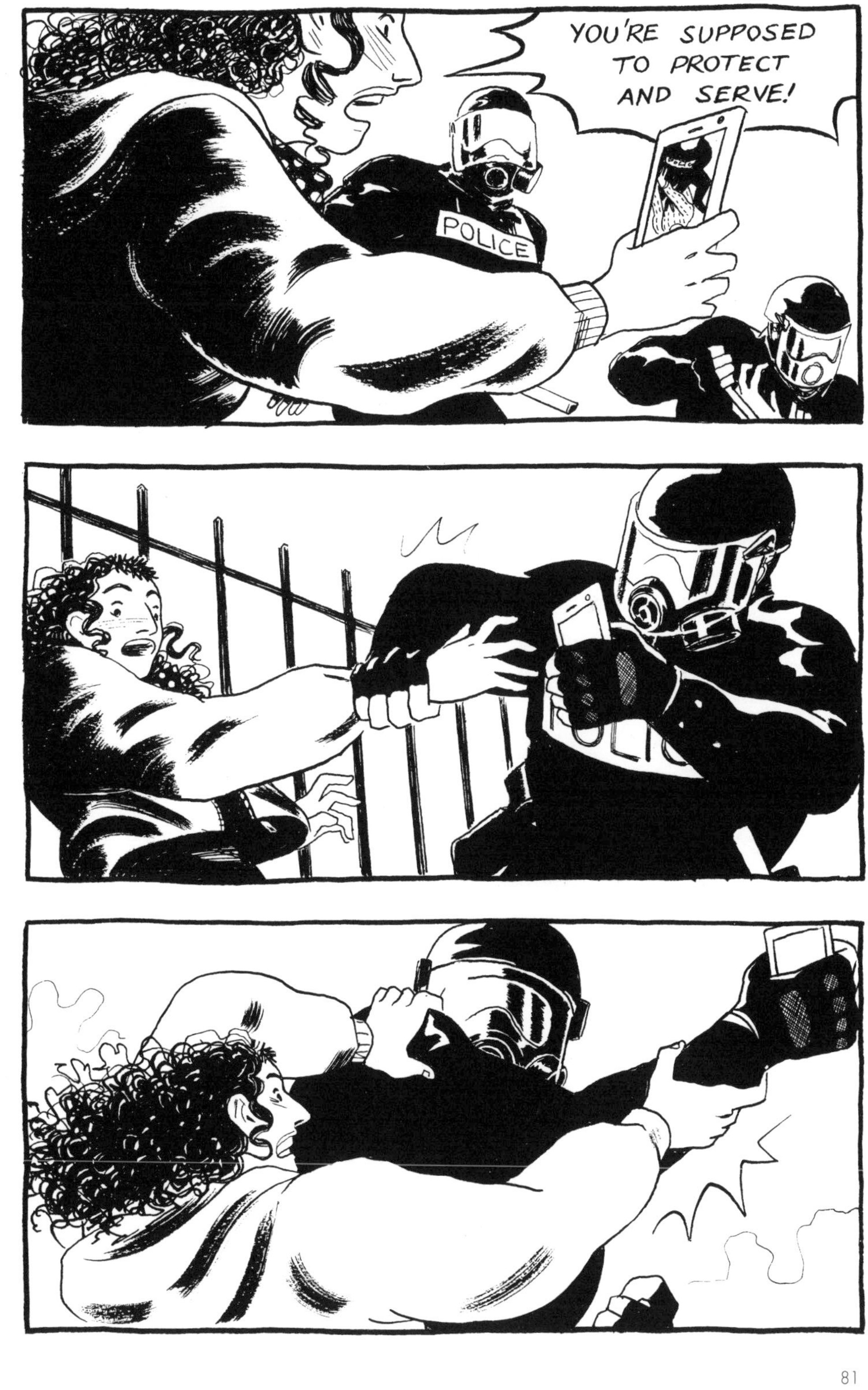
YOU'RE SUPPOSED TO PROTECT AND SERVE!
POLICE

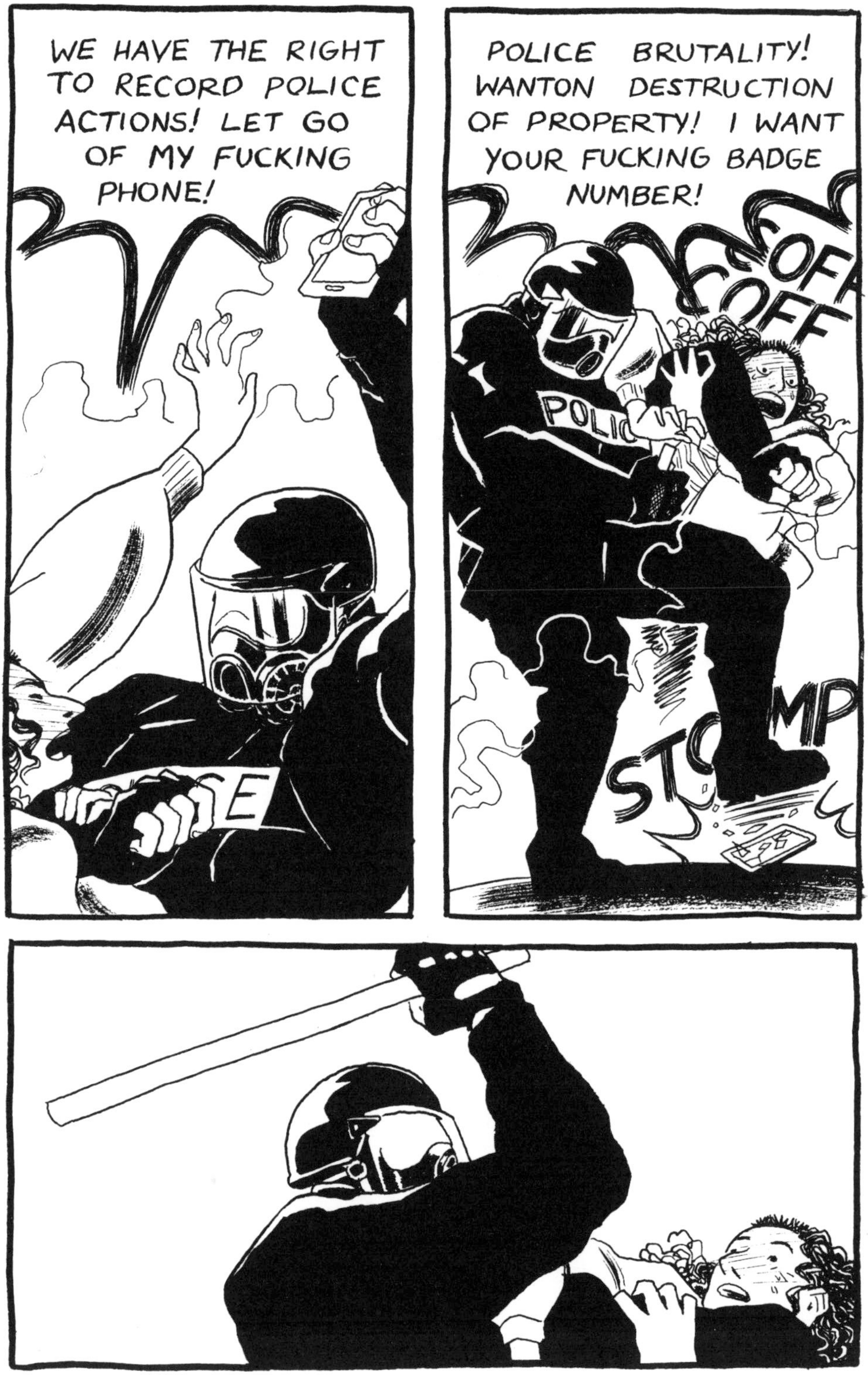
WE HAVE THE RIGHT TO RECORD POLICE ACTIONS! LET GO OF MY FUCKING PHONE!
POLICE BRUTALITY! WANTON DESTRUCTION OF PROPERTY! I WANT YOUR FUCKING BADGE NUMBER!
COFF
COFF
STOMP

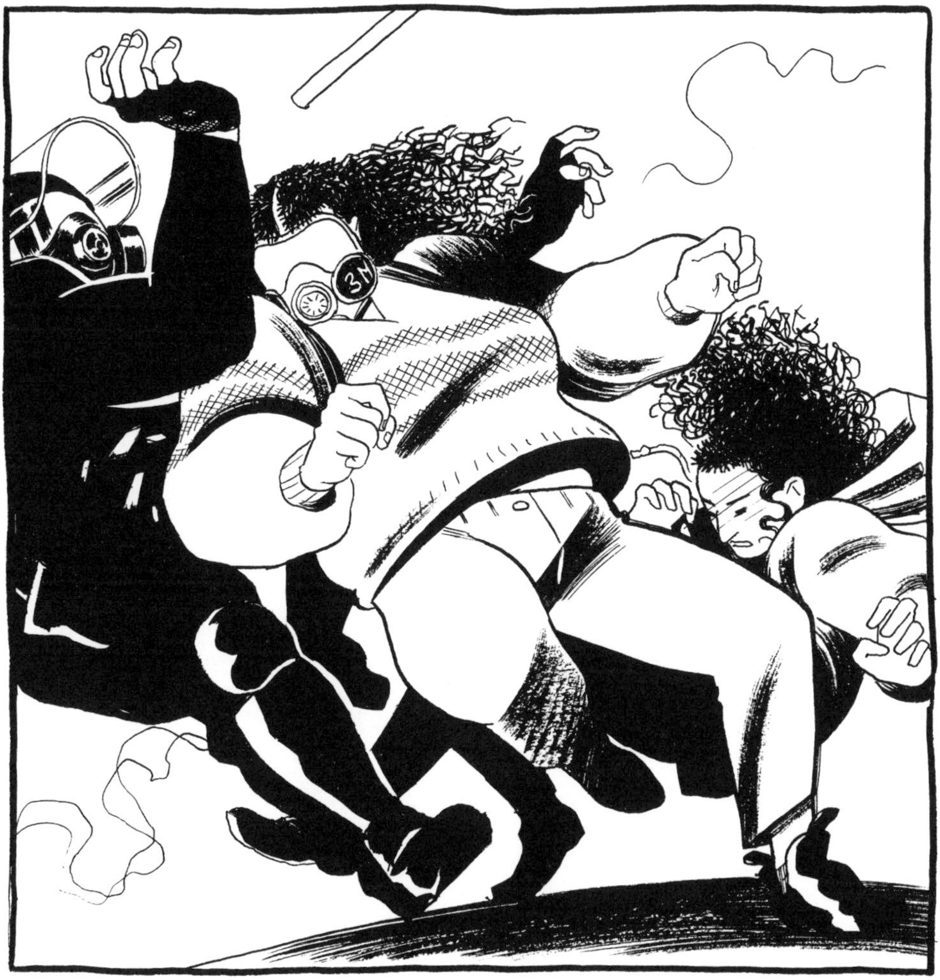
3M

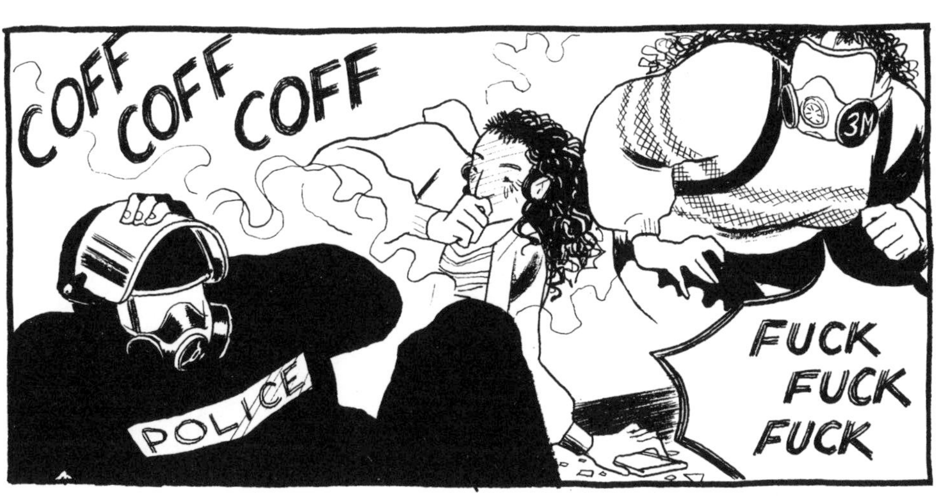
COFF
COFF
COFF
3M
POLICE
FUCK
FUCK
FUCK

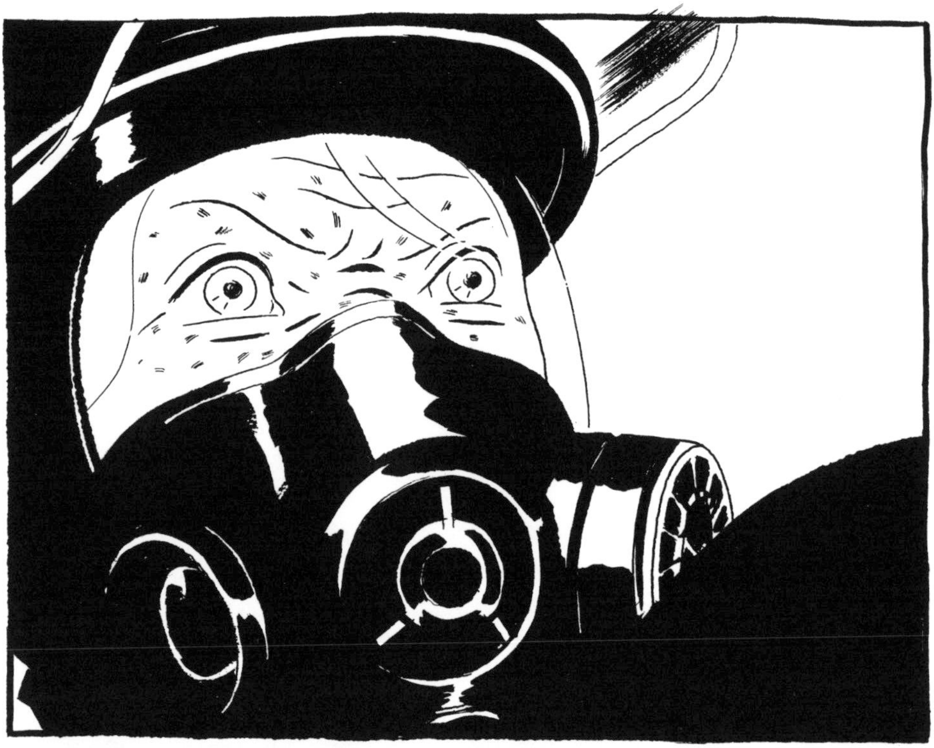

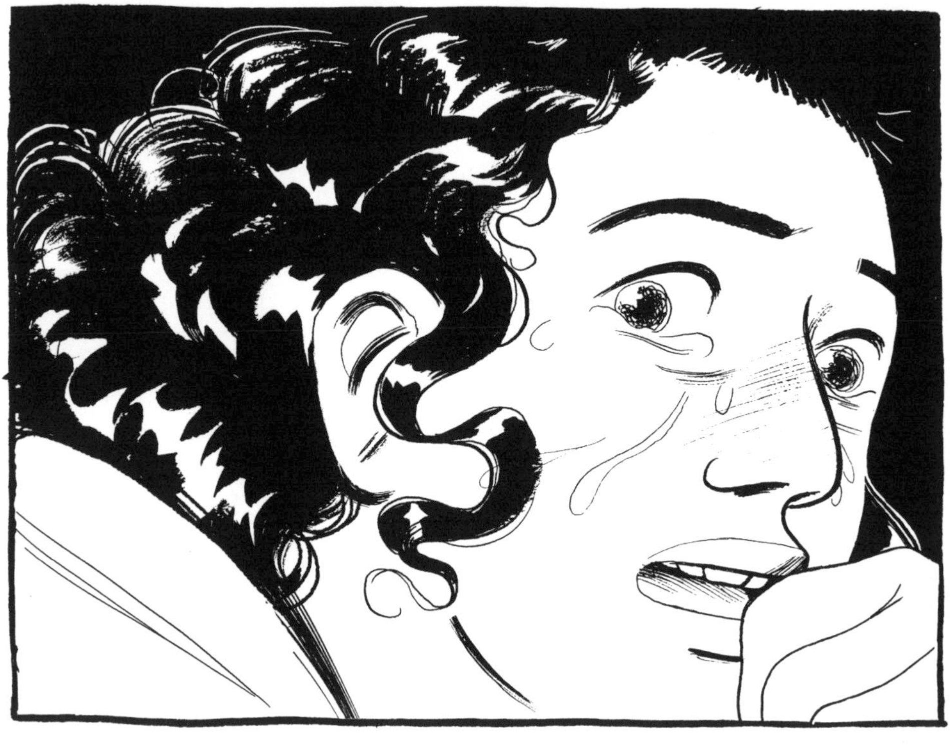

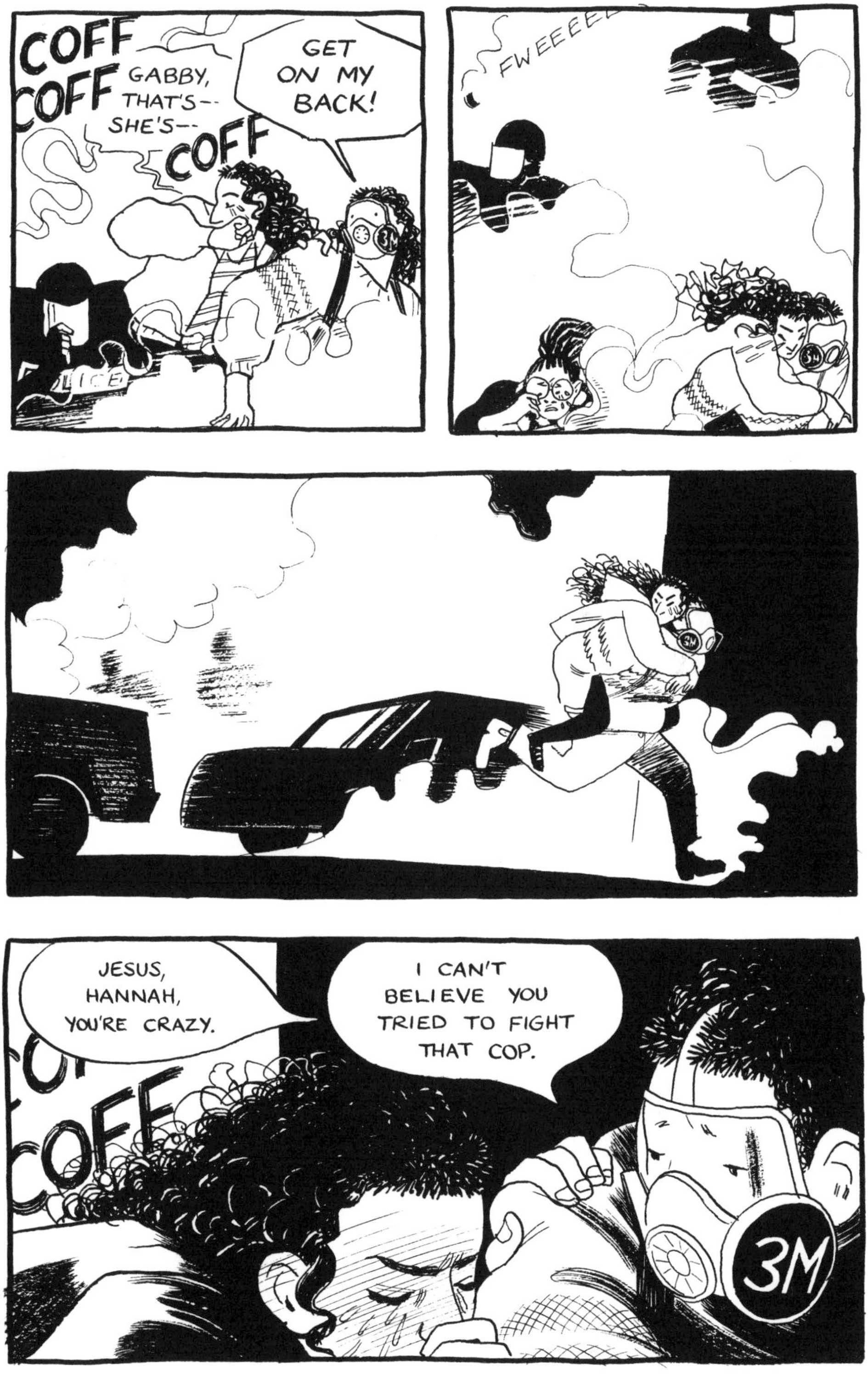
COFF COFF
GABBY, THAT'S-- SHE'S--
COFF
GET ON MY BACK!
FWEEEEE
COFF
JESUS, HANNAH, YOU'RE CRAZY.
I CAN'T BELIEVE YOU TRIED TO FIGHT THAT COP.

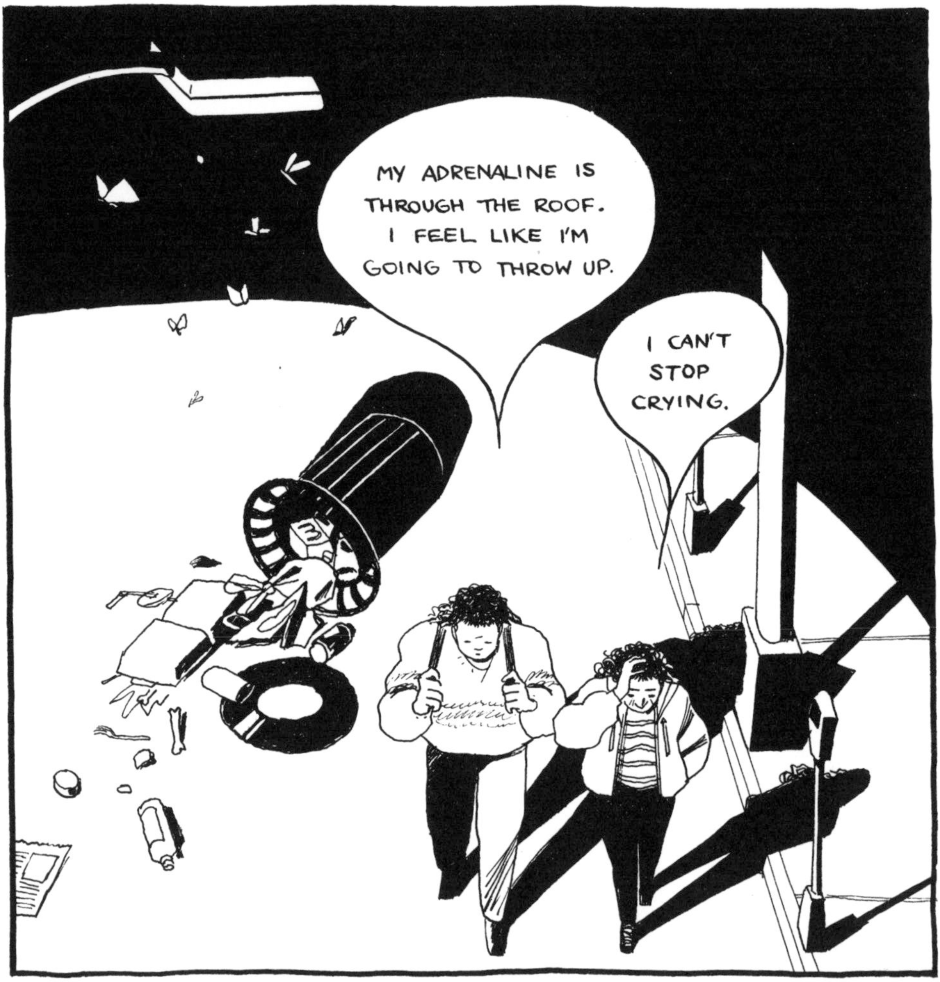
MY ADRENALINE IS THROUGH THE ROOF. I FEEL LIKE I'M GOING TO THROW UP.
I CAN'T STOP CRYING.

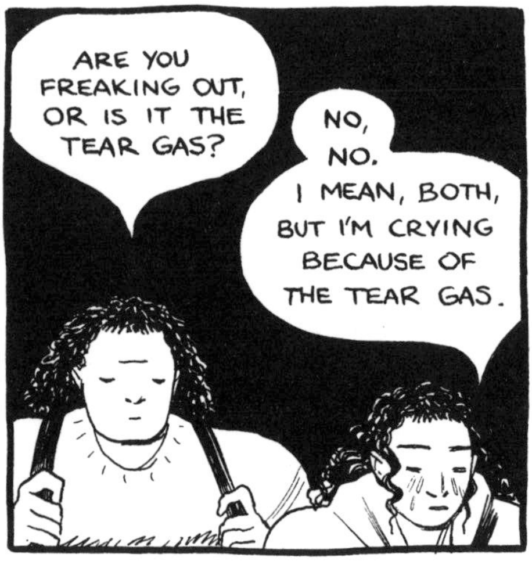
ARE YOU FREAKING OUT, OR IS IT THE TEAR GAS?
NO, NO. I MEAN, BOTH, BUT I'M CRYING BECAUSE OF THE TEAR GAS.

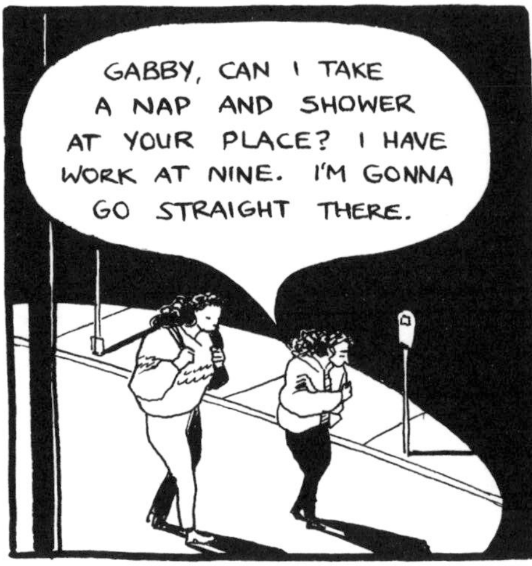
GABBY, CAN I TAKE A NAP AND SHOWER AT YOUR PLACE? I HAVE WORK AT NINE. I'M GONNA GO STRAIGHT THERE.

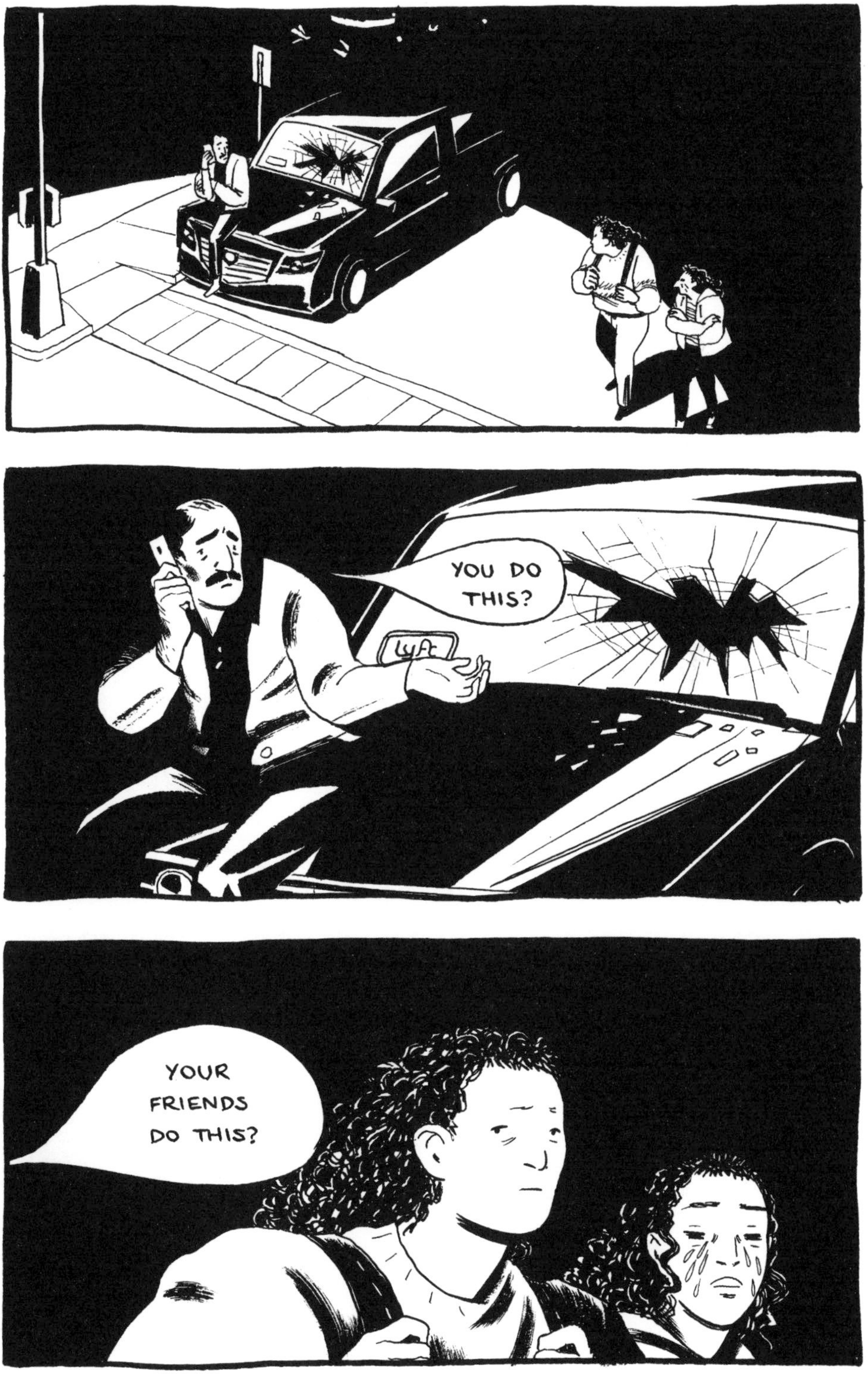
YOU DO THIS?
Lyft
YOUR FRIENDS DO THIS?

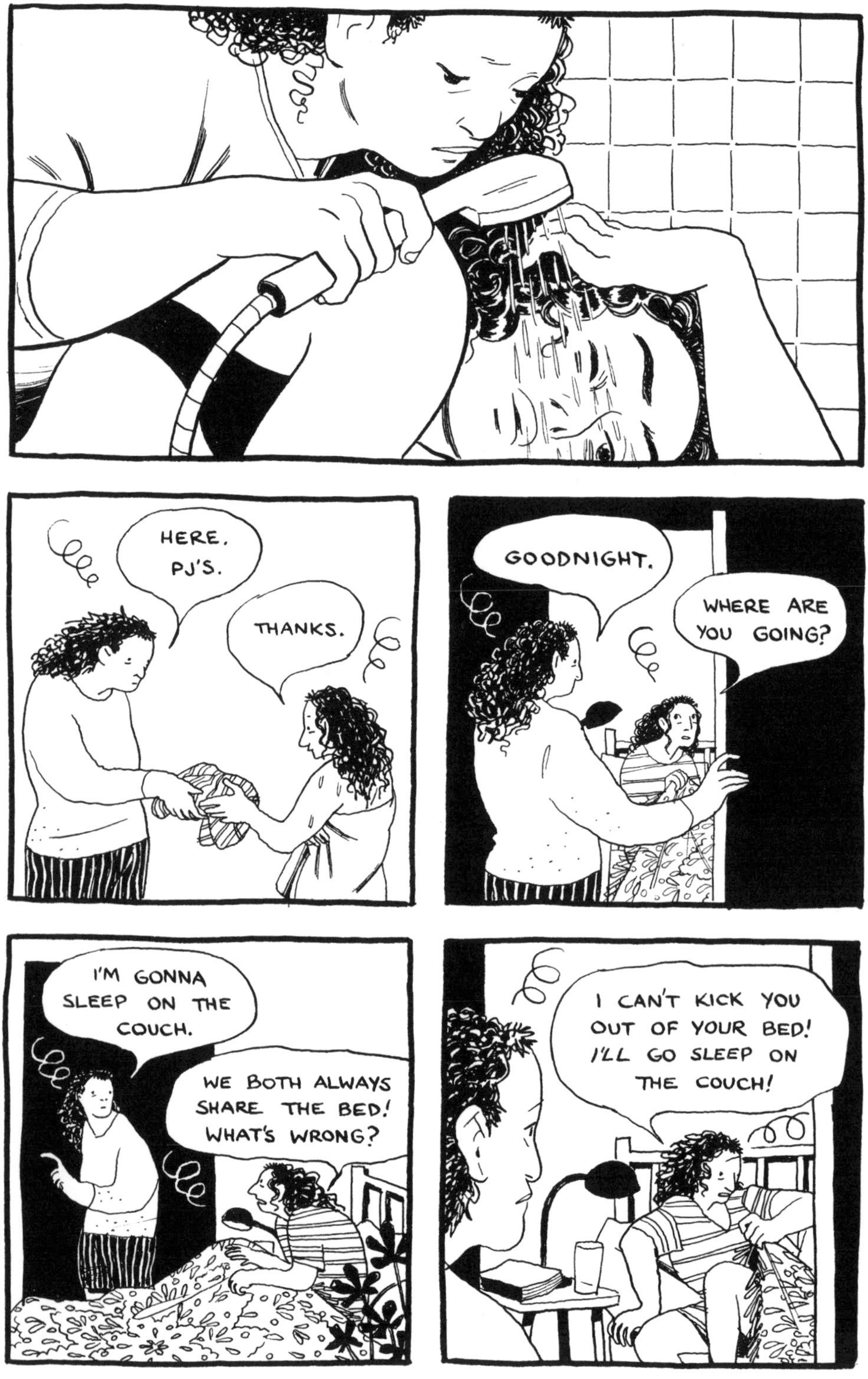

HERE. PJ'S.
THANKS.
GOODNIGHT.
WHERE ARE YOU GOING?
I'M GONNA SLEEP ON THE COUCH.
WE BOTH ALWAYS SHARE THE BED! WHAT'S WRONG?
I CAN'T KICK YOU OUT OF YOUR BED! I'LL GO SLEEP ON THE COUCH!

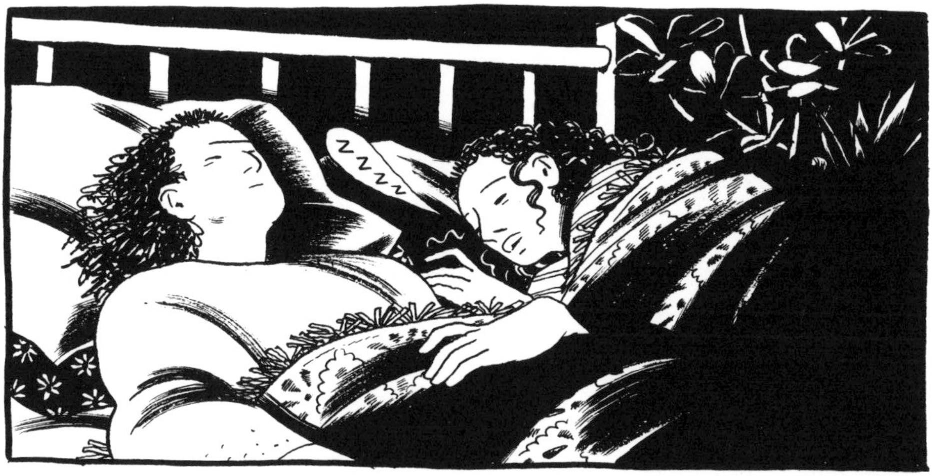
ZZZZ
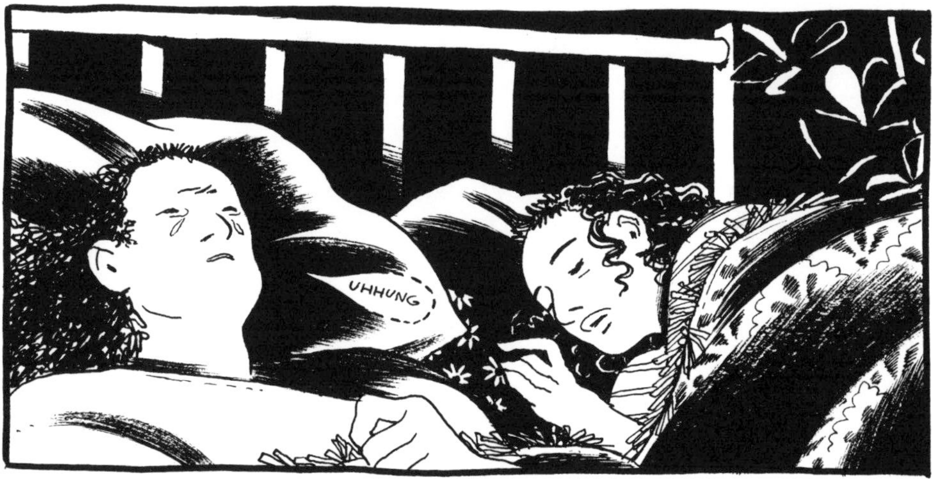
UHHUNG
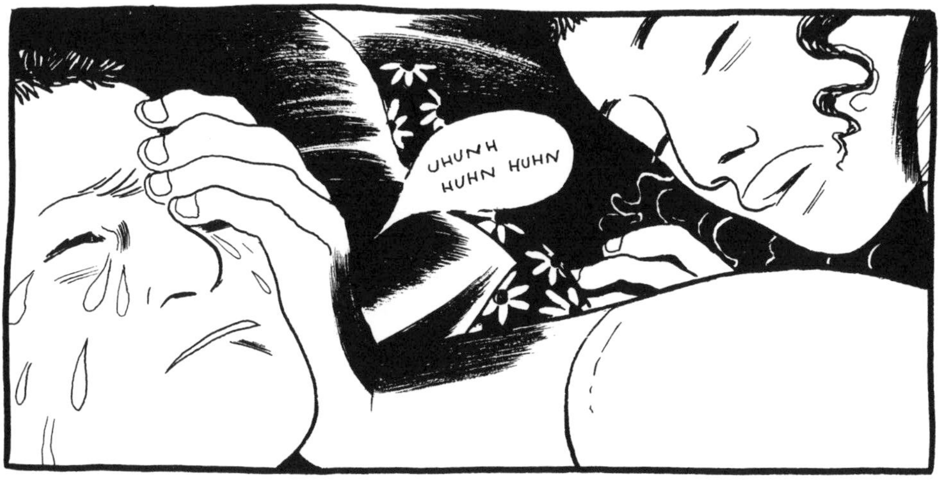
UHUNH HUHN HUHN

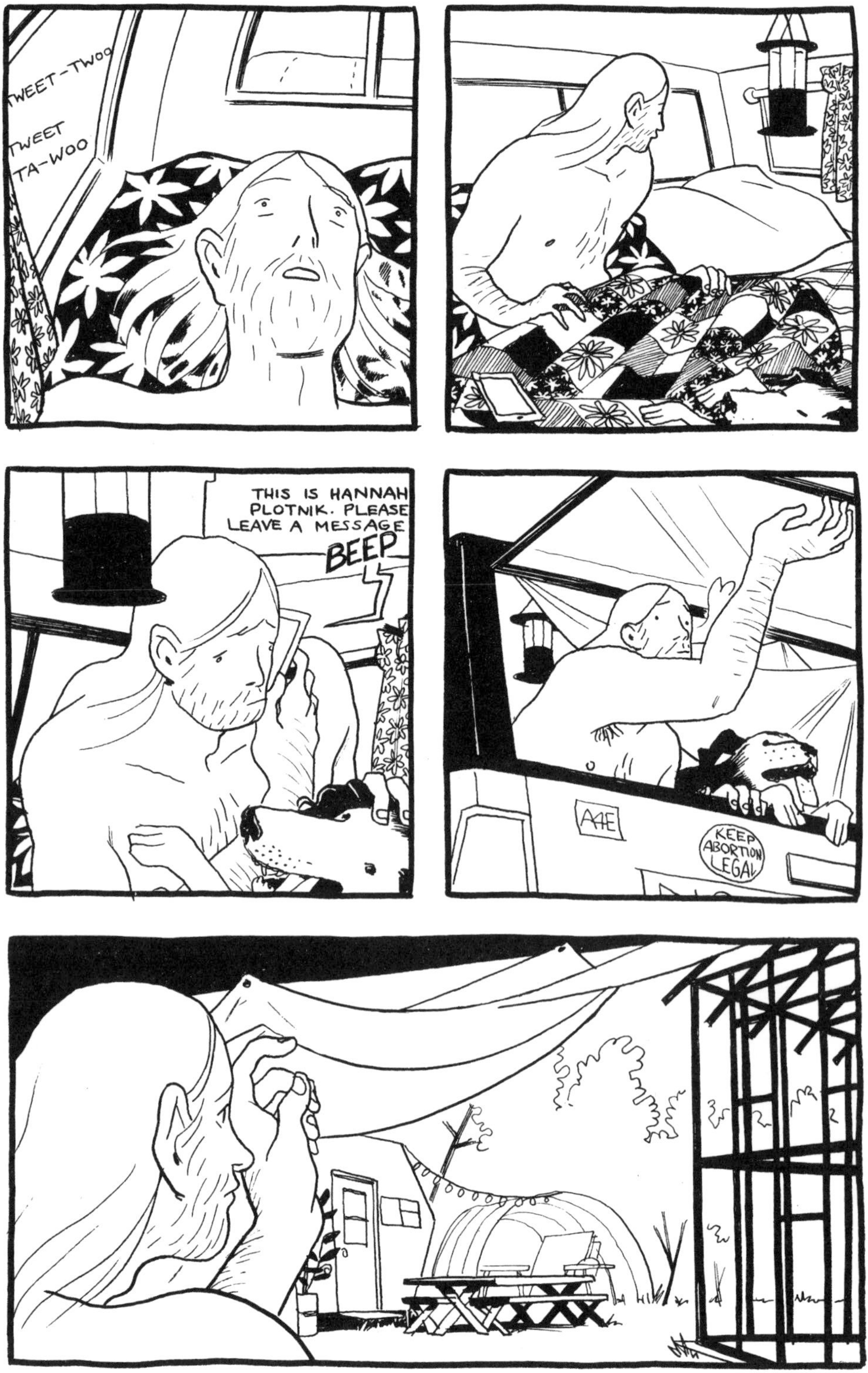
TWEET-TWOO
TWEET
TA-WOO
THIS IS HANNAH PLOTNIK. PLEASE LEAVE A MESSAGE
BEEP
A4E
KEEP ABORTION LEGAL

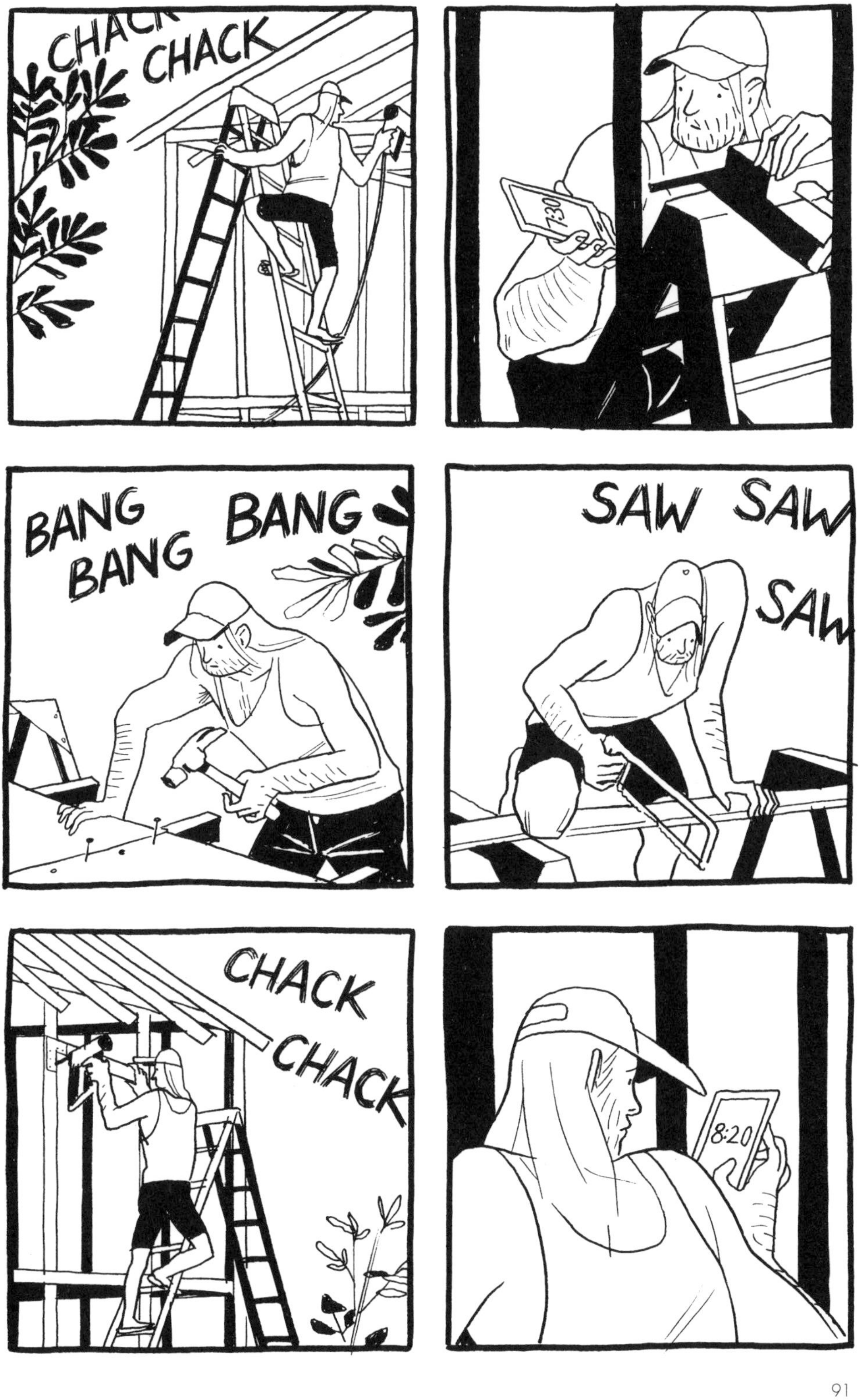
CHACK CHACK
7:30
BANG BANG BANG
SAW SAW SAW
CHACK CHACK
8:20

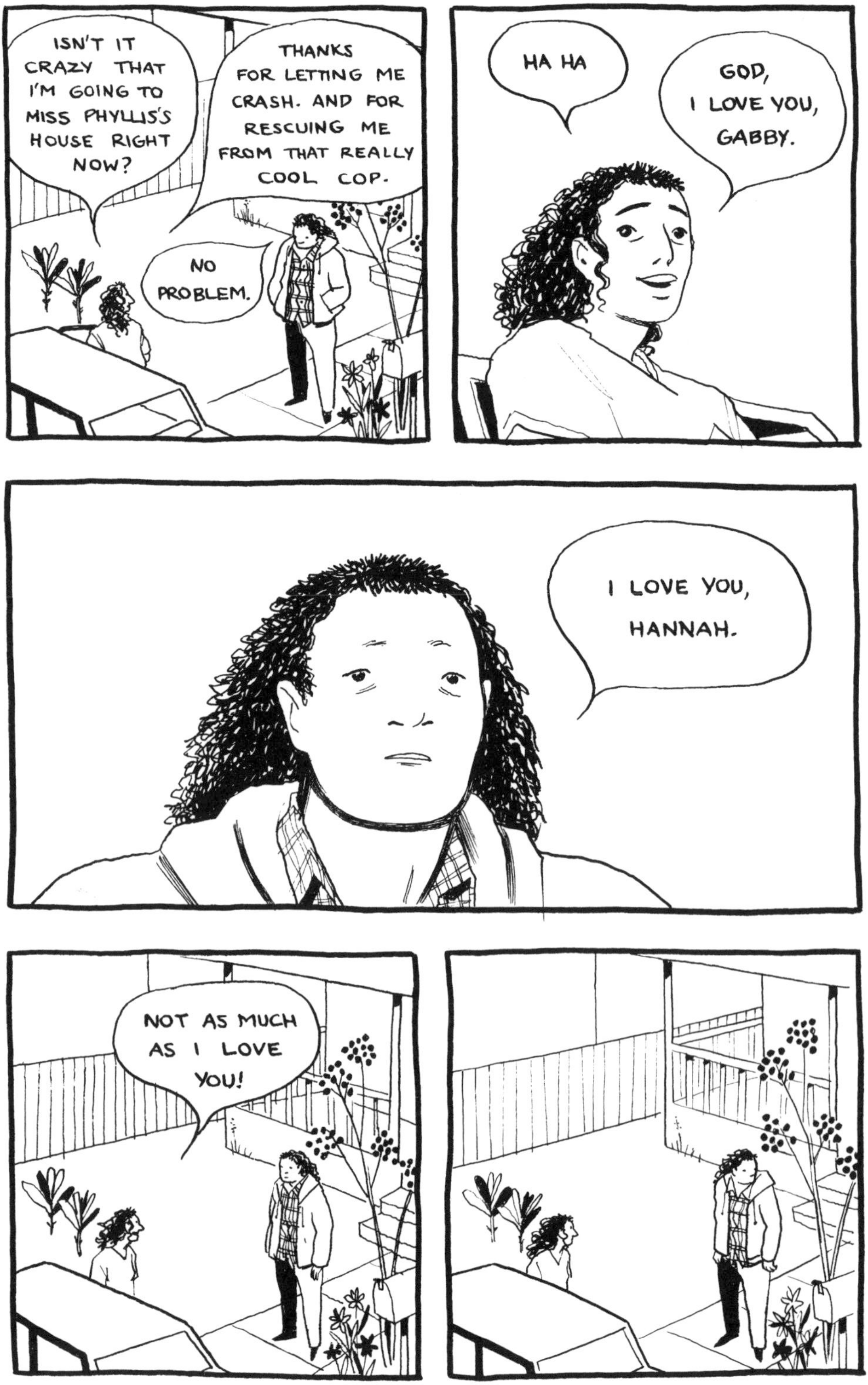
ISN'T IT CRAZY THAT I'M GOING TO MISS PHYLLIS'S HOUSE RIGHT NOW?
THANKS FOR LETTING ME CRASH. AND FOR RESCUING ME FROM THAT REALLY COOL COP.
NO PROBLEM.
HA HA
GOD, I LOVE YOU, GABBY.
I LOVE YOU, HANNAH.
NOT AS MUCH AS I LOVE YOU!

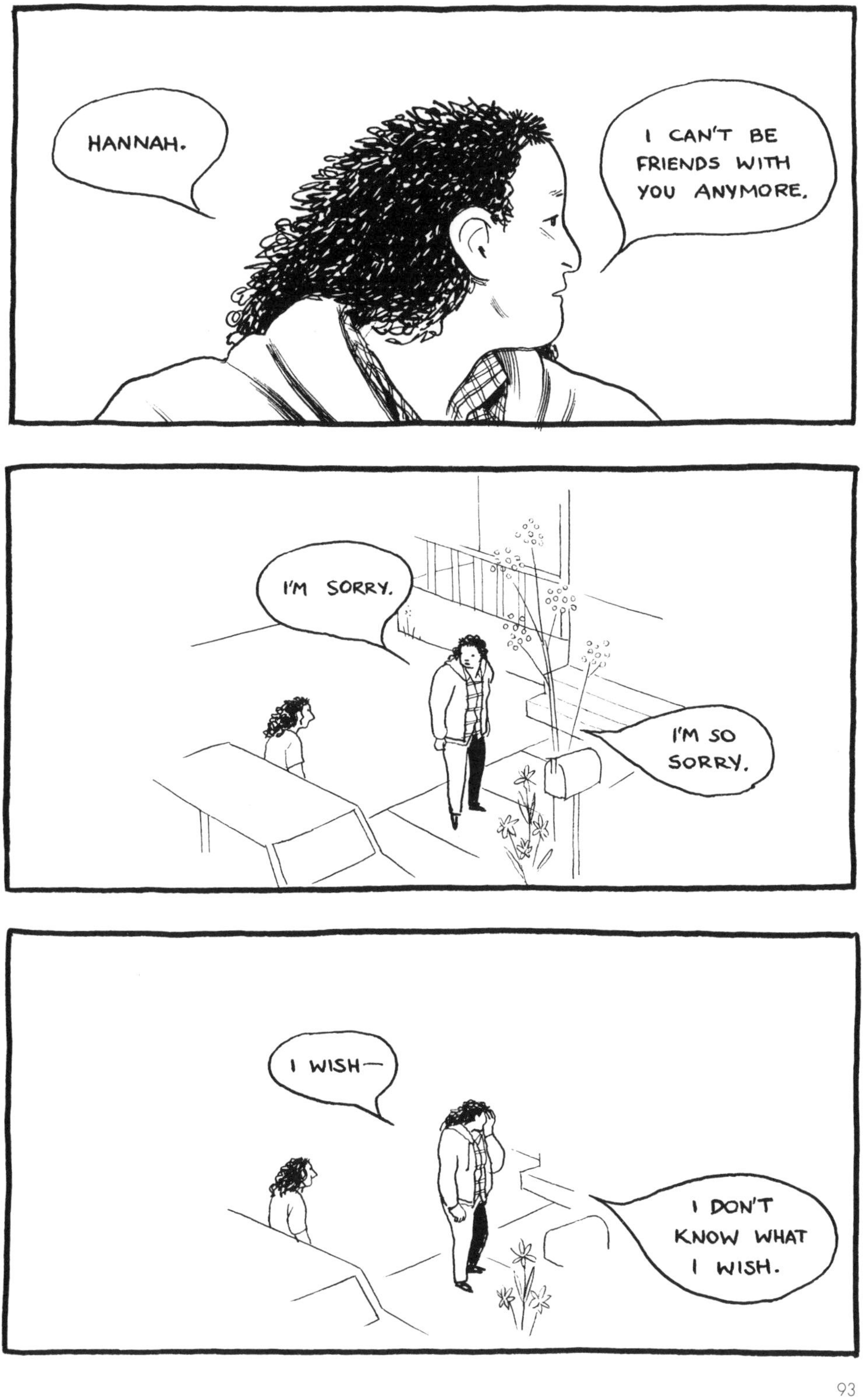
HANNAH.
I CAN'T BE FRIENDS WITH YOU ANYMORE.
I'M SORRY.
I'M SO SORRY.
I WISH—
I DON'T KNOW WHAT I WISH.

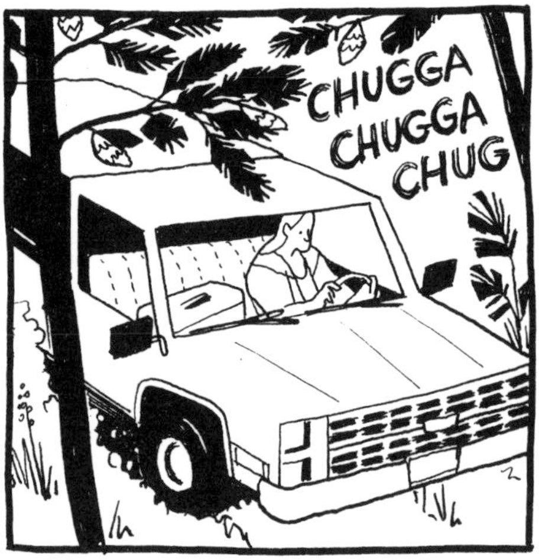
CHUGGA CHUGGA CHUG

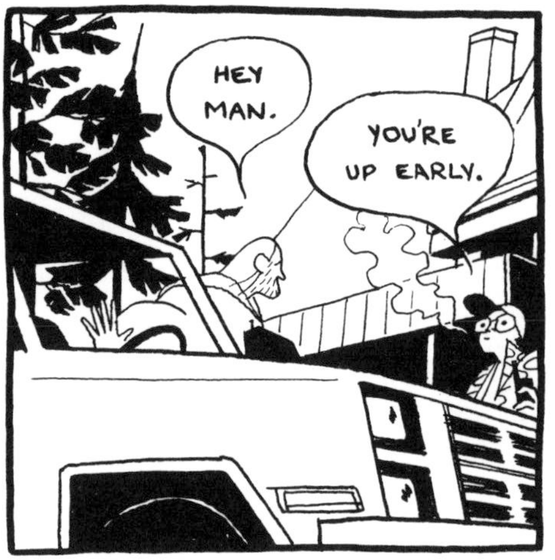
HEY MAN.
YOU'RE UP EARLY.

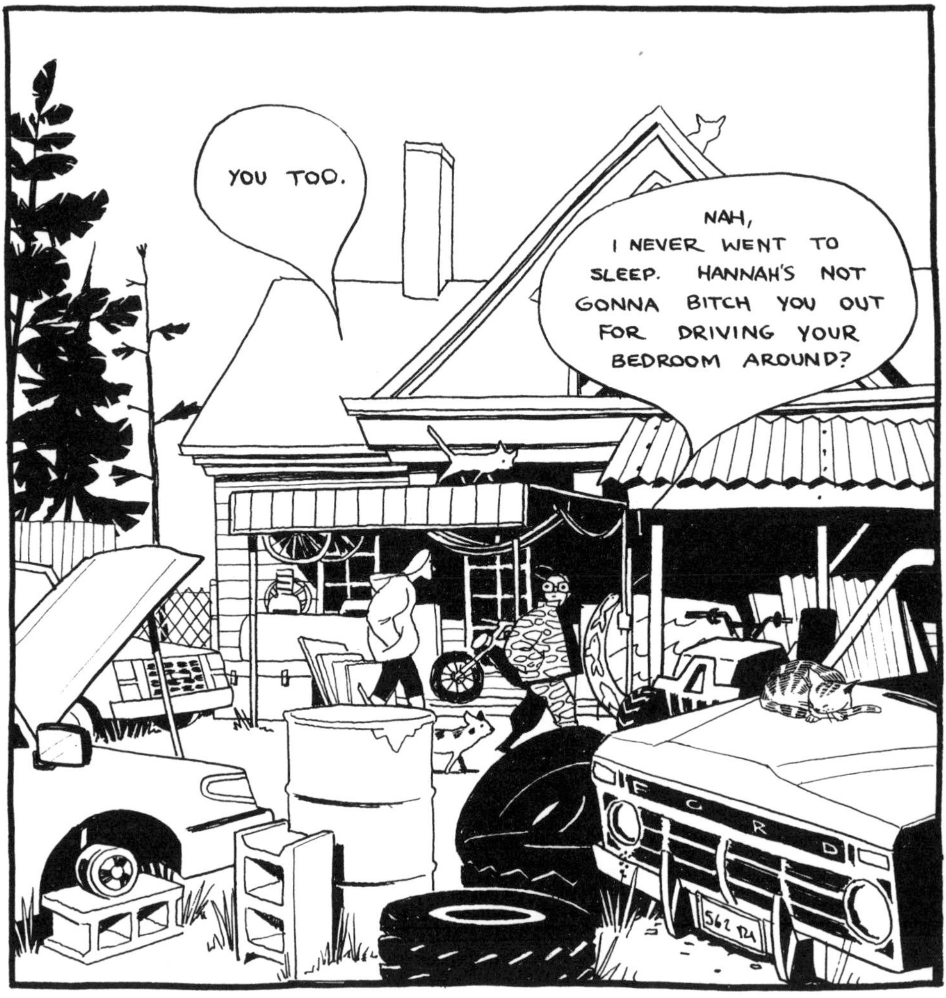
YOU TOO.
NAH, I NEVER WENT TO SLEEP. HANNAH'S NOT GONNA BITCH YOU OUT FOR DRIVING YOUR BEDROOM AROUND?
FORD

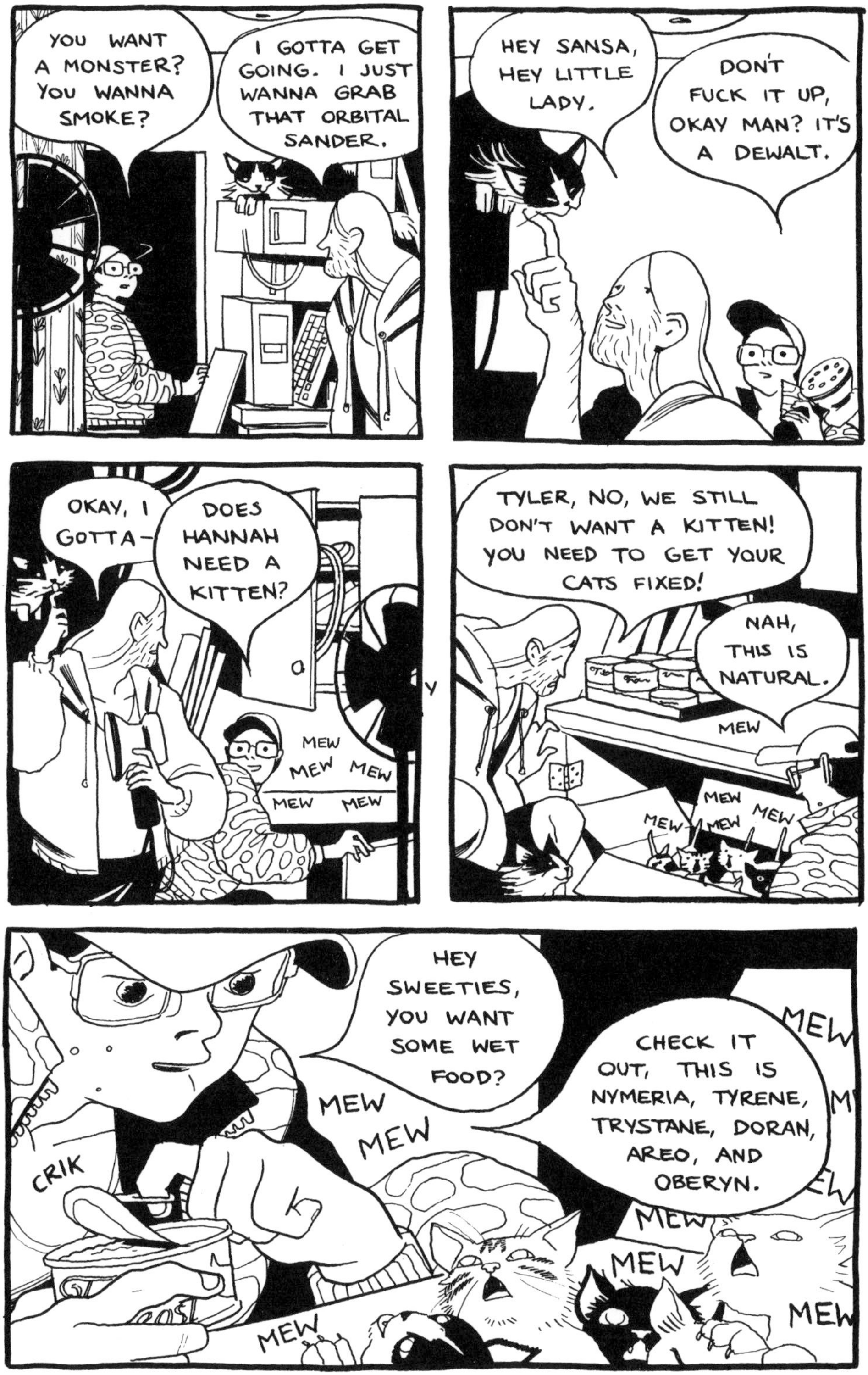

YOU WANT A MONSTER? YOU WANNA SMOKE?
I GOTTA GET GOING. I JUST WANNA GRAB THAT ORBITAL SANDER.
HEY SANSA, HEY LITTLE LADY.
DON'T FUCK IT UP, OKAY MAN? IT'S A DEWALT.
OKAY, I GOTTA–
DOES HANNAH NEED A KITTEN?
MEW
MEW MEW
MEW MEW
TYLER, NO, WE STILL DON'T WANT A KITTEN! YOU NEED TO GET YOUR CATS FIXED!
NAH, THIS IS NATURAL.
MEW
MEW MEW
MEW MEW
HEY SWEETIES, YOU WANT SOME WET FOOD?
CHECK IT OUT, THIS IS NYMERIA, TYRENE, TRYSTANE, DORAN, AREO, AND OBERYN.
CRIK
MEW
MEW
MEW
MEW
MEW
MEW
MEW

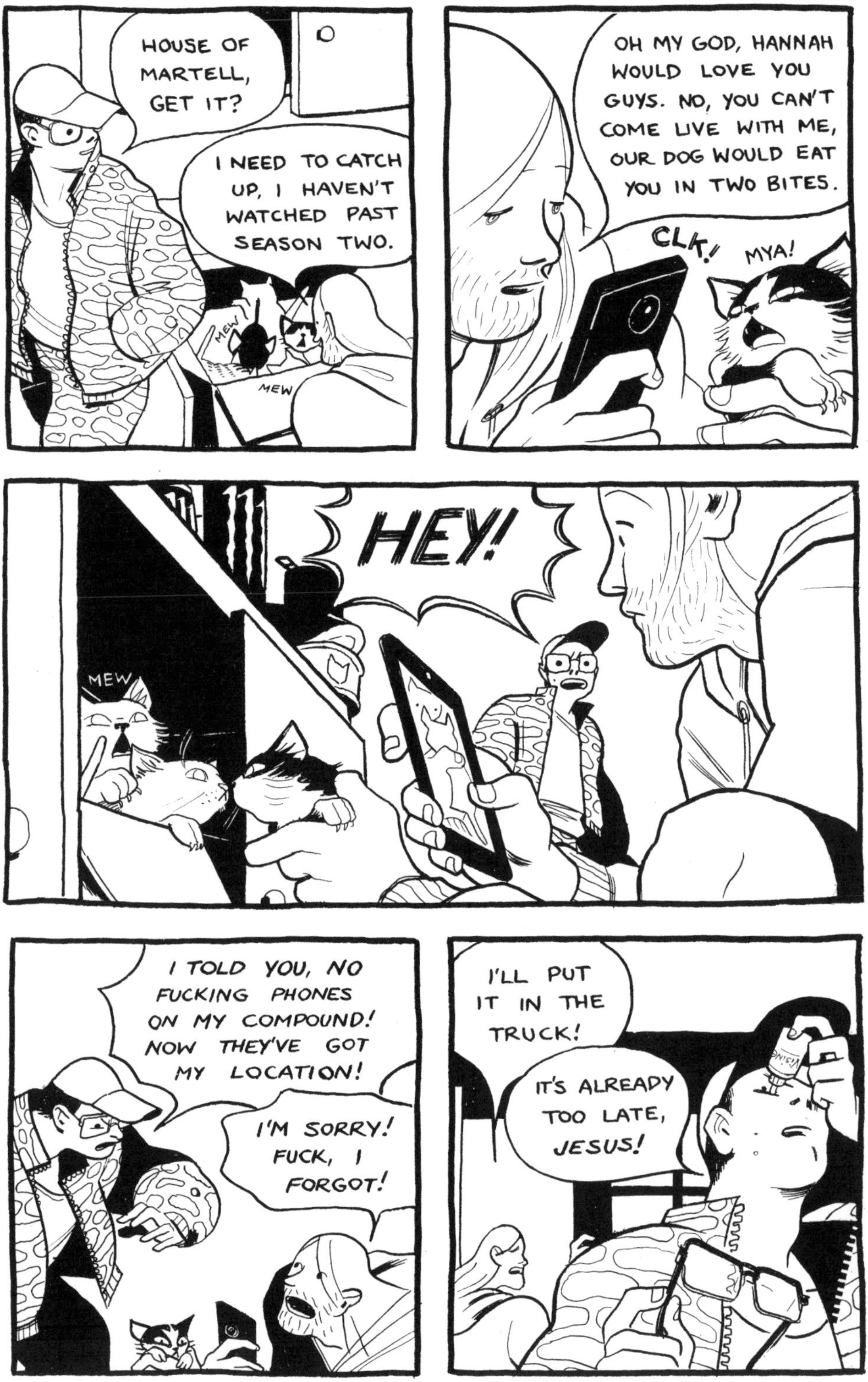
HOUSE OF MARTELL, GET IT?
I NEED TO CATCH UP, I HAVEN'T WATCHED PAST SEASON TWO.
MEW
MEW
OH MY GOD, HANNAH WOULD LOVE YOU GUYS. NO, YOU CAN'T COME LIVE WITH ME, OUR DOG WOULD EAT YOU IN TWO BITES.
CLK!
MYA!
HEY!
MEW
I TOLD YOU, NO FUCKING PHONES ON MY COMPOUND! NOW THEY'VE GOT MY LOCATION!
I'M SORRY! FUCK, I FORGOT!
I'LL PUT IT IN THE TRUCK!
IT'S ALREADY TOO LATE, JESUS!

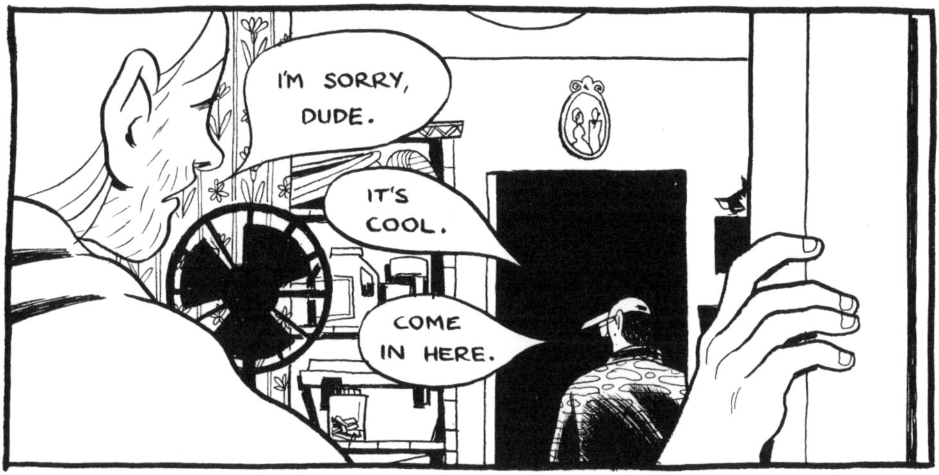
I'M SORRY, DUDE.
IT'S COOL.
COME IN HERE.

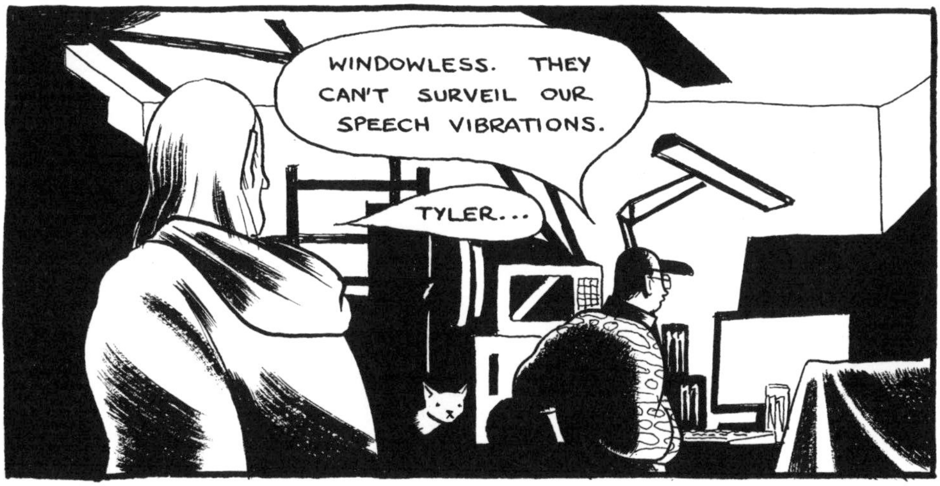
WINDOWLESS. THEY CAN'T SURVEIL OUR SPEECH VIBRATIONS.
TYLER...

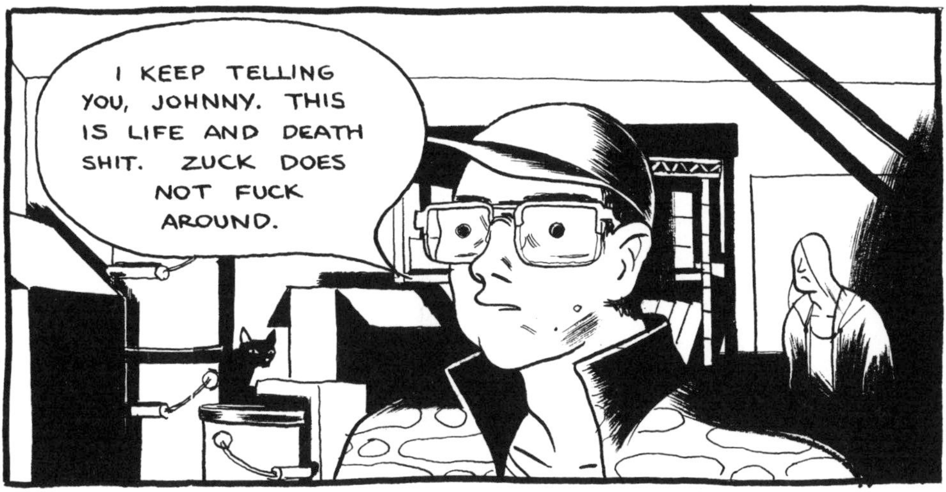
I KEEP TELLING YOU, JOHNNY. THIS IS LIFE AND DEATH SHIT. ZUCK DOES NOT FUCK AROUND.

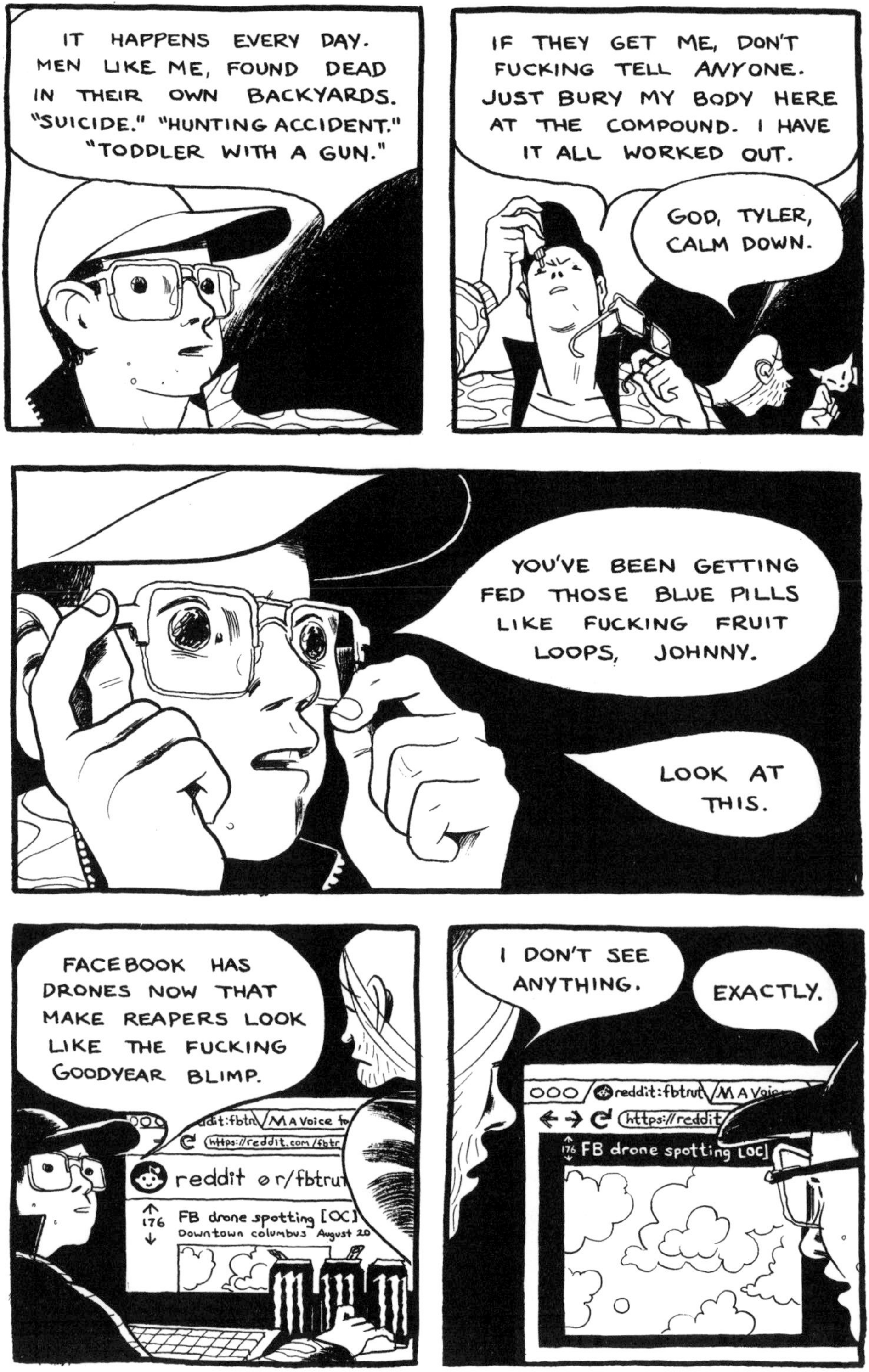
IT HAPPENS EVERY DAY. MEN LIKE ME, FOUND DEAD IN THEIR OWN BACKYARDS. "SUICIDE." "HUNTING ACCIDENT." "TODDLER WITH A GUN."
IF THEY GET ME, DON'T FUCKING TELL ANYONE. JUST BURY MY BODY HERE AT THE COMPOUND. I HAVE IT ALL WORKED OUT.
GOD, TYLER, CALM DOWN.
YOU'VE BEEN GETTING FED THOSE BLUE PILLS LIKE FUCKING FRUIT LOOPS, JOHNNY.
LOOK AT THIS.
FACEBOOK HAS DRONES NOW THAT MAKE REAPERS LOOK LIKE THE FUCKING GOODYEAR BLIMP.
176
FB drone spotting [OC]
Downtown columbus August 20
I DON'T SEE ANYTHING.
EXACTLY.
FB drone spotting [OC]

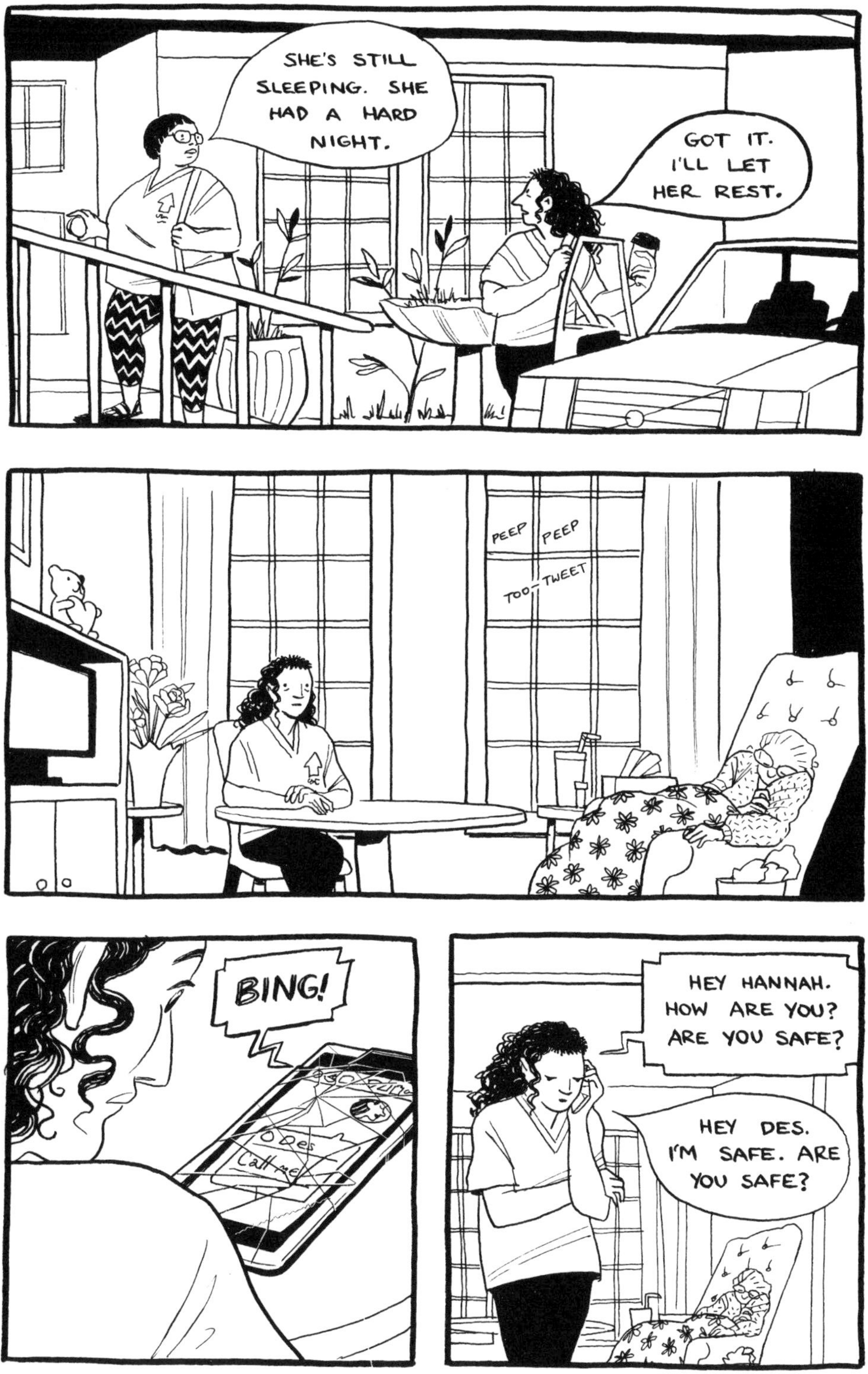
SHE'S STILL SLEEPING. SHE HAD A HARD NIGHT.
GOT IT. I'LL LET HER REST.
PEEP PEEP
TOO-TWEET
BING!
Des
Call me
HEY HANNAH. HOW ARE YOU? ARE YOU SAFE?
HEY DES. I'M SAFE. ARE YOU SAFE?

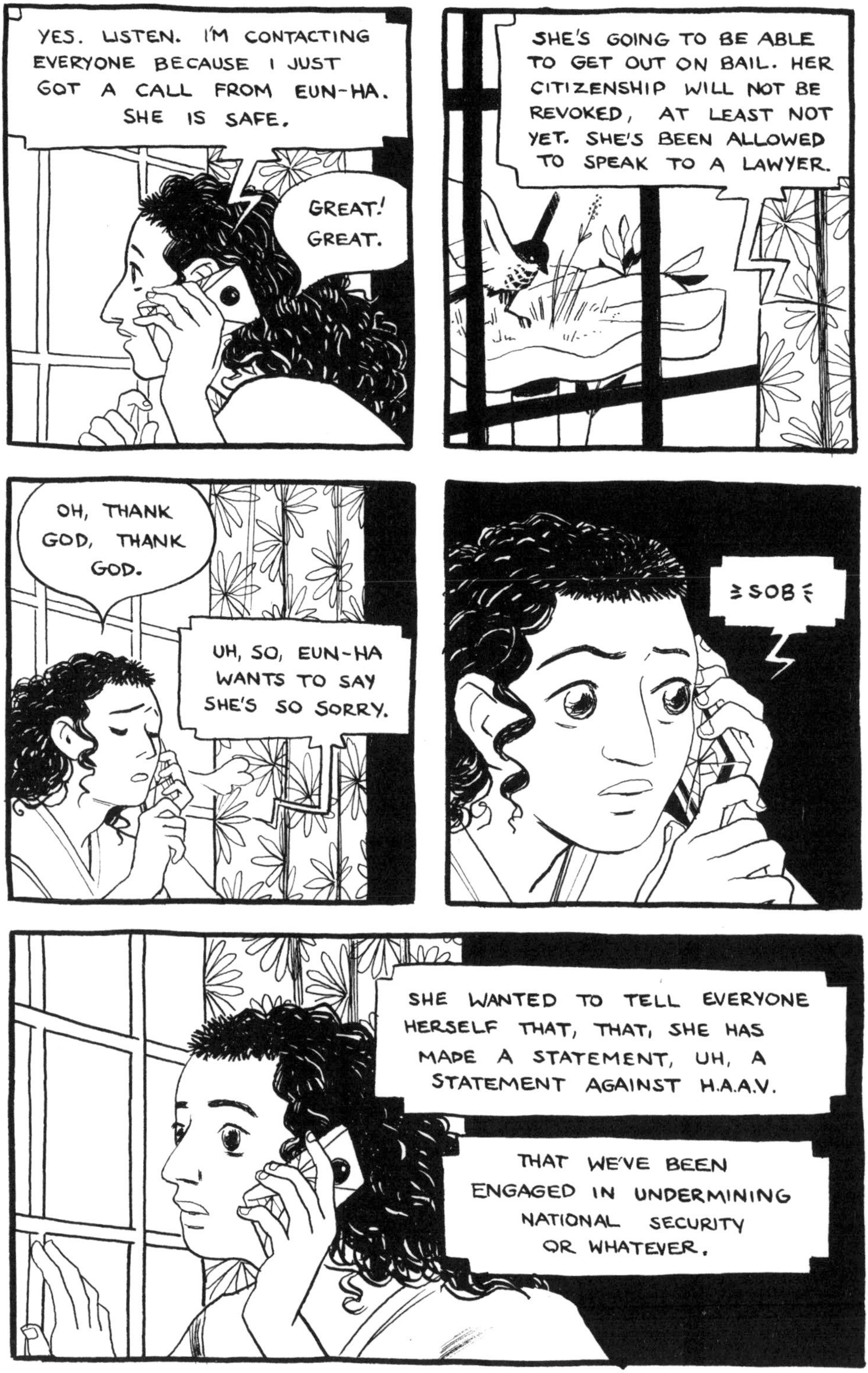
YES. LISTEN. I'M CONTACTING EVERYONE BECAUSE I JUST GOT A CALL FROM EUN-HA. SHE IS SAFE.
GREAT! GREAT.
SHE'S GOING TO BE ABLE TO GET OUT ON BAIL. HER CITIZENSHIP WILL NOT BE REVOKED, AT LEAST NOT YET. SHE'S BEEN ALLOWED TO SPEAK TO A LAWYER.
OH, THANK GOD, THANK GOD.
UH, SO, EUN-HA WANTS TO SAY SHE'S SO SORRY.
SOB
SHE WANTED TO TELL EVERYONE HERSELF THAT, THAT, SHE HAS MADE A STATEMENT, UH, A STATEMENT AGAINST H.A.A.V.
THAT WE'VE BEEN ENGAGED IN UNDERMINING NATIONAL SECURITY OR WHATEVER.

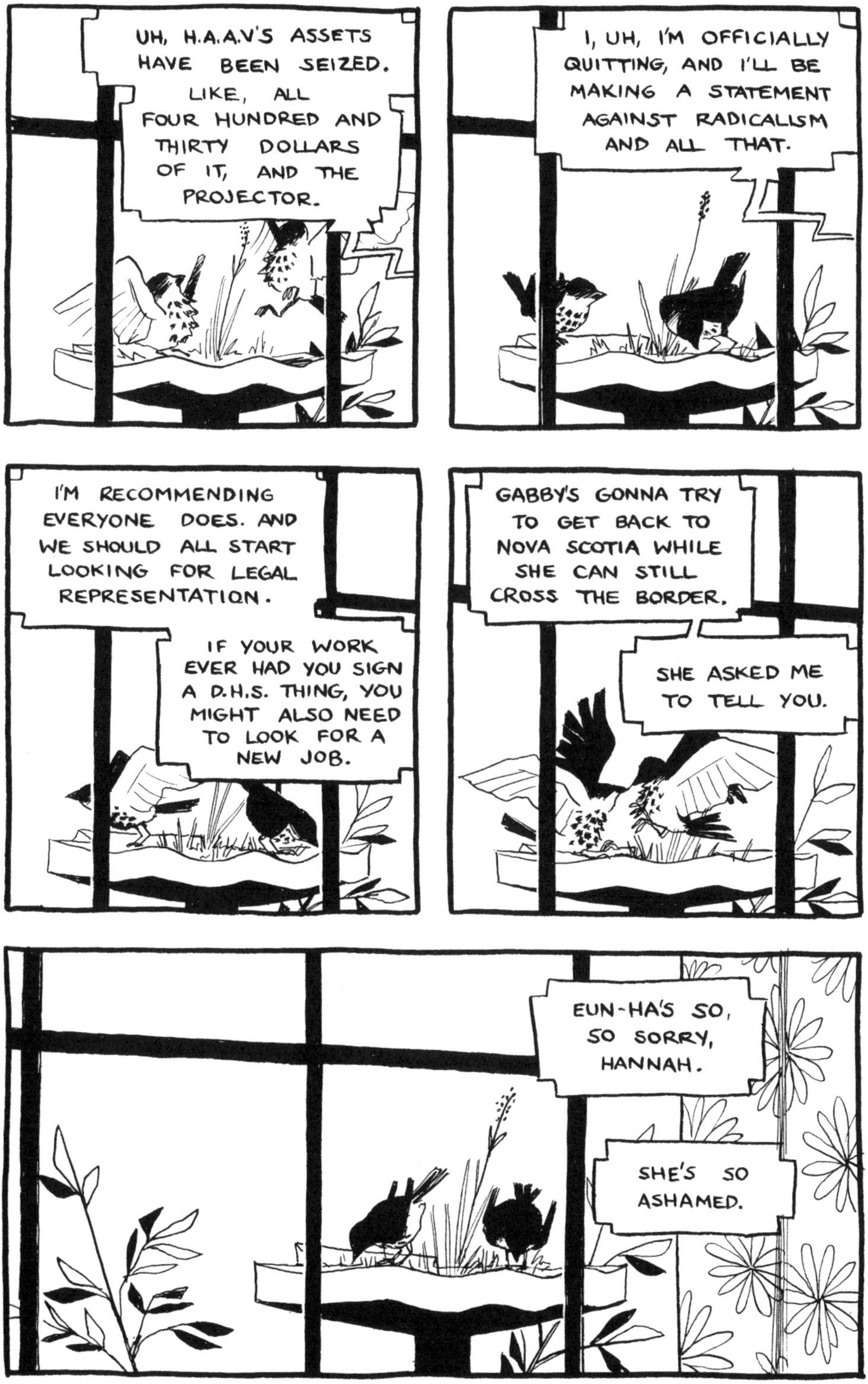
UH, H.A.A.V'S ASSETS HAVE BEEN SEIZED.
LIKE, ALL FOUR HUNDRED AND THIRTY DOLLARS OF IT, AND THE PROJECTOR.
I, UH, I'M OFFICIALLY QUITTING, AND I'LL BE MAKING A STATEMENT AGAINST RADICALISM AND ALL THAT.
I'M RECOMMENDING EVERYONE DOES. AND WE SHOULD ALL START LOOKING FOR LEGAL REPRESENTATION.
IF YOUR WORK EVER HAD YOU SIGN A D.H.S. THING, YOU MIGHT ALSO NEED TO LOOK FOR A NEW JOB.
GABBY'S GONNA TRY TO GET BACK TO NOVA SCOTIA WHILE SHE CAN STILL CROSS THE BORDER.
SHE ASKED ME TO TELL YOU.
EUN-HA'S SO, SO SORRY, HANNAH.
SHE'S SO ASHAMED.

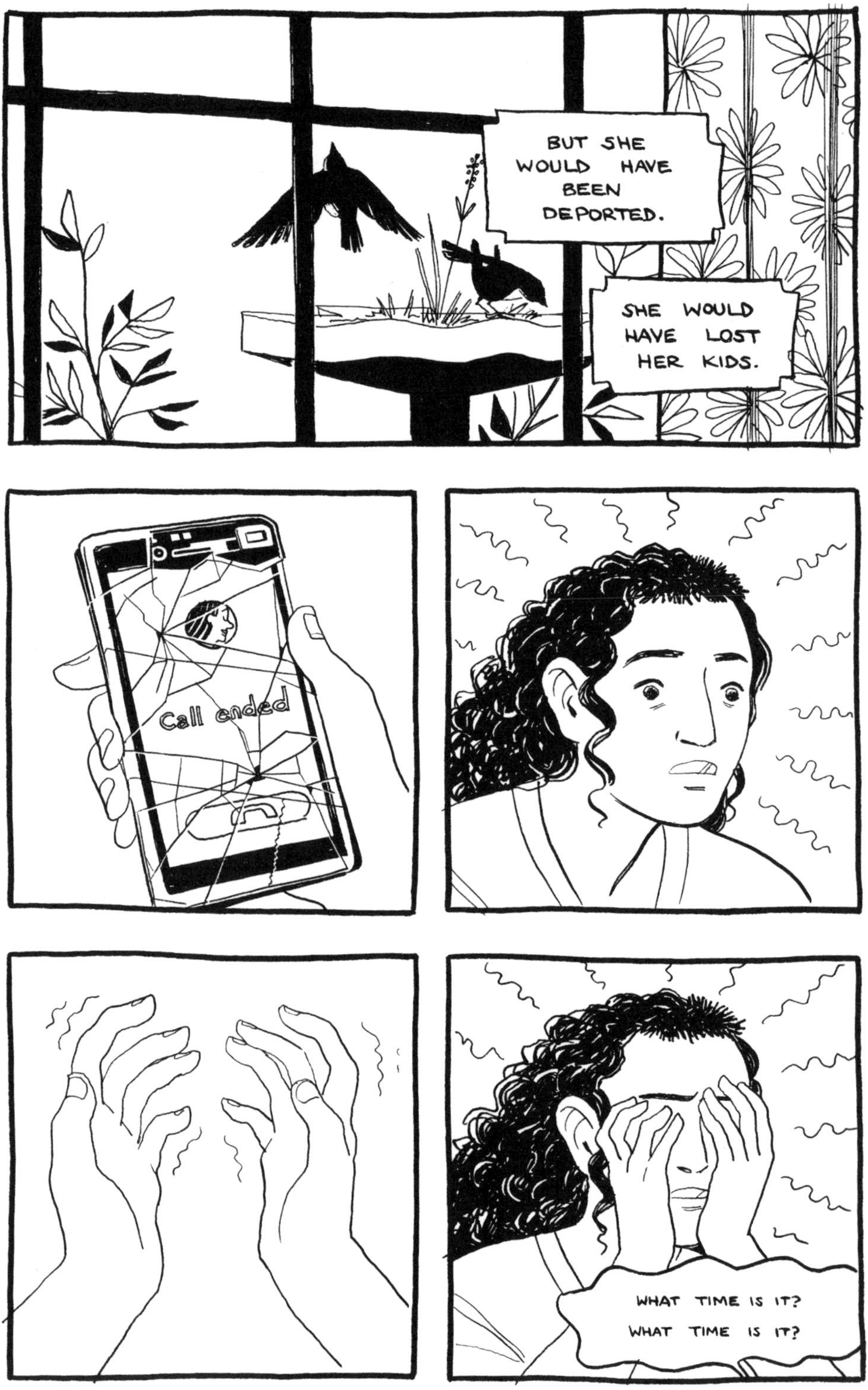
BUT SHE WOULD HAVE BEEN DEPORTED.
SHE WOULD HAVE LOST HER KIDS.
Call ended
WHAT TIME IS IT?
WHAT TIME IS IT?

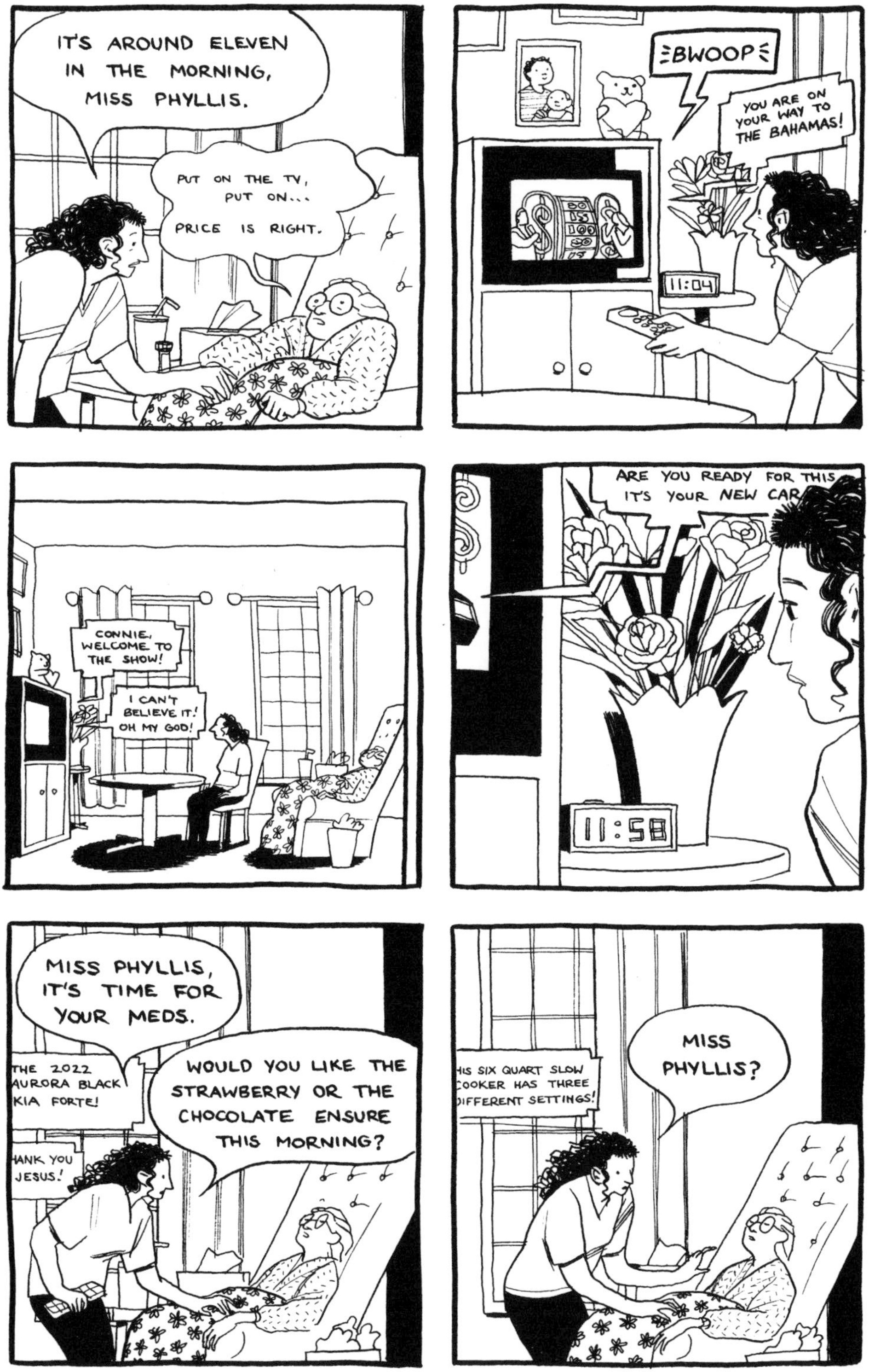
IT'S AROUND ELEVEN IN THE MORNING, MISS PHYLLIS.
PUT ON THE TV, PUT ON... PRICE IS RIGHT.
BWOOP
YOU ARE ON YOUR WAY TO THE BAHAMAS!
11:04
CONNIE, WELCOME TO THE SHOW!
I CAN'T BELIEVE IT! OH MY GOD!
ARE YOU READY FOR THIS IT'S YOUR NEW CAR
11:58
MISS PHYLLIS, IT'S TIME FOR YOUR MEDS.
THE 2022 AURORA BLACK KIA FORTE!
WOULD YOU LIKE THE STRAWBERRY OR THE CHOCOLATE ENSURE THIS MORNING?
HANK YOU JESUS!
HIS SIX QUART SLOW COOKER HAS THREE DIFFERENT SETTINGS!
MISS PHYLLIS?

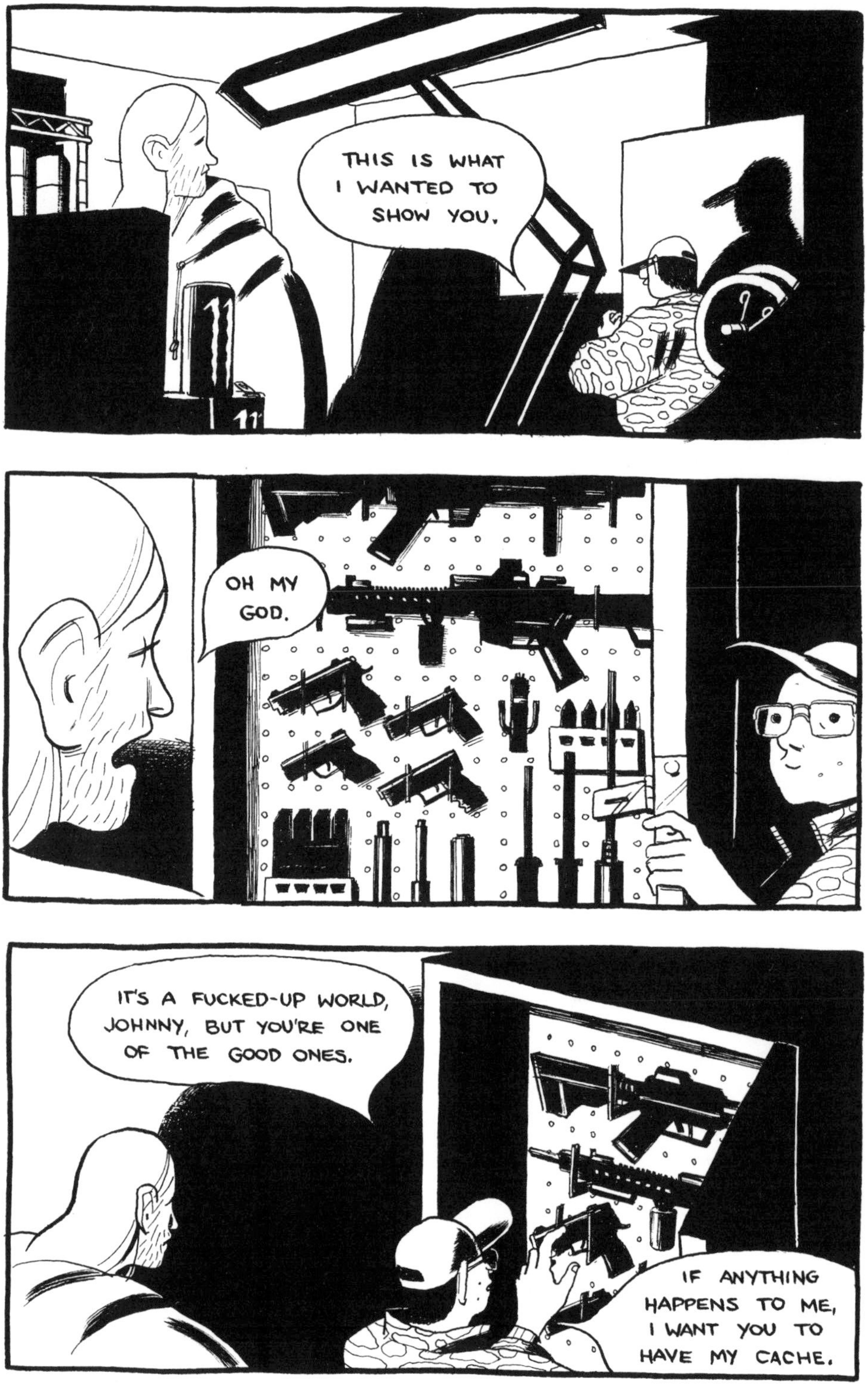
THIS IS WHAT I WANTED TO SHOW YOU.
OH MY GOD.
IT'S A FUCKED-UP WORLD, JOHNNY, BUT YOU'RE ONE OF THE GOOD ONES.
IF ANYTHING HAPPENS TO ME, I WANT YOU TO HAVE MY CACHE.

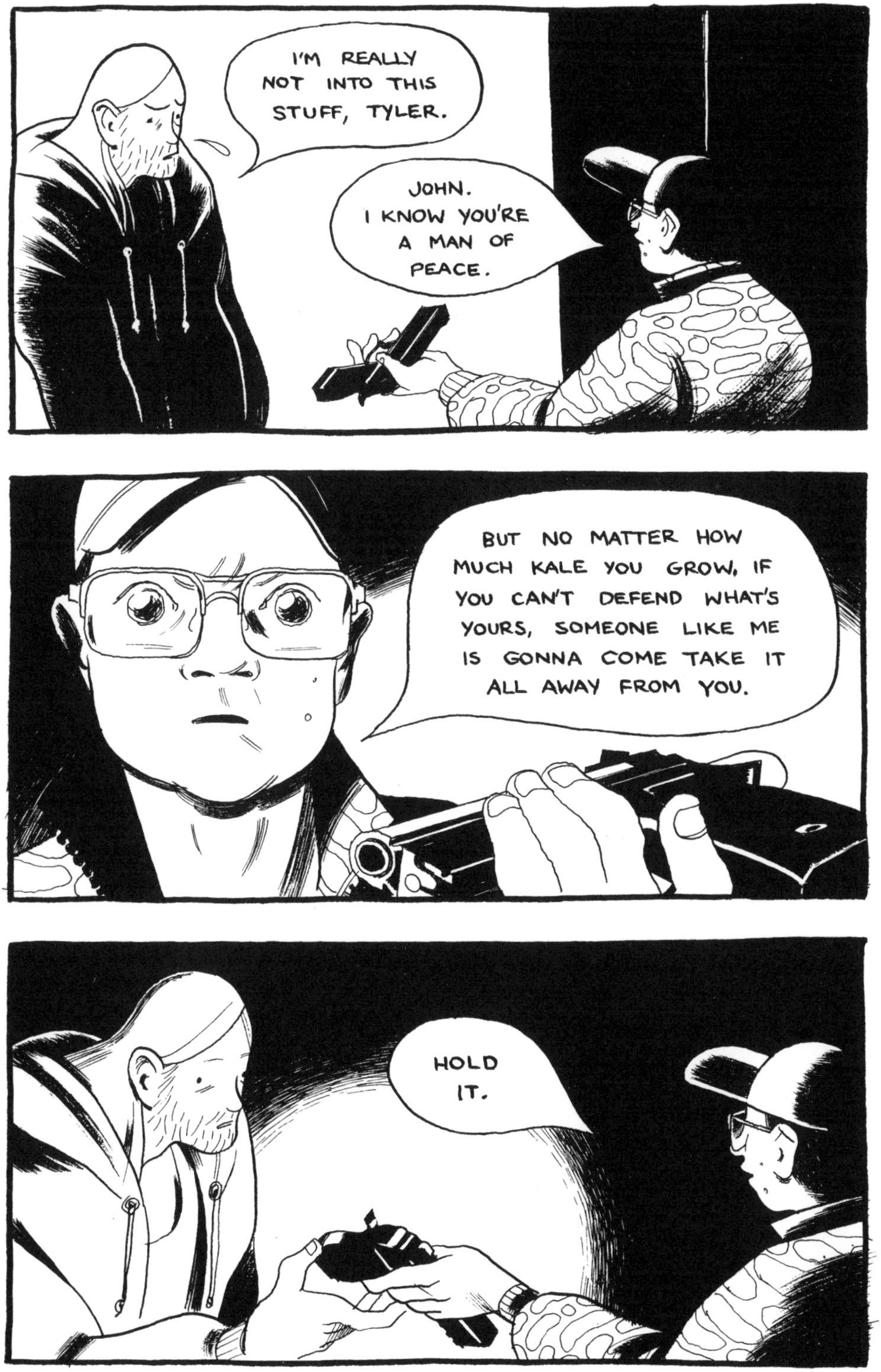
I'M REALLY NOT INTO THIS STUFF, TYLER.
JOHN. I KNOW YOU'RE A MAN OF PEACE.
BUT NO MATTER HOW MUCH KALE YOU GROW, IF YOU CAN'T DEFEND WHAT'S YOURS, SOMEONE LIKE ME IS GONNA COME TAKE IT ALL AWAY FROM YOU.
HOLD IT.

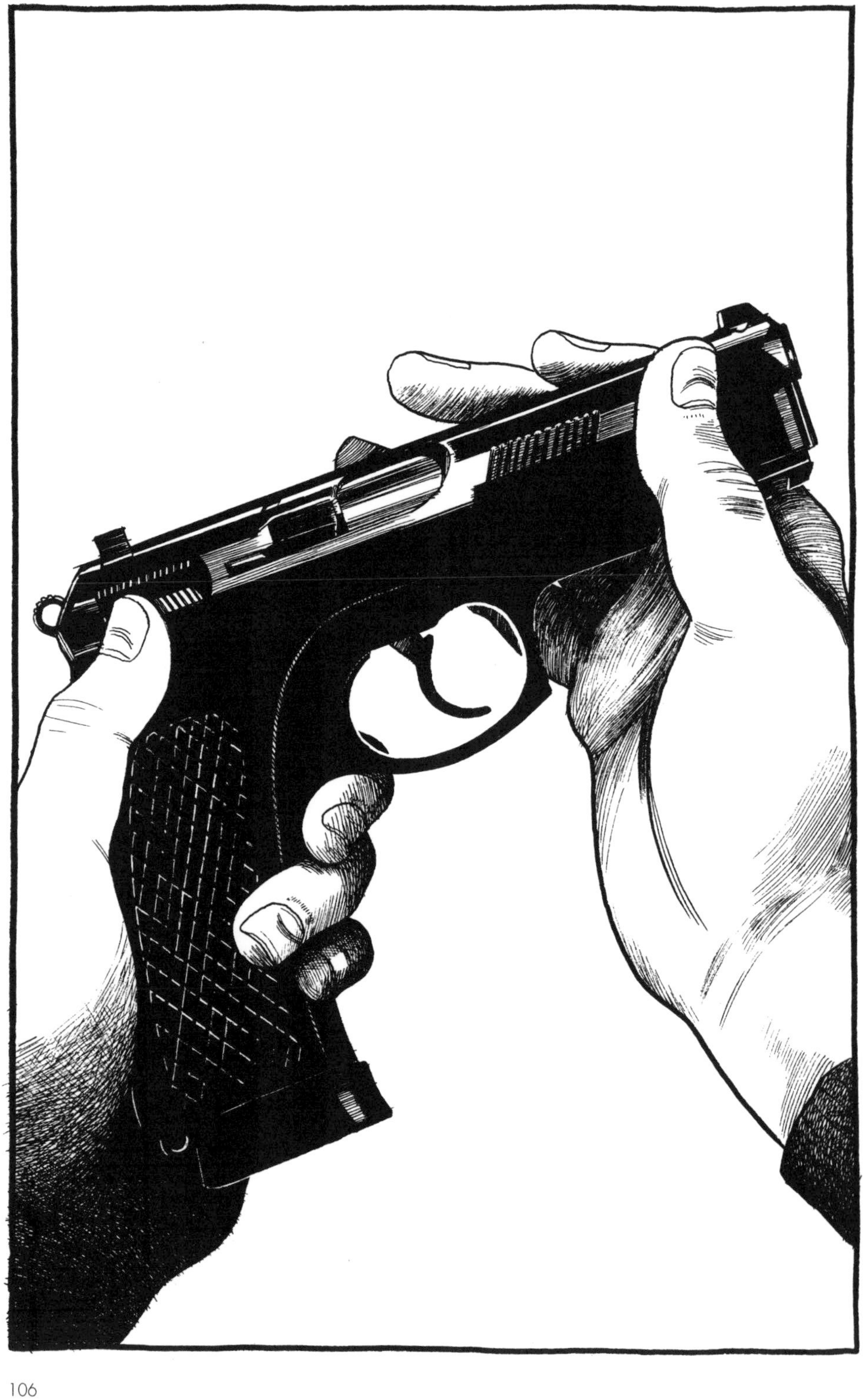

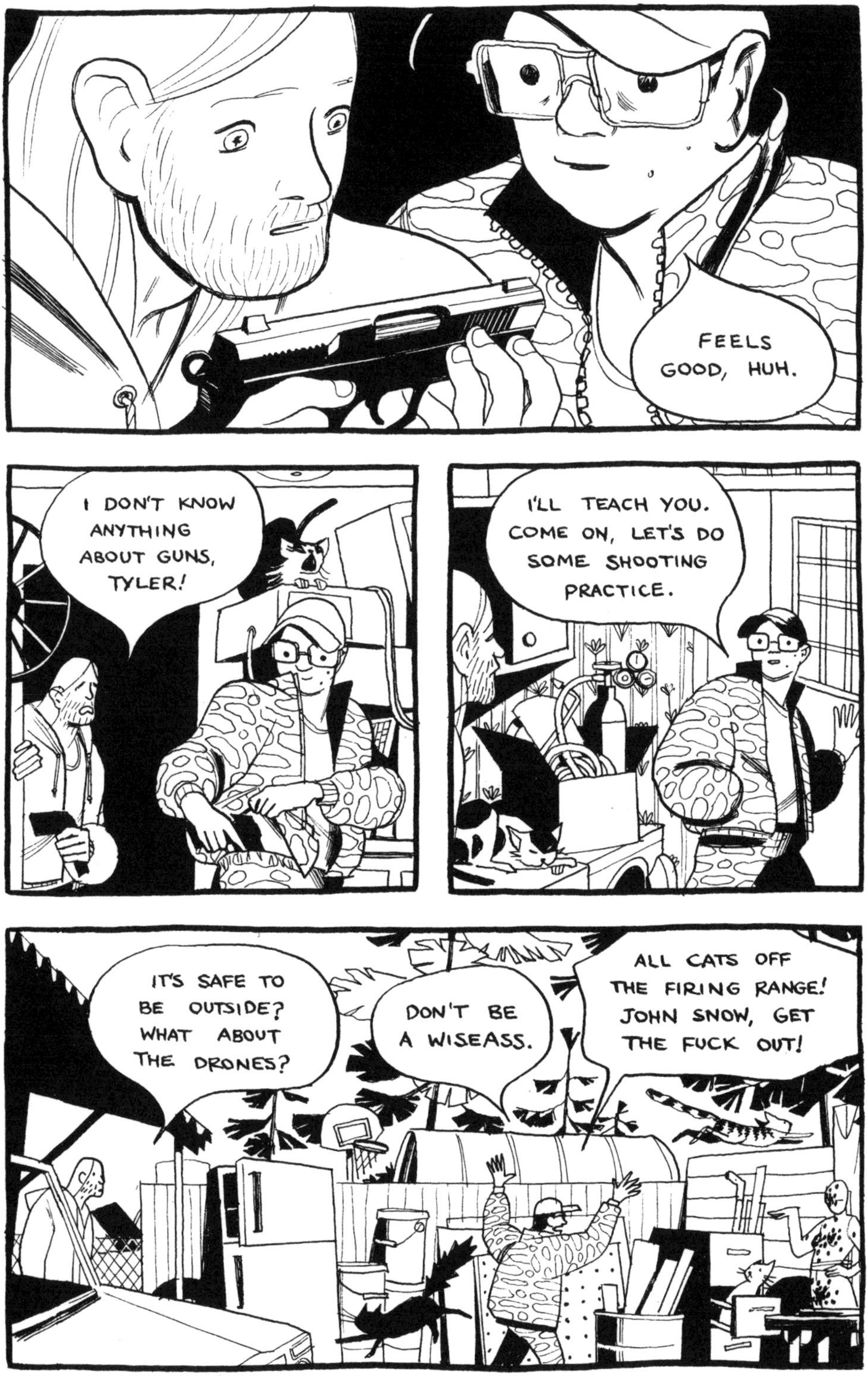
FEELS GOOD, HUH.
I DON'T KNOW ANYTHING ABOUT GUNS, TYLER!
I'LL TEACH YOU. COME ON, LET'S DO SOME SHOOTING PRACTICE.
IT'S SAFE TO BE OUTSIDE? WHAT ABOUT THE DRONES?
DON'T BE A WISEASS.
ALL CATS OFF THE FIRING RANGE! JOHN SNOW, GET THE FUCK OUT!

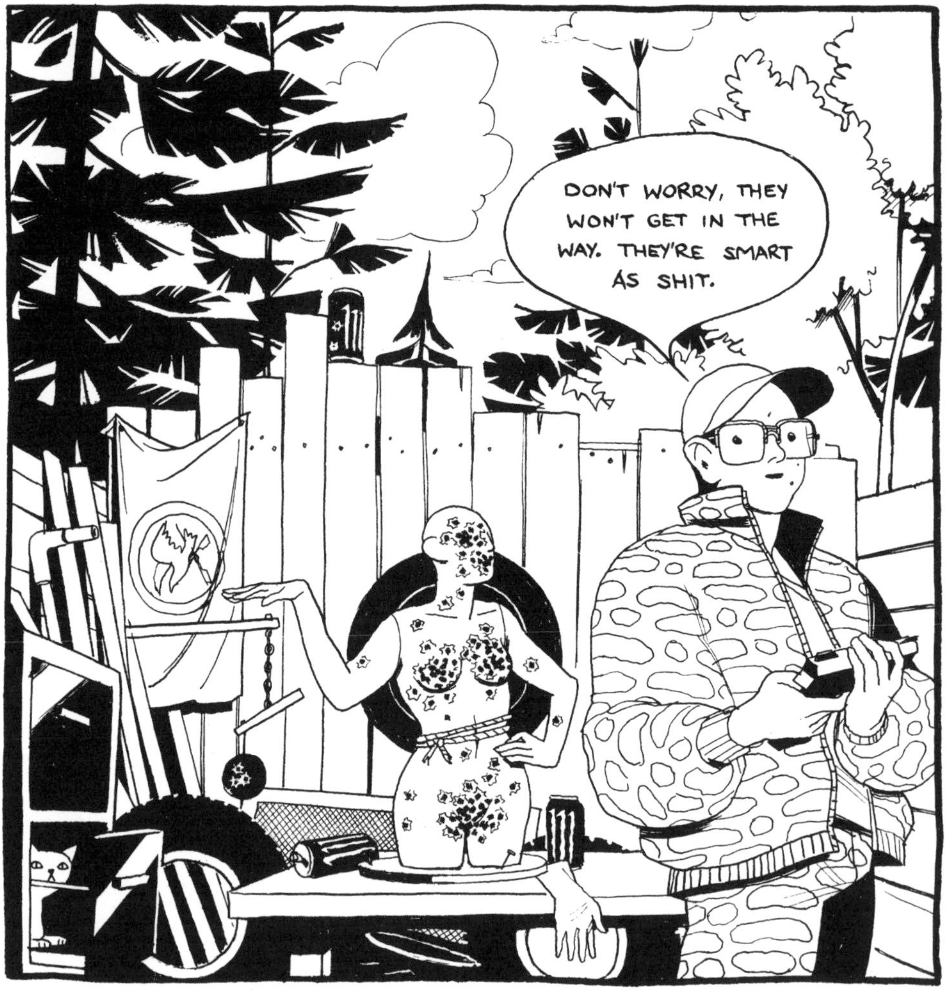
DON'T WORRY, THEY WON'T GET IN THE WAY. THEY'RE SMART AS SHIT.

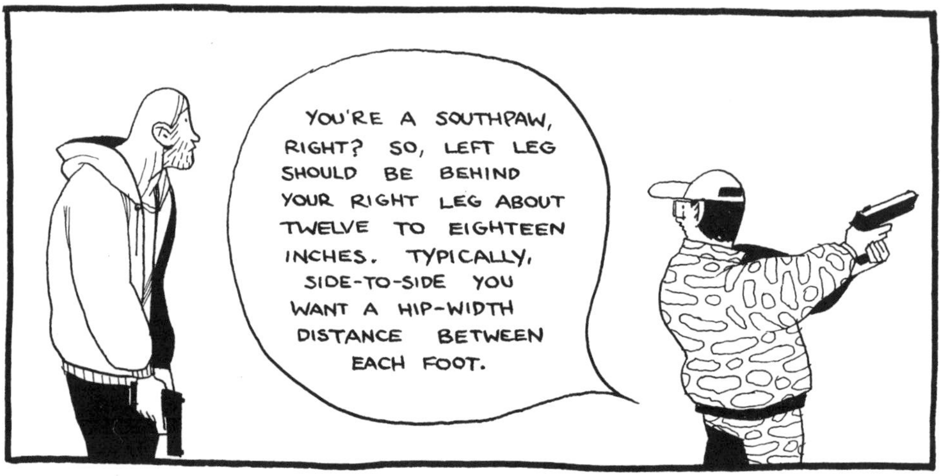
YOU'RE A SOUTHPAW, RIGHT? SO, LEFT LEG SHOULD BE BEHIND YOUR RIGHT LEG ABOUT TWELVE TO EIGHTEEN INCHES. TYPICALLY, SIDE-TO-SIDE YOU WANT A HIP-WIDTH DISTANCE BETWEEN EACH FOOT.

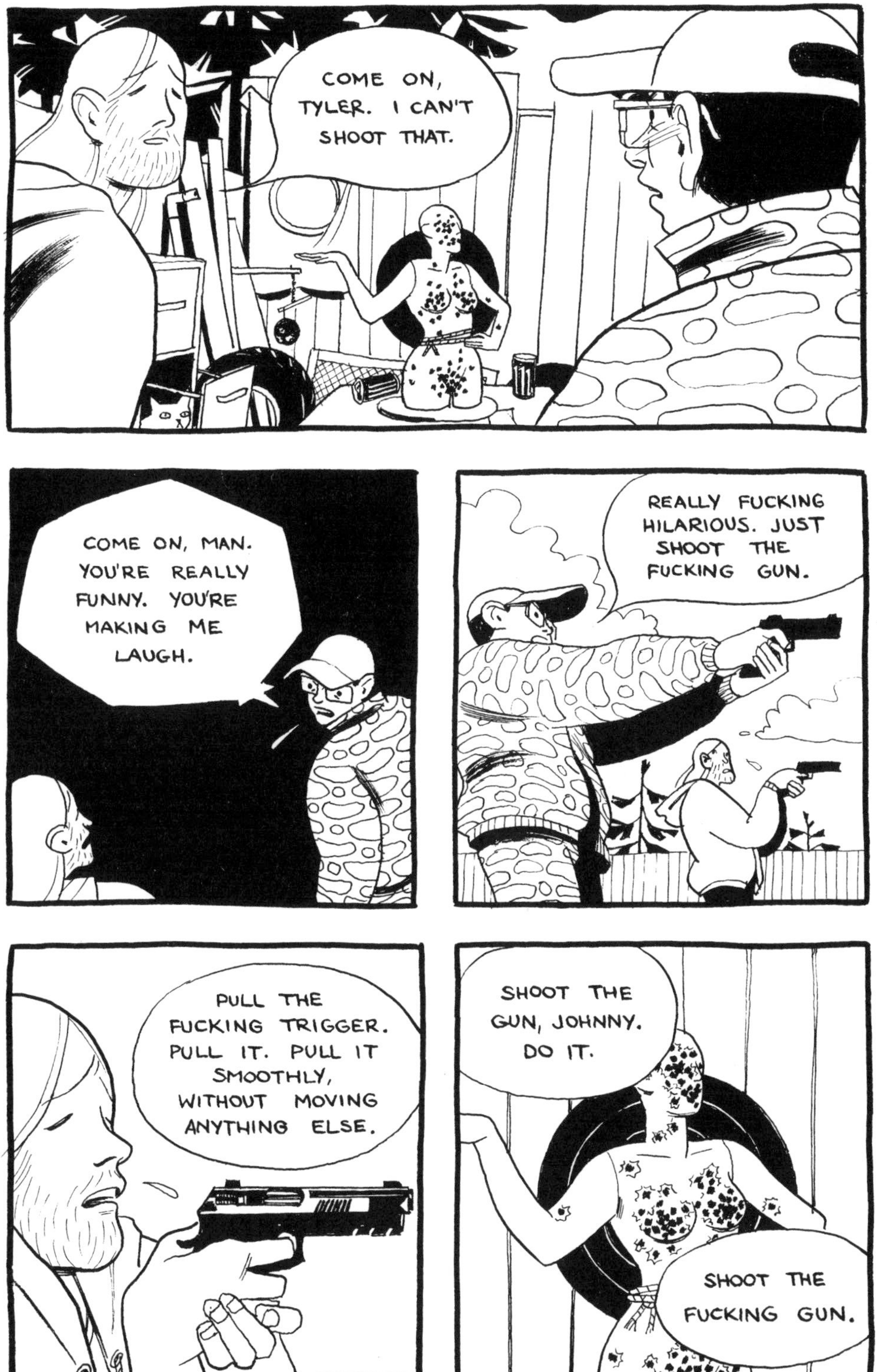
COME ON, TYLER. I CAN'T SHOOT THAT.
COME ON, MAN. YOU'RE REALLY FUNNY. YOU'RE MAKING ME LAUGH.
REALLY FUCKING HILARIOUS. JUST SHOOT THE FUCKING GUN.
PULL THE FUCKING TRIGGER. PULL IT. PULL IT SMOOTHLY, WITHOUT MOVING ANYTHING ELSE.
SHOOT THE GUN, JOHNNY. DO IT.
SHOOT THE FUCKING GUN.

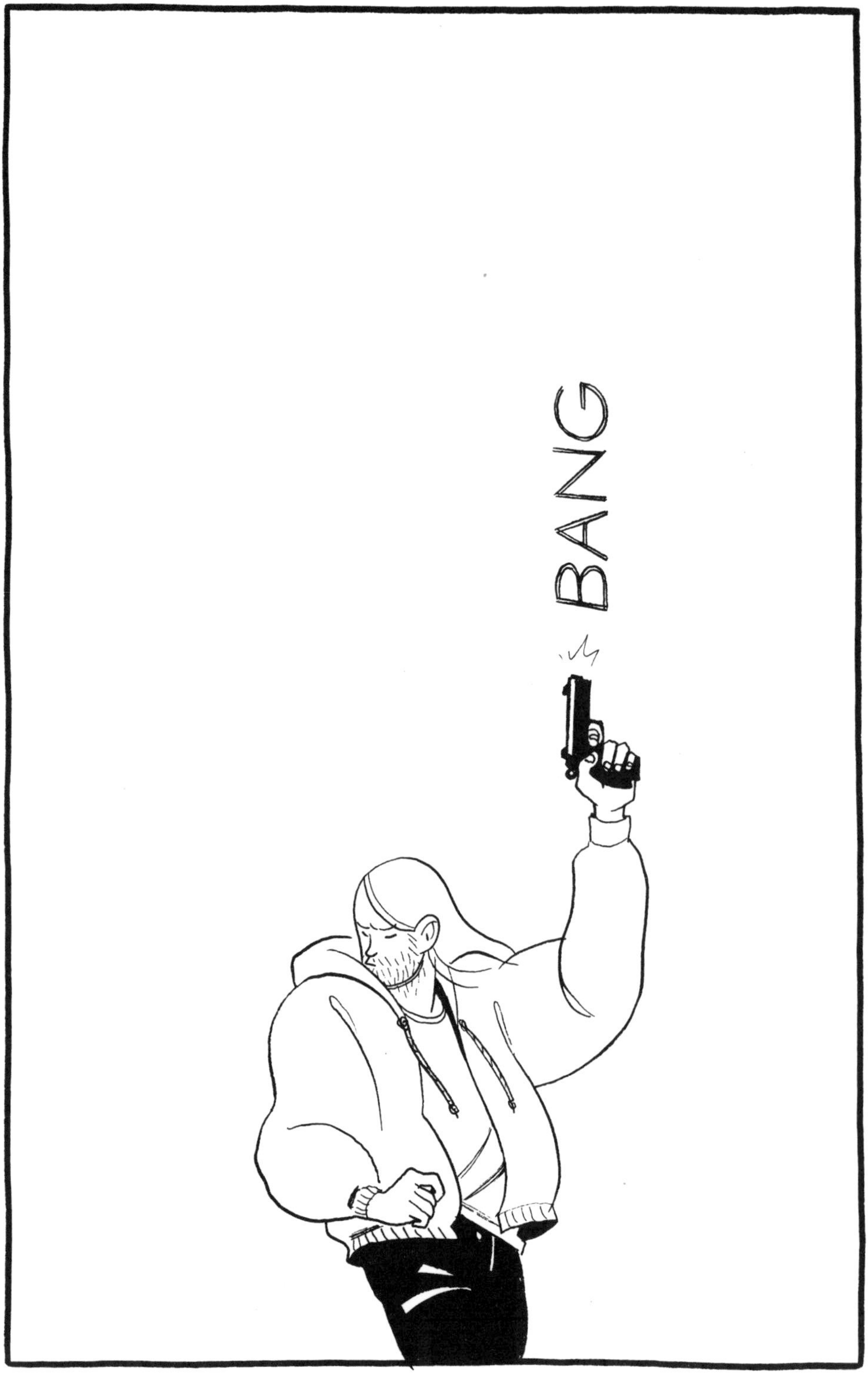
BANG

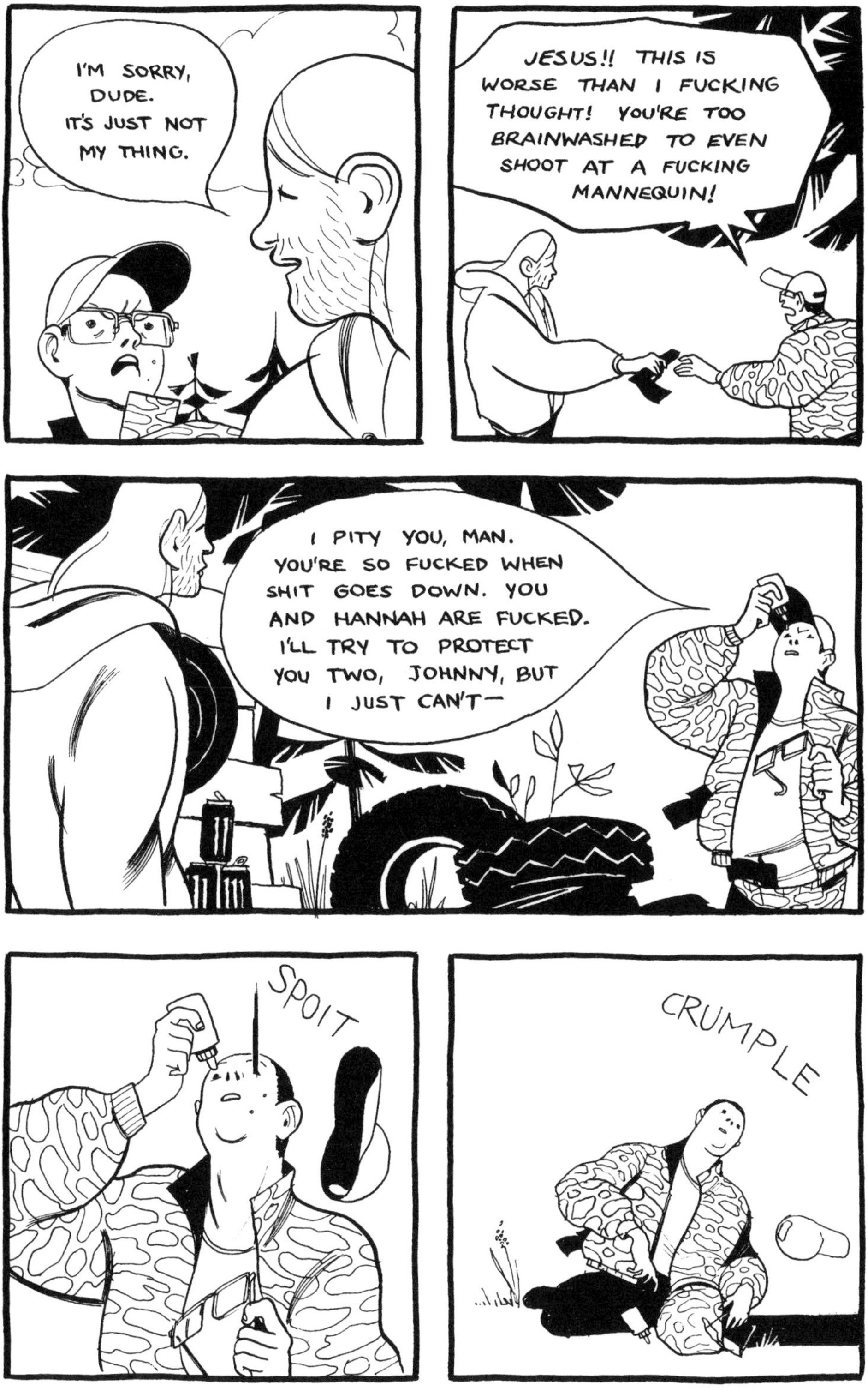
I'M SORRY, DUDE. IT'S JUST NOT MY THING.
JESUS!! THIS IS WORSE THAN I FUCKING THOUGHT! YOU'RE TOO BRAINWASHED TO EVEN SHOOT AT A FUCKING MANNEQUIN!
I PITY YOU, MAN. YOU'RE SO FUCKED WHEN SHIT GOES DOWN. YOU AND HANNAH ARE FUCKED. I'LL TRY TO PROTECT YOU TWO, JOHNNY, BUT I JUST CAN'T—
SPOIT
CRUMPLE

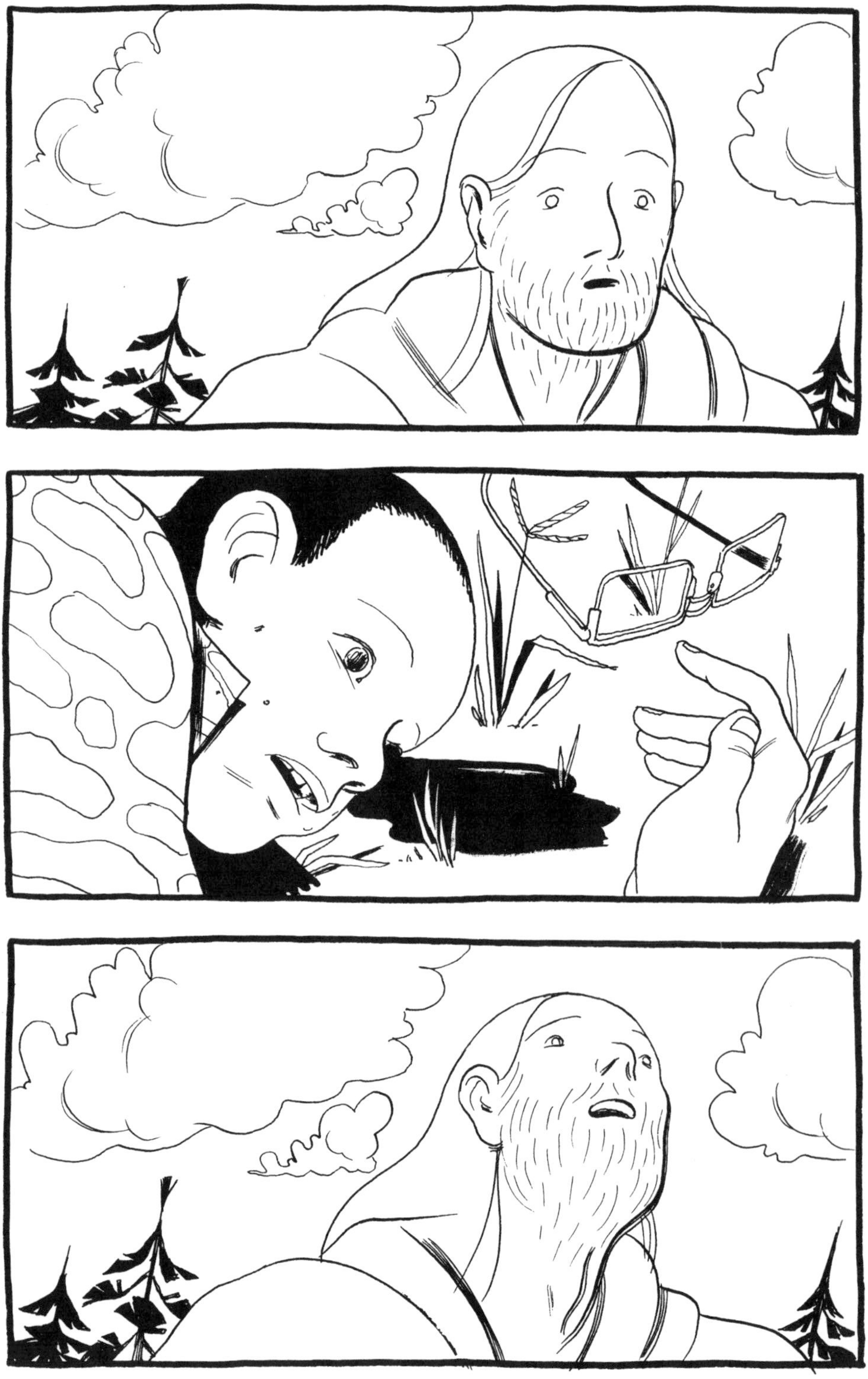

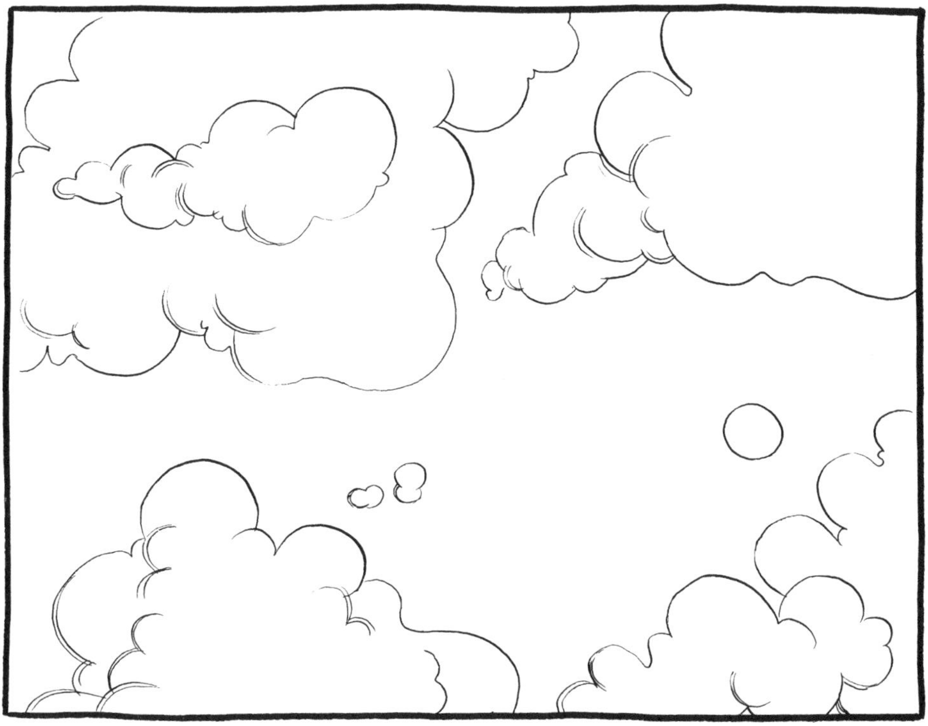

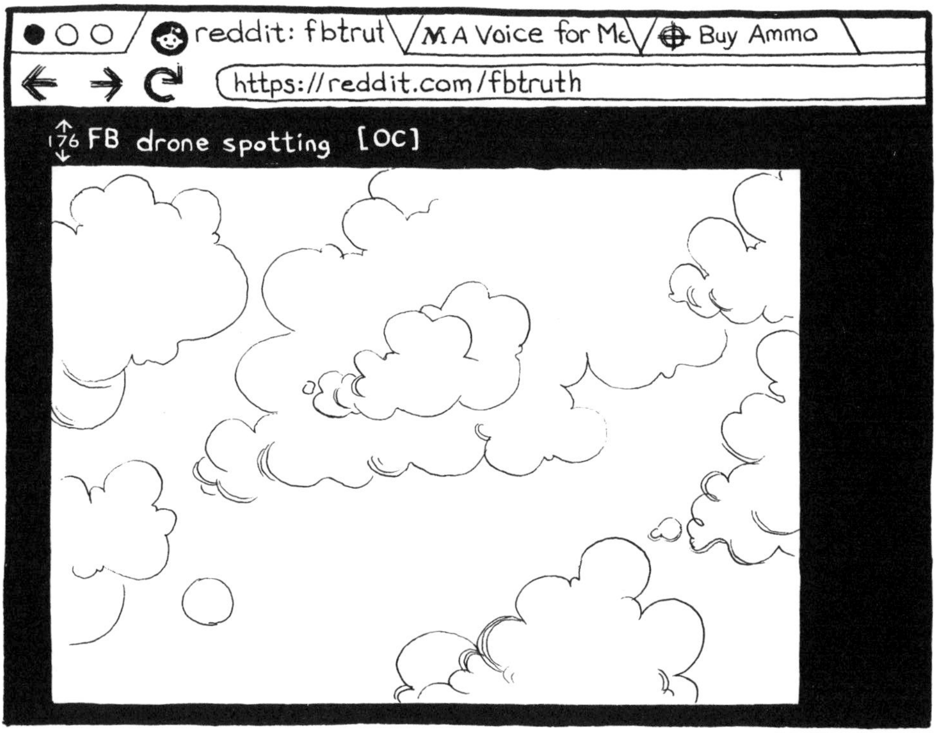
reddit: fbtrut
A Voice for Me
Buy Ammo
https://reddit.com/fbtruth
176 FB drone spotting [OC]

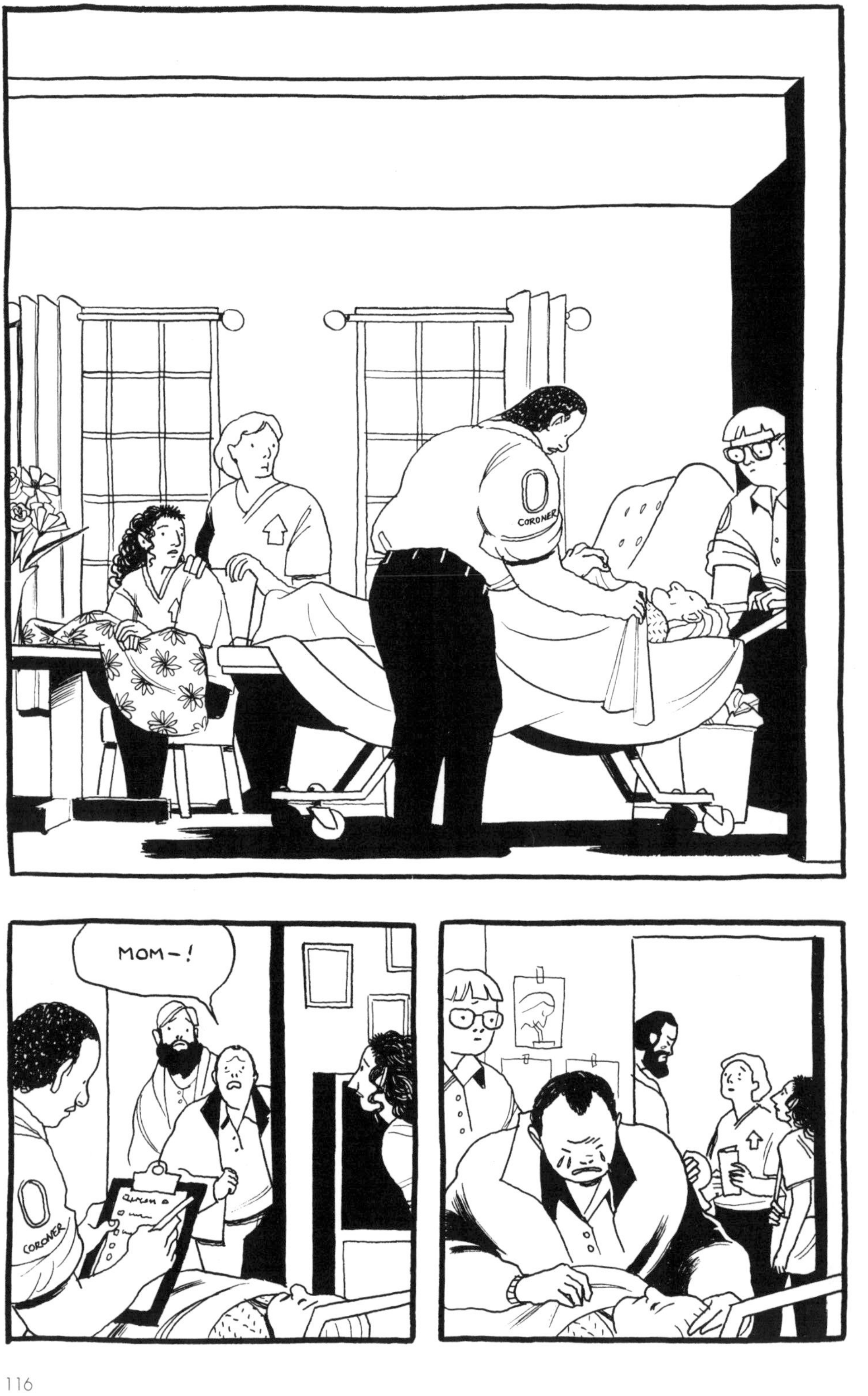
CORONER
MOM–!
CORONER

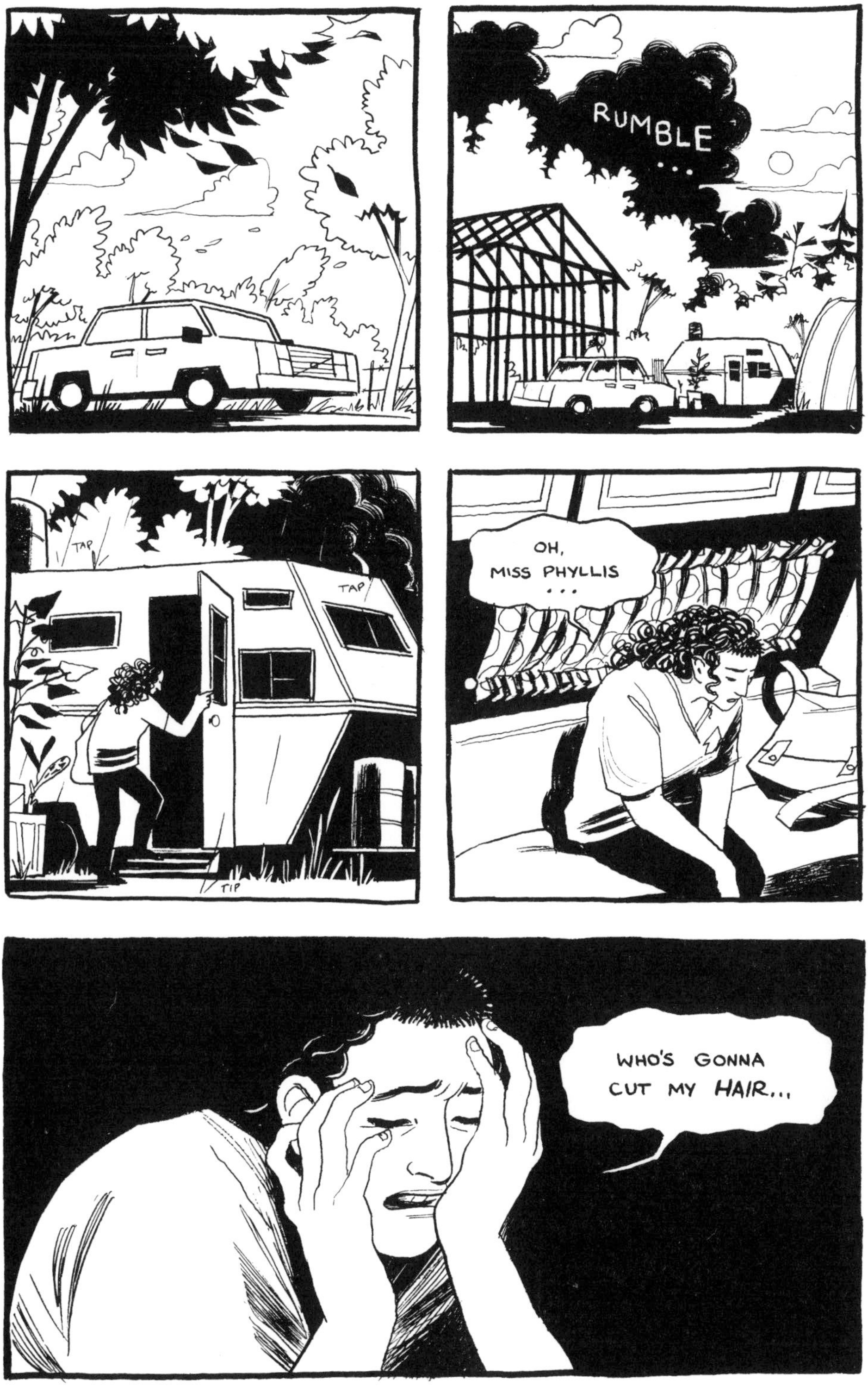
RUMBLE...
TAP
TAP
TIP
OH, MISS PHYLLIS...
WHO'S GONNA CUT MY HAIR...

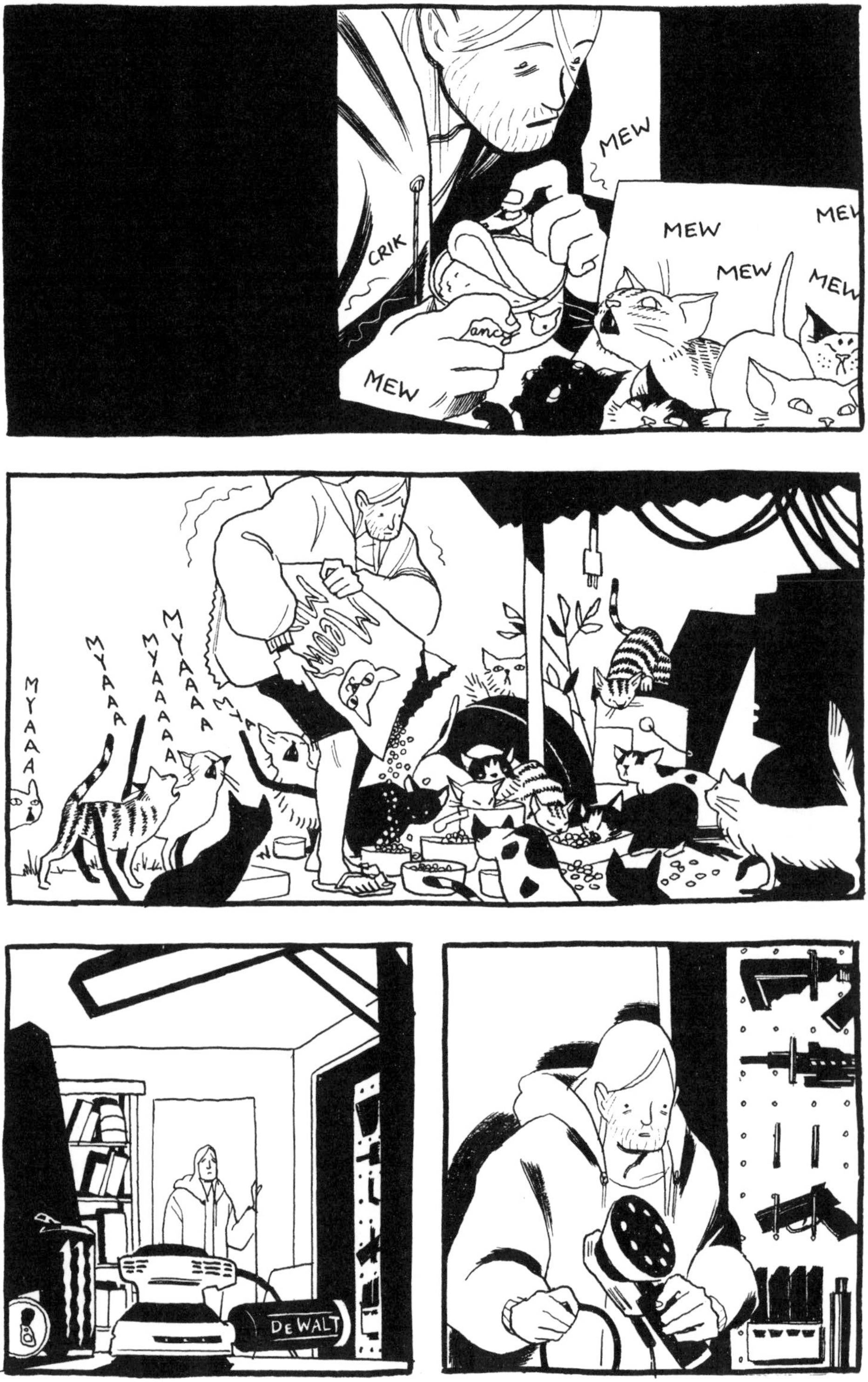
MEW
MEW
MEW
CRIK
MEW
MEW
MEW
MEW
MYAAAA
MYAAA
MYAAAAAA
MYAAAAA
MYA
DEWALT

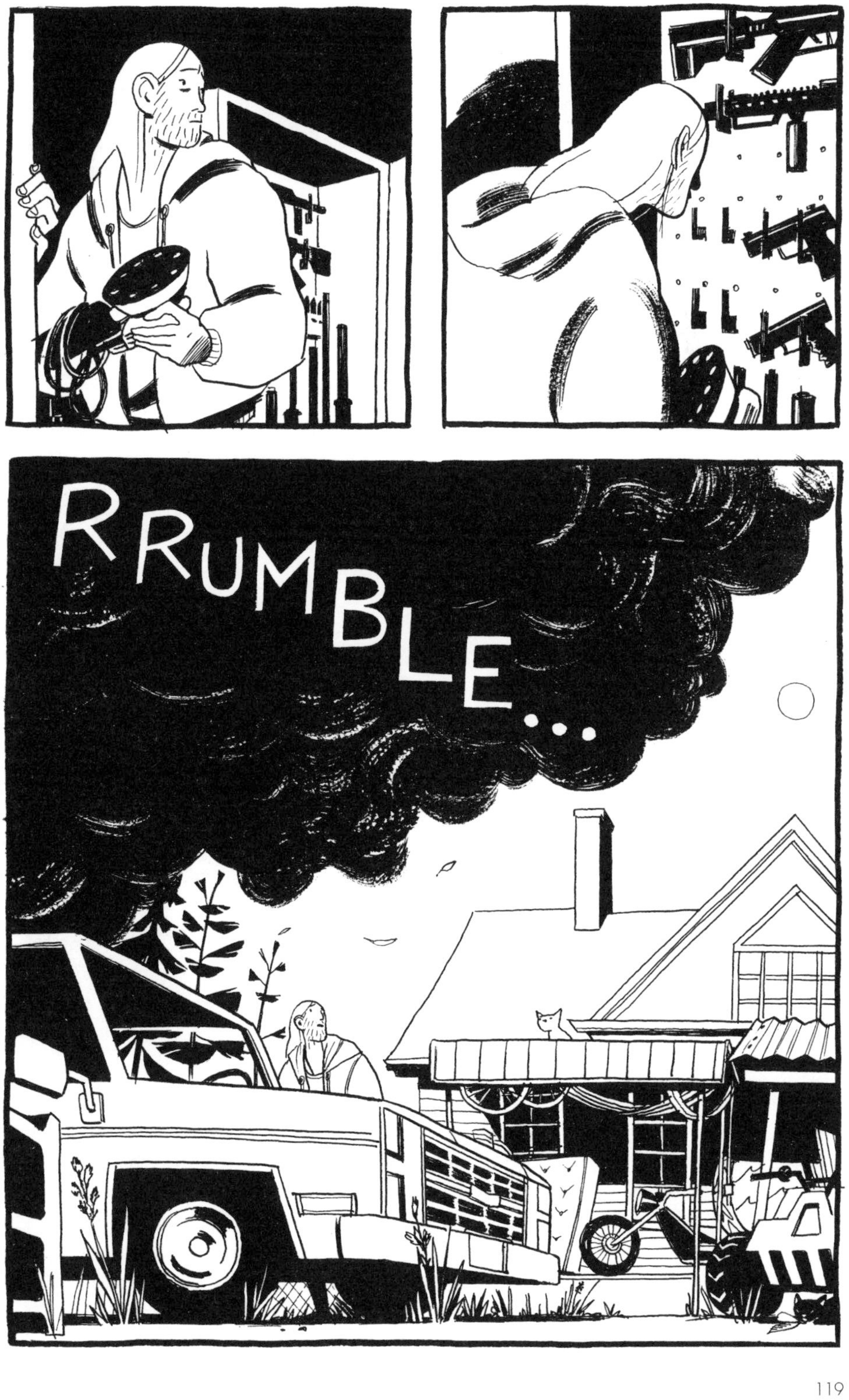
RRUMBLE...

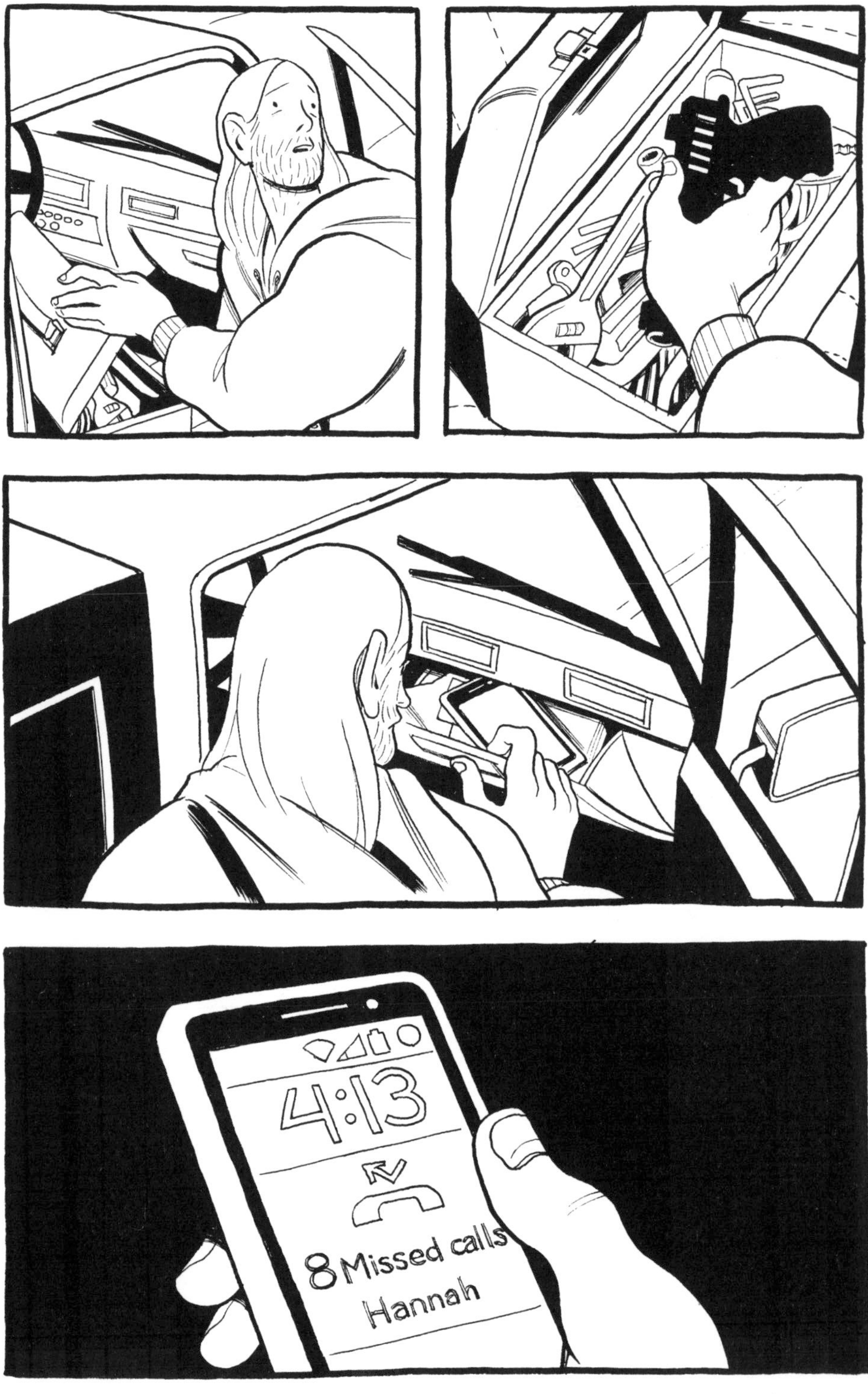
4:13
8 Missed calls
Hannah

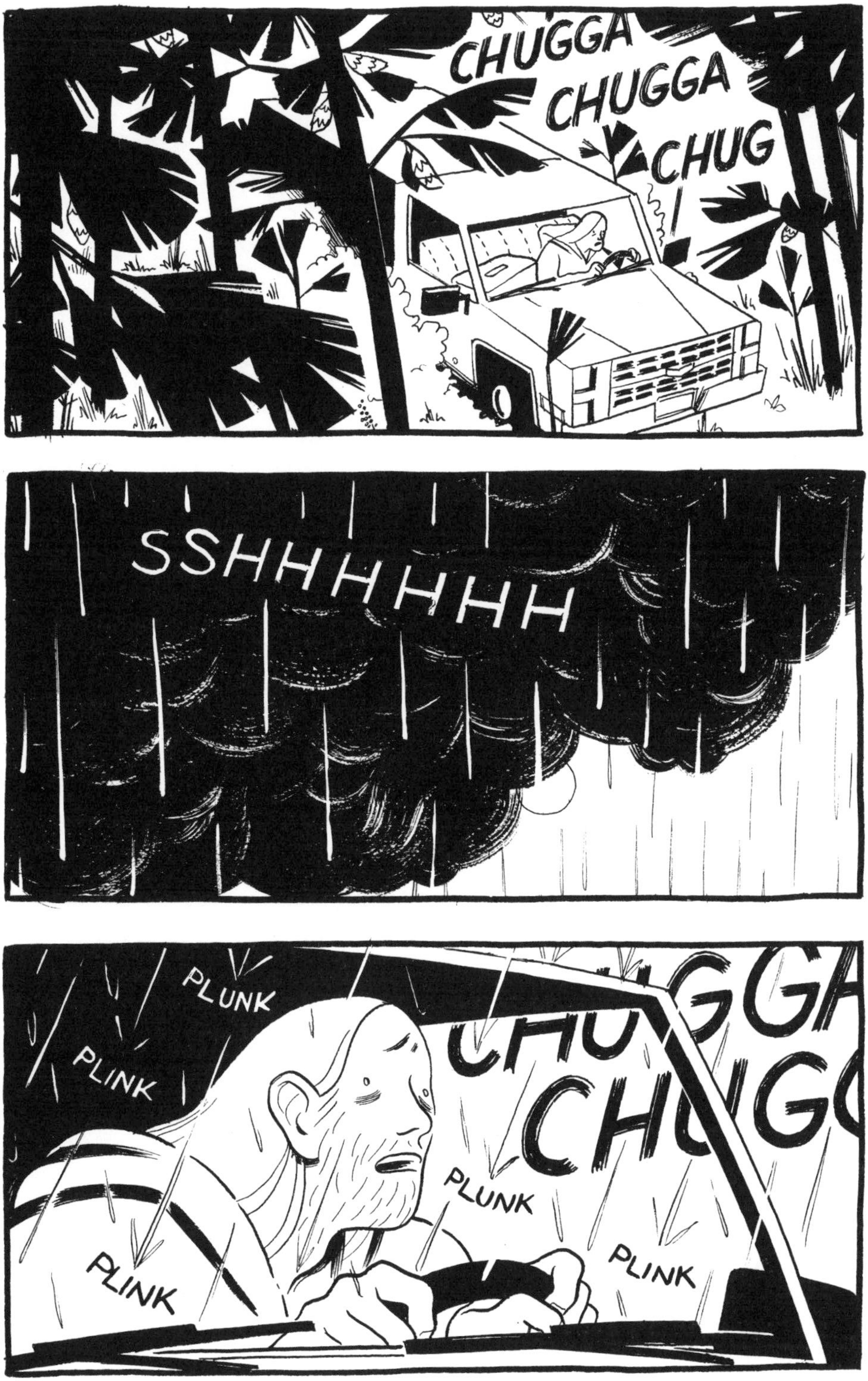
CHUGGA
CHUGGA
CHUG
SSHHHHHHH
PLUNK
PLINK
PLUNK
PLINK
PLINK

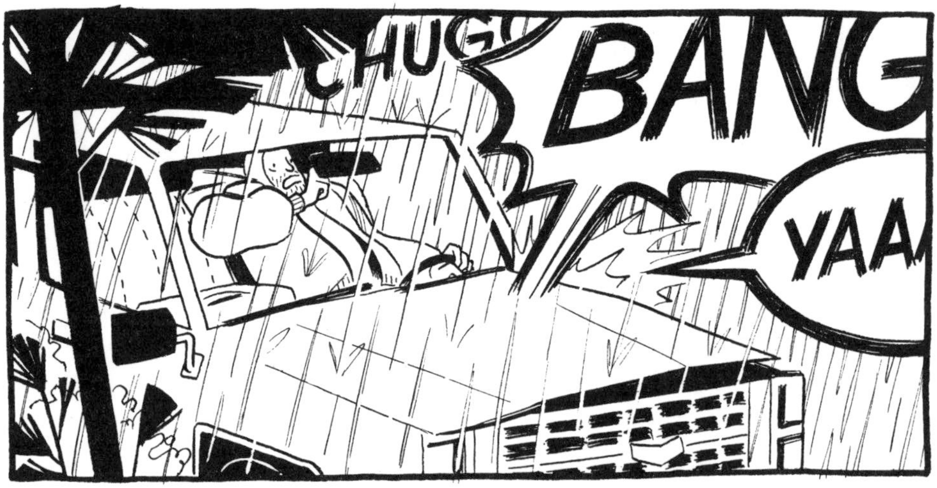
CHUG
BANG
YAA

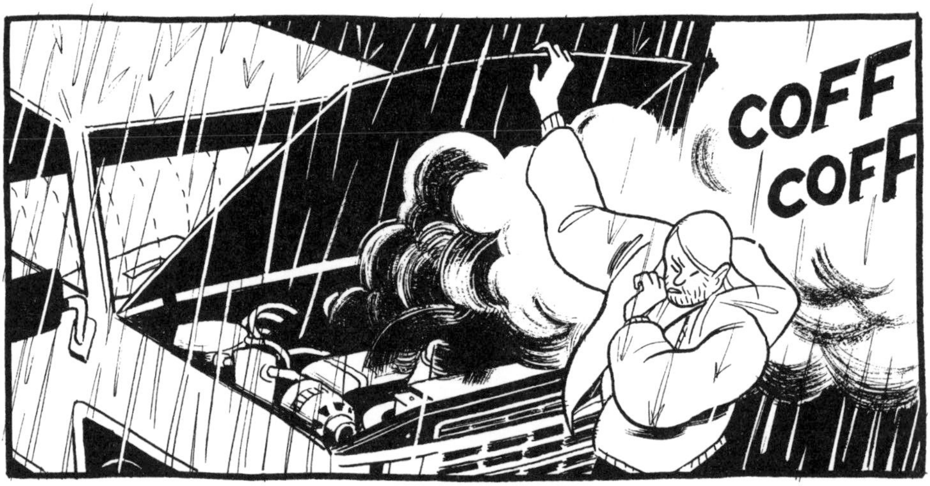
COFF
COFF

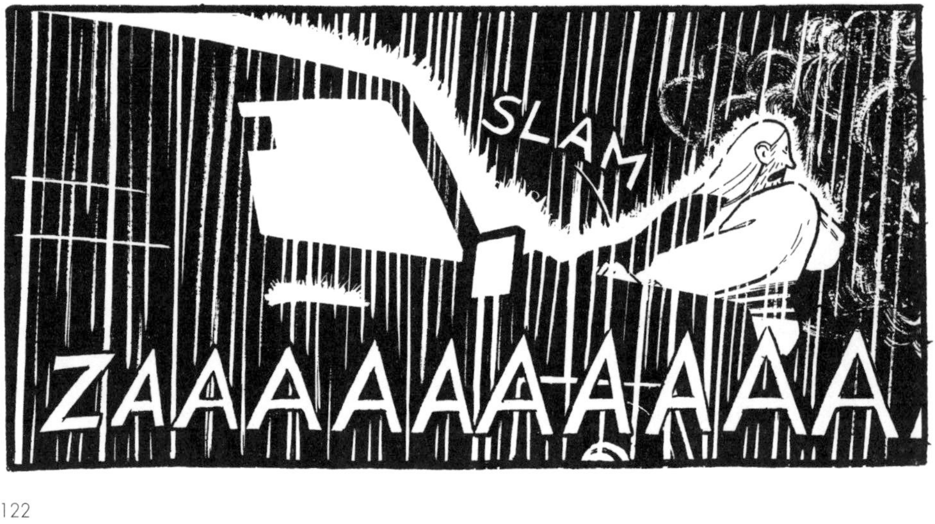
SLAM
ZAAAAAAAAAA

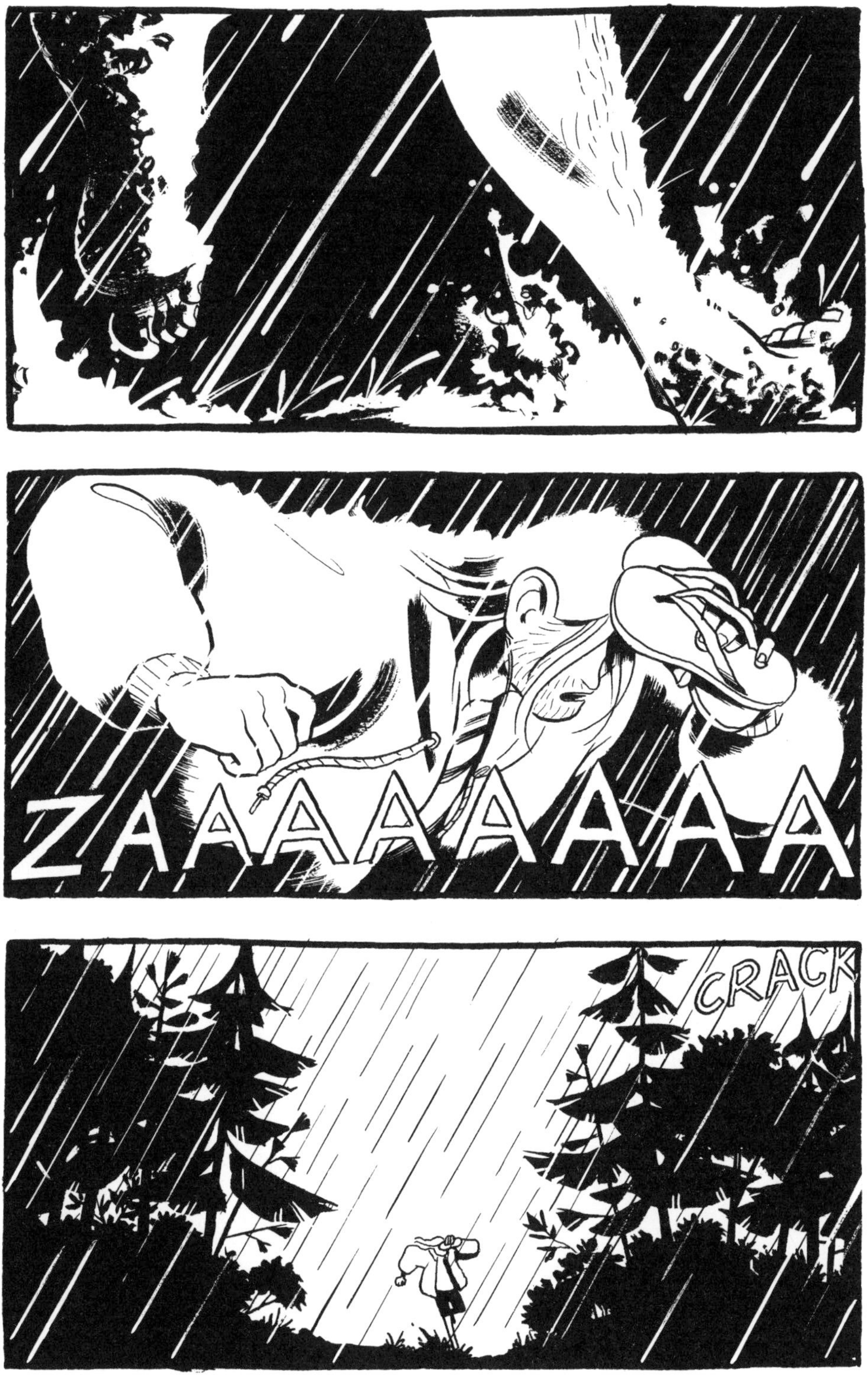
ZAAAAAAAAA
CRACK

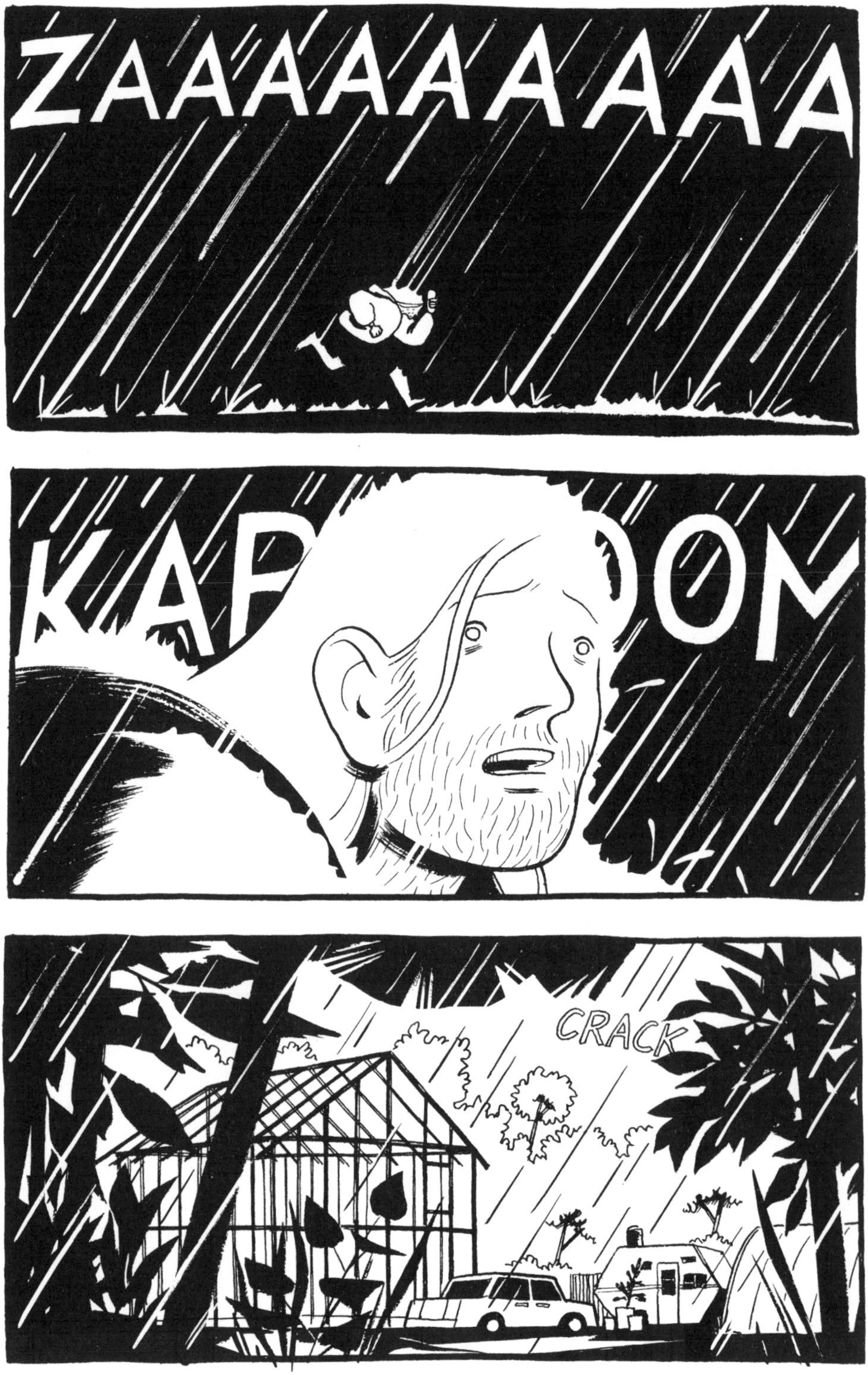
ZAAAAAAAAA
CRACK

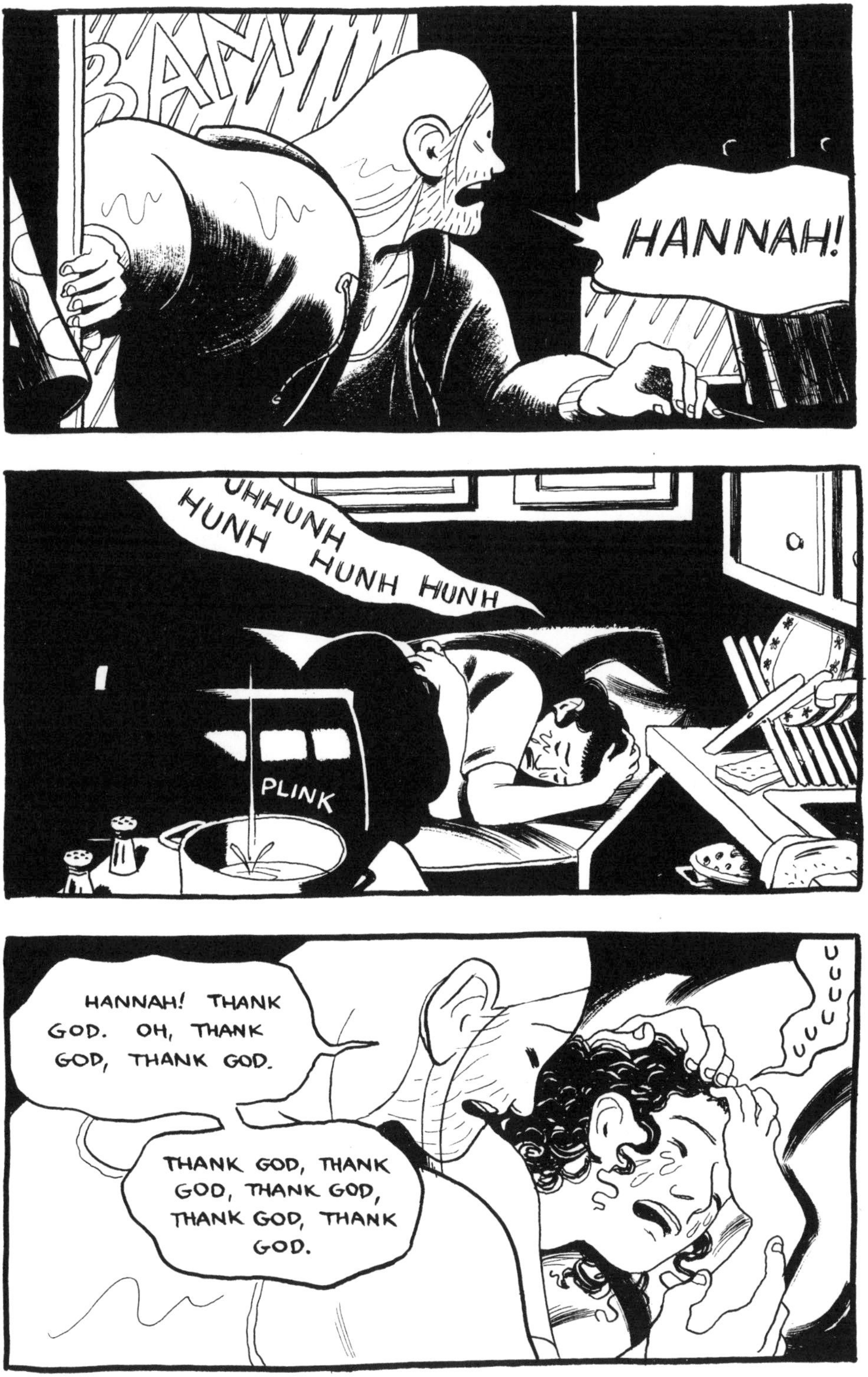
BAM!
HANNAH!
UHHUNH
HUNH HUNH HUNH
PLINK
HANNAH! THANK GOD. OH, THANK GOD, THANK GOD.
UUUUUU
THANK GOD, THANK GOD, THANK GOD, THANK GOD, THANK GOD.

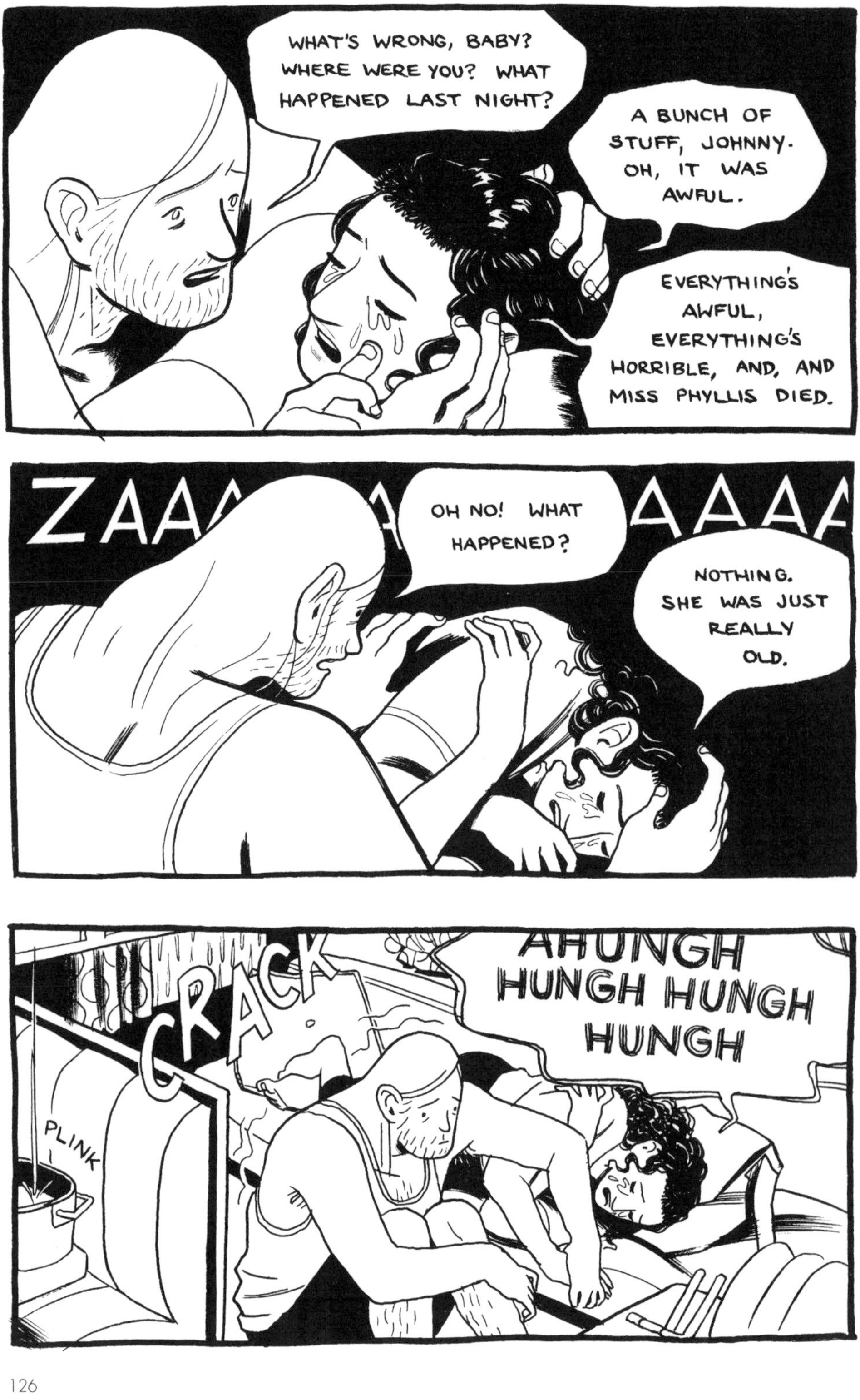
WHAT'S WRONG, BABY? WHERE WERE YOU? WHAT HAPPENED LAST NIGHT?
A BUNCH OF STUFF, JOHNNY. OH, IT WAS AWFUL.
EVERYTHING'S AWFUL, EVERYTHING'S HORRIBLE, AND, AND MISS PHYLLIS DIED.
OH NO! WHAT HAPPENED?
NOTHING. SHE WAS JUST REALLY OLD.
CRACK
AHUNGH HUNGH HUNGH HUNGH
PLINK

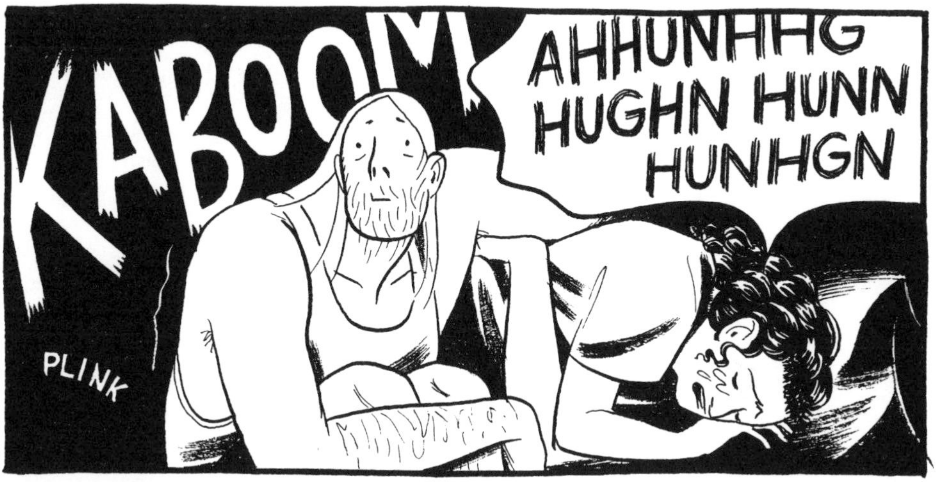
KABOOM
AHHUNHHG HUGHN HUNN HUNHGN
PLINK

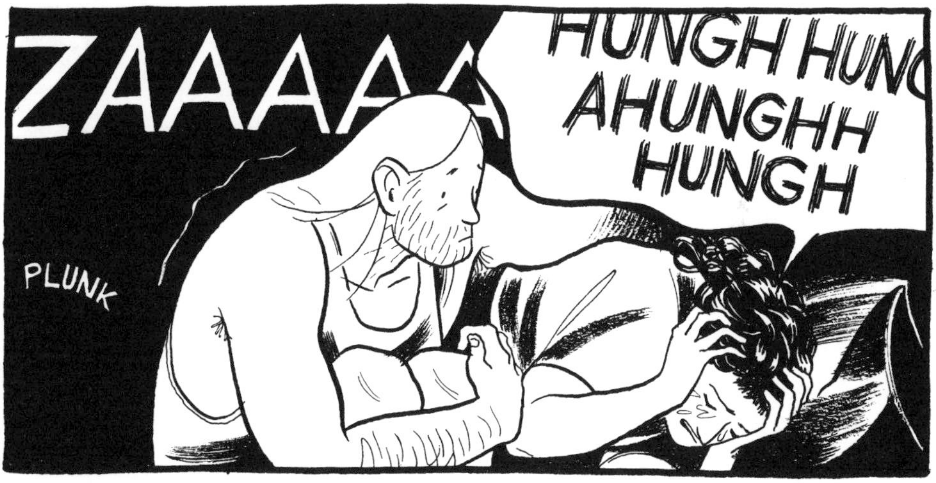
ZAAAAA
HUNGH HUNG AHUNGHH HUNGH
PLUNK

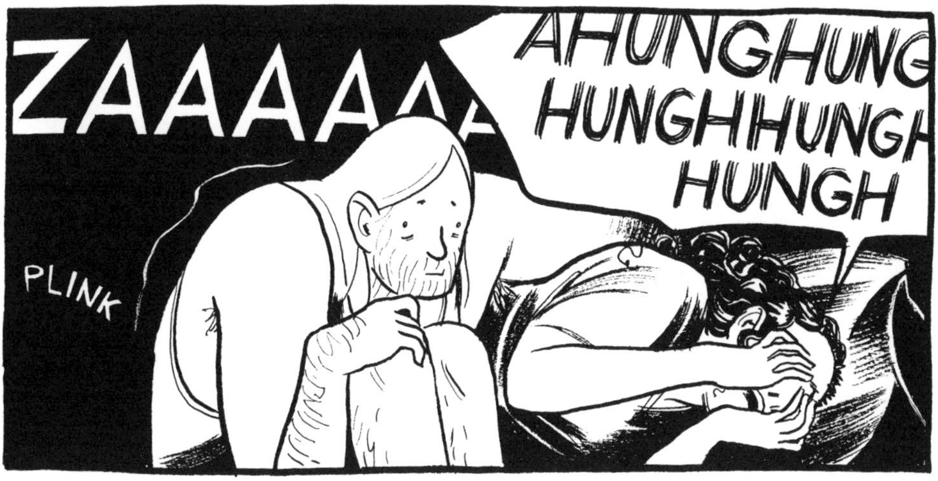
ZAAAAA
AHUNGHUNG HUNGHHUNGH HUNGH
PLINK

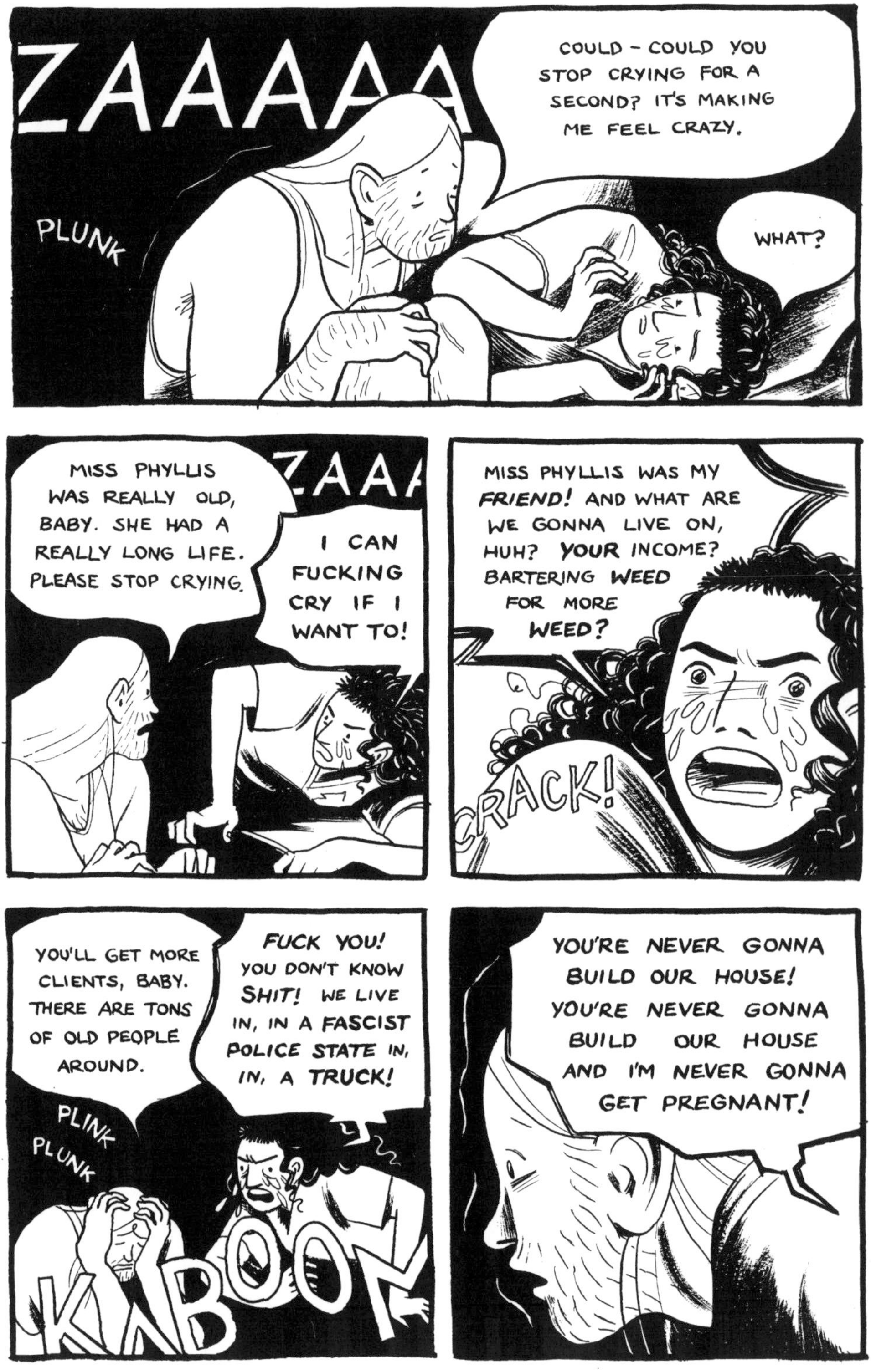
ZAAAAA
COULD - COULD YOU STOP CRYING FOR A SECOND? IT'S MAKING ME FEEL CRAZY.
PLUNK
WHAT?
MISS PHYLLIS WAS REALLY OLD, BABY. SHE HAD A REALLY LONG LIFE. PLEASE STOP CRYING.
ZAAA
I CAN FUCKING CRY IF I WANT TO!
MISS PHYLLIS WAS MY FRIEND! AND WHAT ARE WE GONNA LIVE ON, HUH? YOUR INCOME? BARTERING WEED FOR MORE WEED?
CRACK!
YOU'LL GET MORE CLIENTS, BABY. THERE ARE TONS OF OLD PEOPLE AROUND.
FUCK YOU! YOU DON'T KNOW SHIT! WE LIVE IN, IN A FASCIST POLICE STATE IN, IN, A TRUCK!
PLINK
PLUNK
KABOOM
YOU'RE NEVER GONNA BUILD OUR HOUSE! YOU'RE NEVER GONNA BUILD OUR HOUSE AND I'M NEVER GONNA GET PREGNANT!

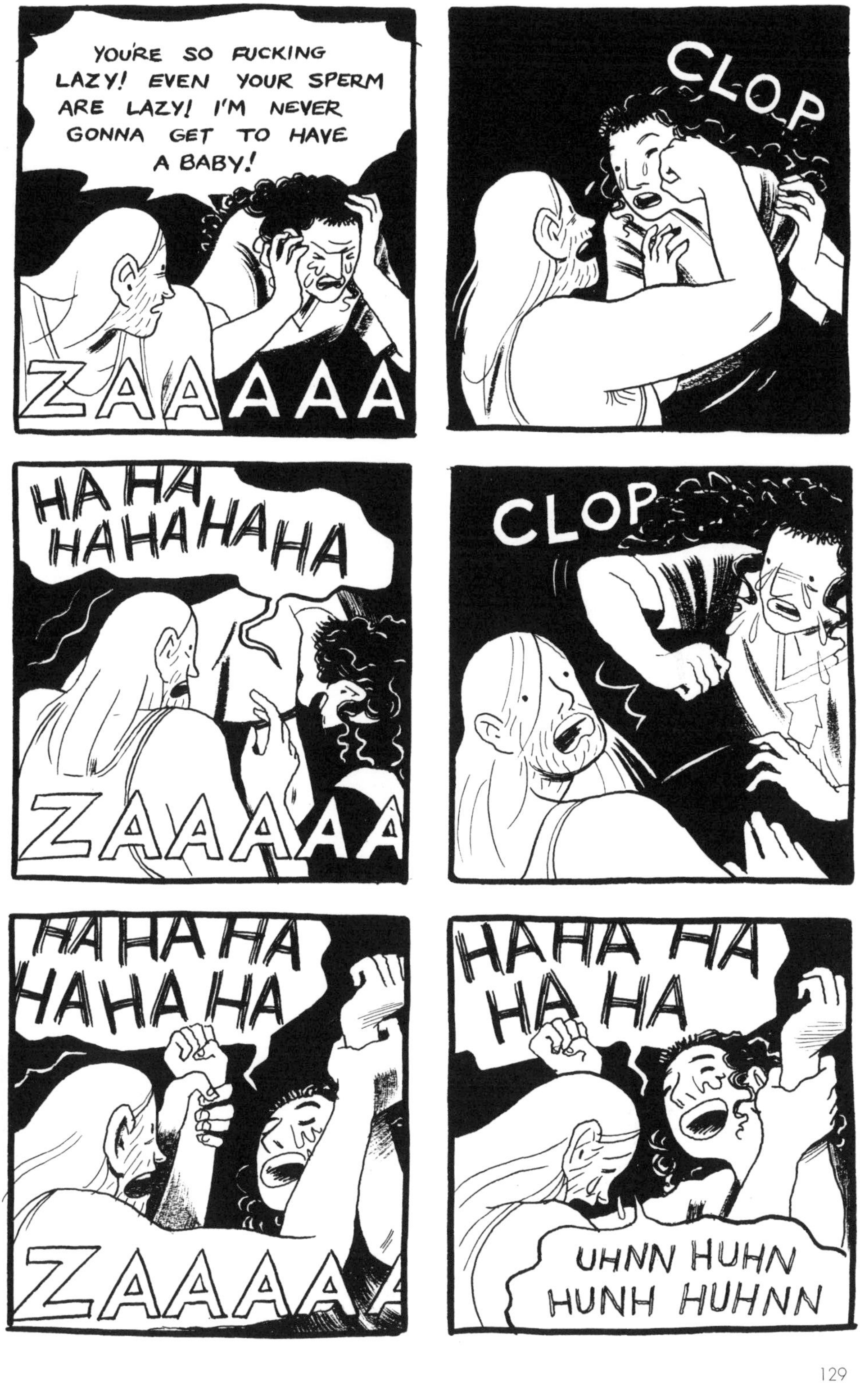
YOU'RE SO FUCKING LAZY! EVEN YOUR SPERM ARE LAZY! I'M NEVER GONNA GET TO HAVE A BABY!
ZAAAAA
CLOP
HA HA HA HA HA HA HA
ZAAAAA
CLOP
HA HA HA HA HA HA HA
ZAAAAA
HA HA HA HA HA HA
UHNN HUHN HUNH HUHNN

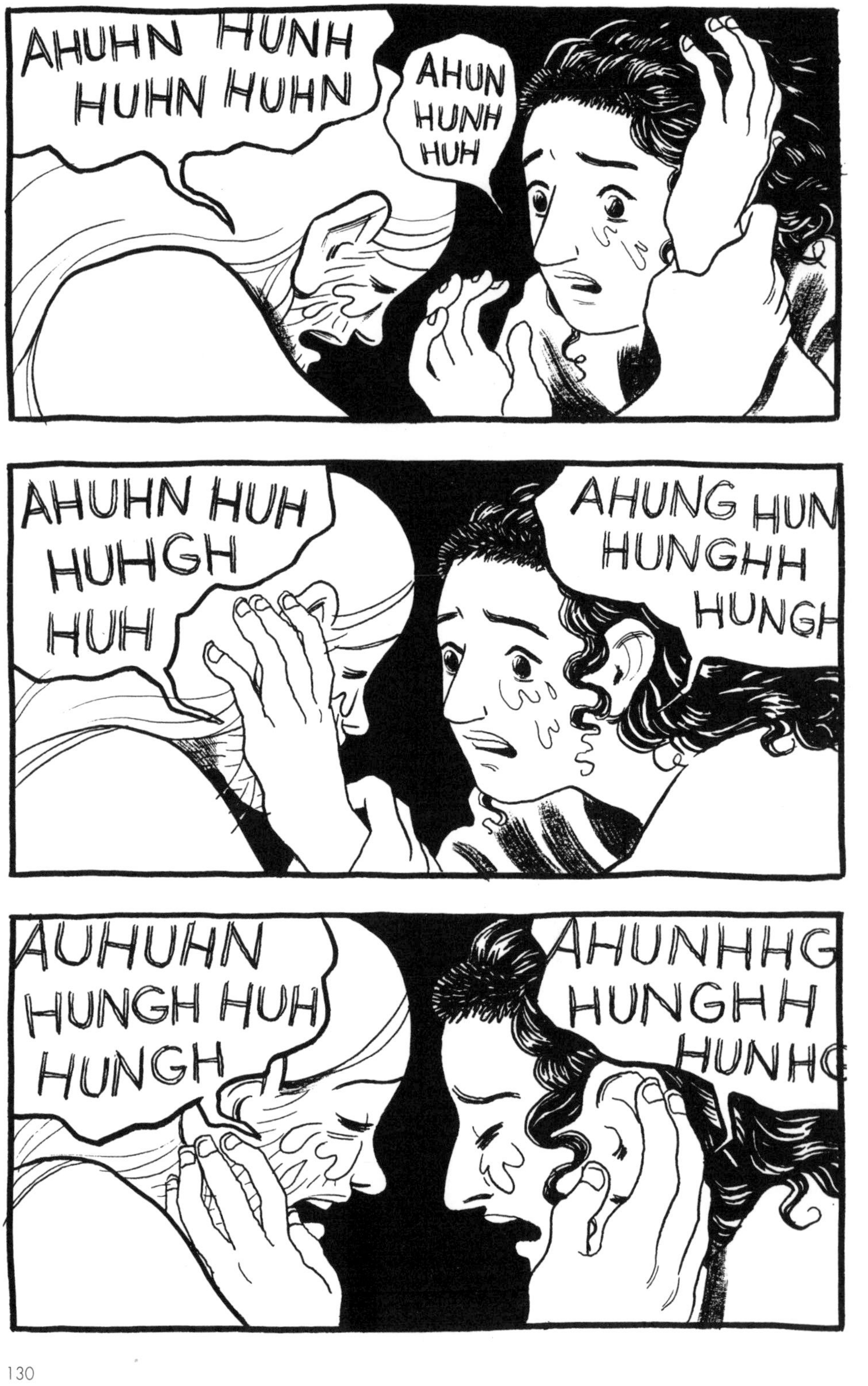
AHUHN HUNH HUHN HUHN
AHUN HUNH HUH
AHUHN HUH HUHGH HUH
AHUNG HUN HUNGHH HUNG
AUHUHN HUNGH HUH HUNGH
AHUNHHG HUNGHH HUNH

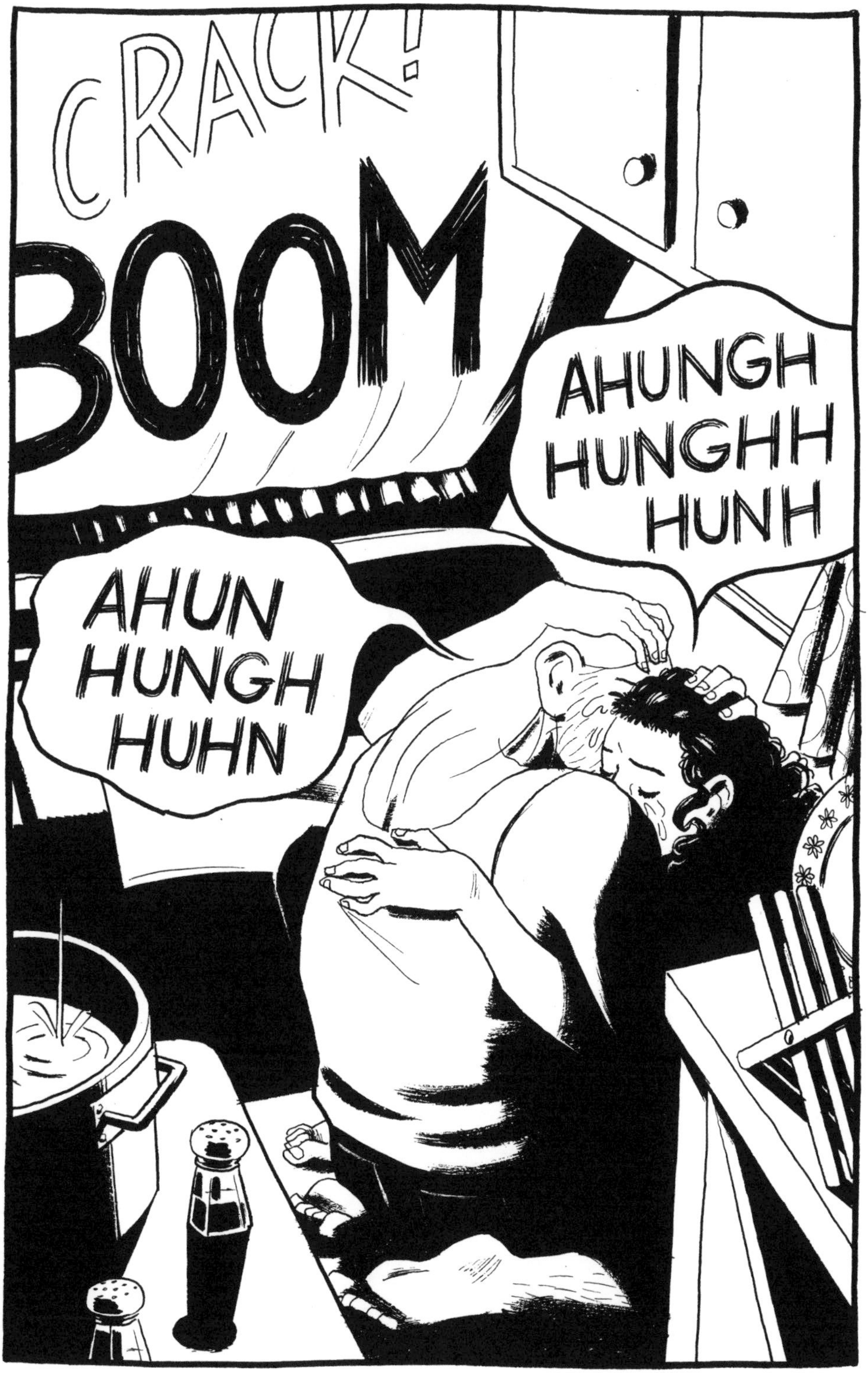
CRACK!
BOOM
AHUNGH HUNGHH HUNH
AHUN HUNGH HUHN

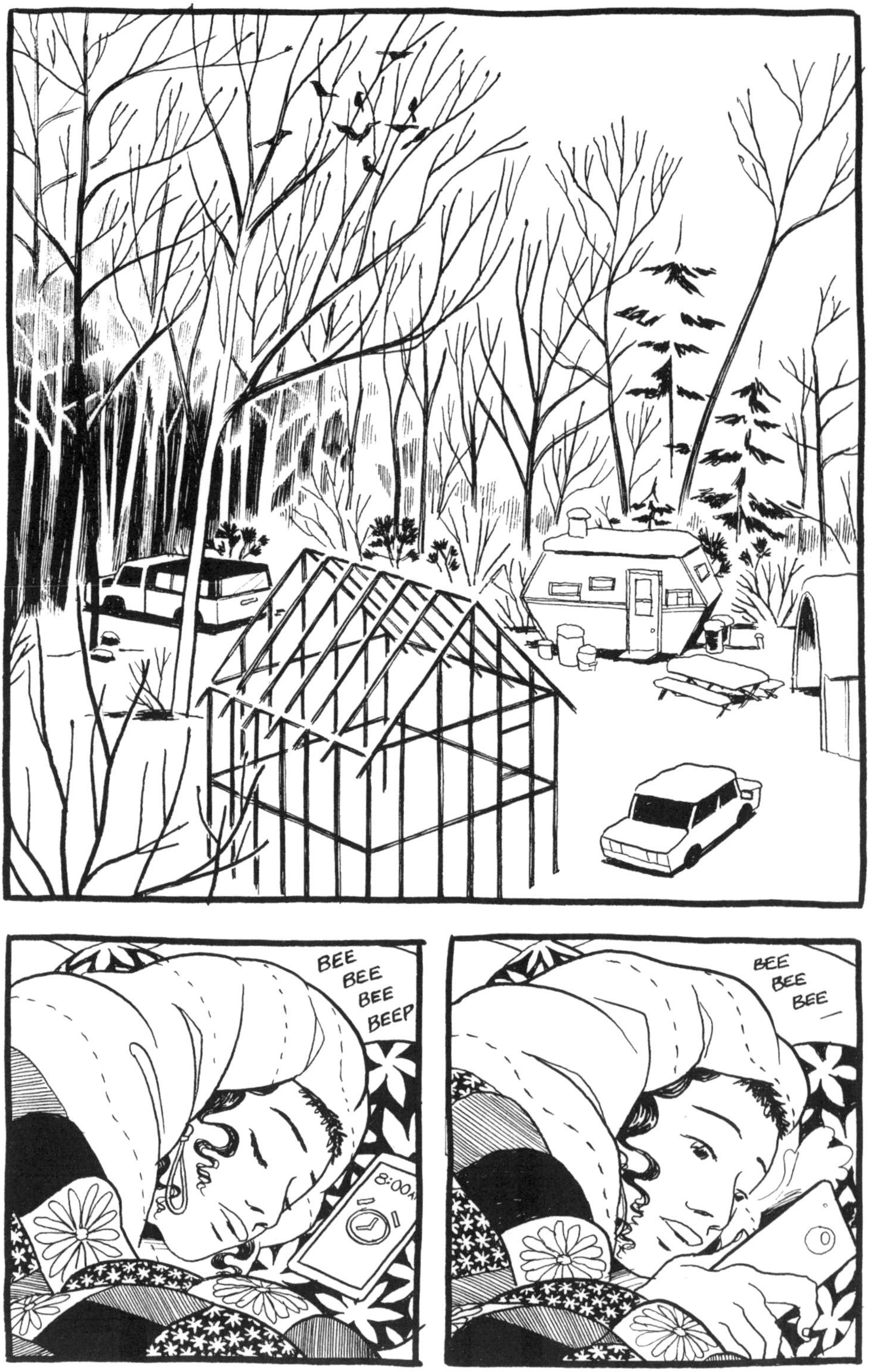
BEE
BEE
BEE
BEEP
8:00
BEE
BEE
BEE

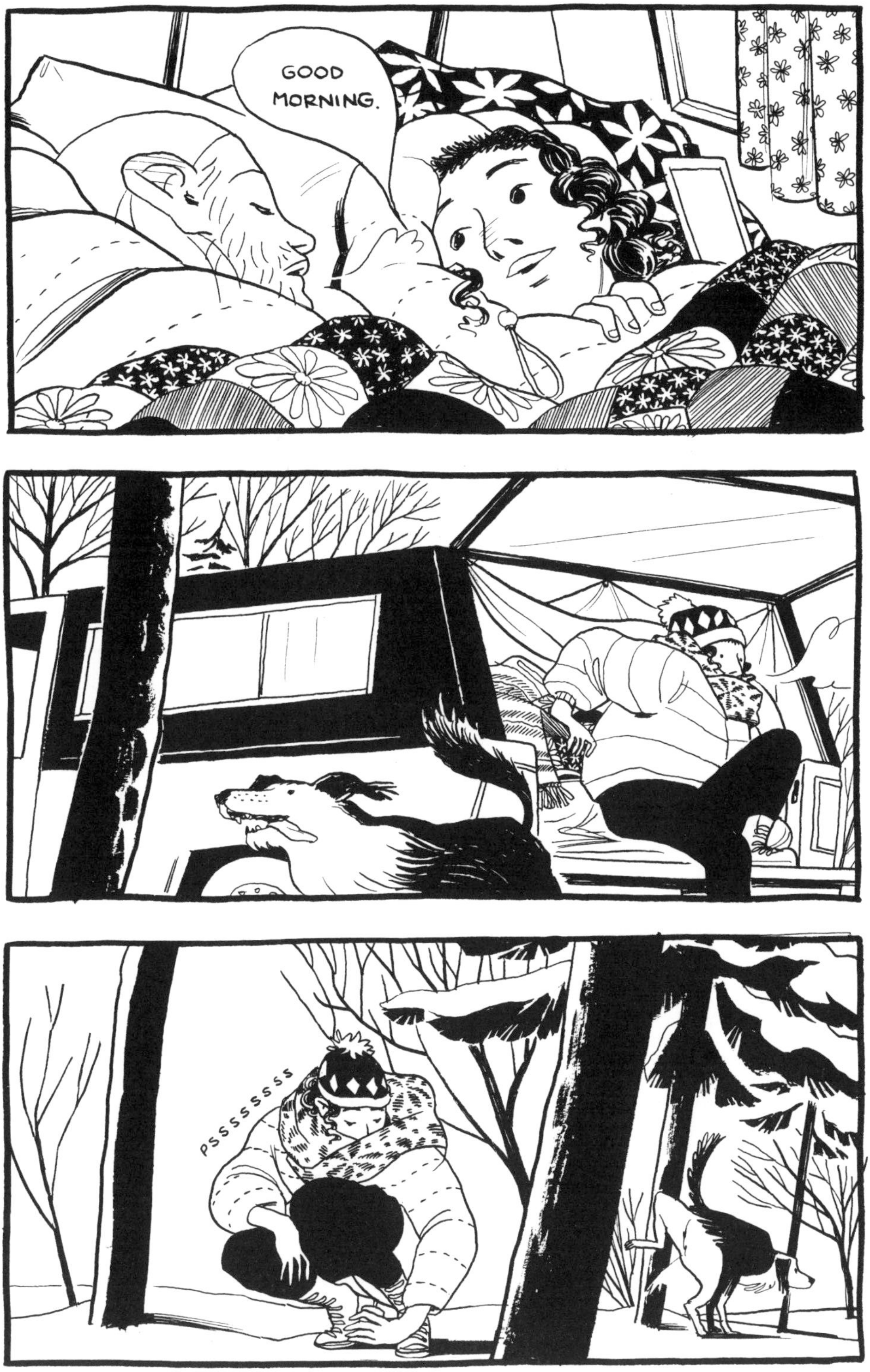
GOOD MORNING.
PSSSSSSSS

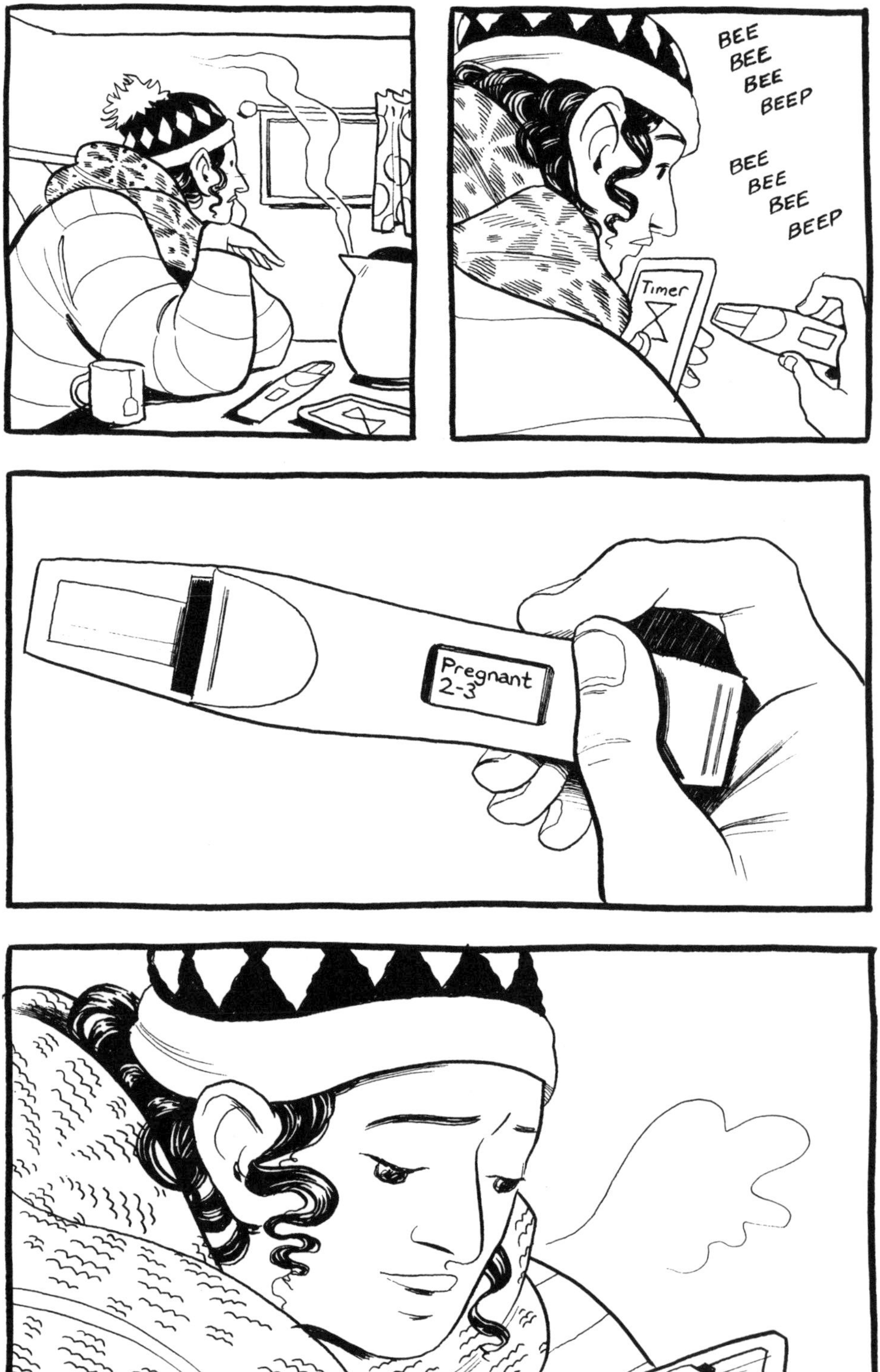
BEE
BEE
BEE
BEEP
BEE
BEE
BEE
BEEP
Timer
Pregnant
2-3

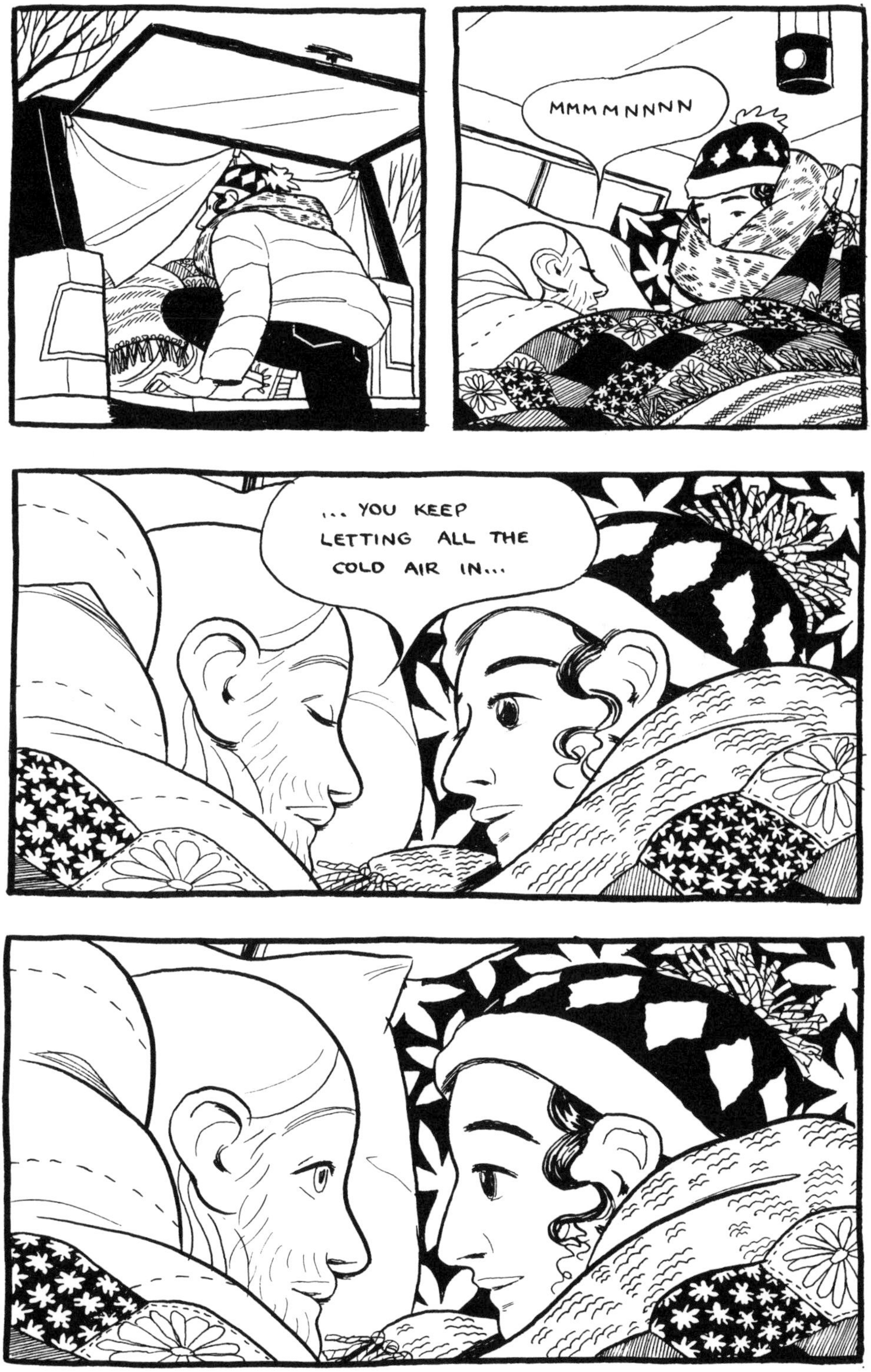
MMMMNNNN
... YOU KEEP LETTING ALL THE COLD AIR IN...

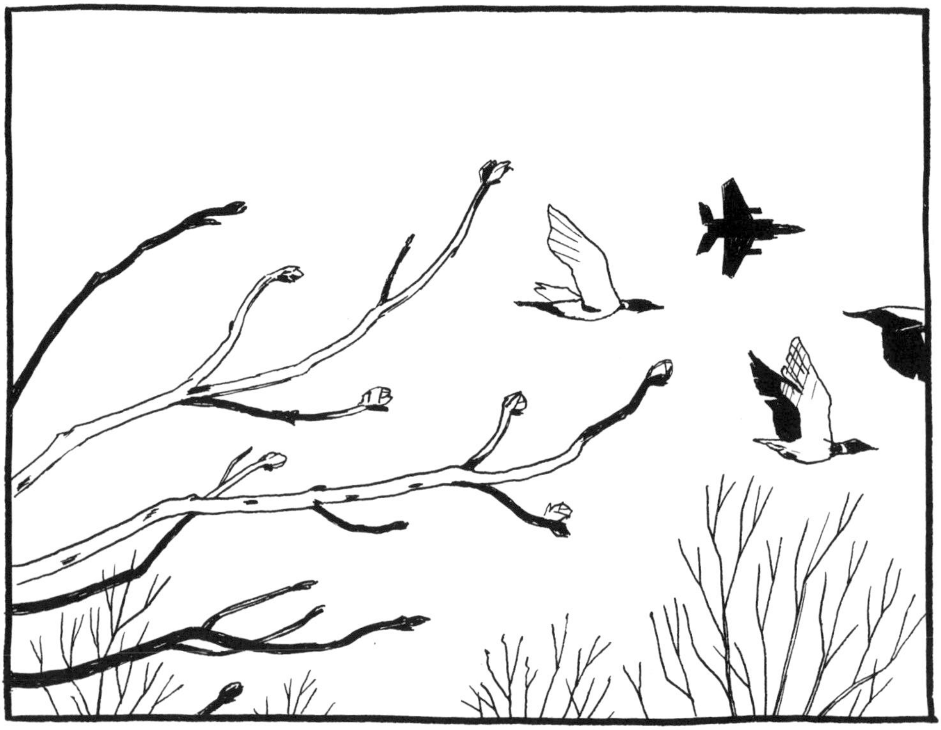

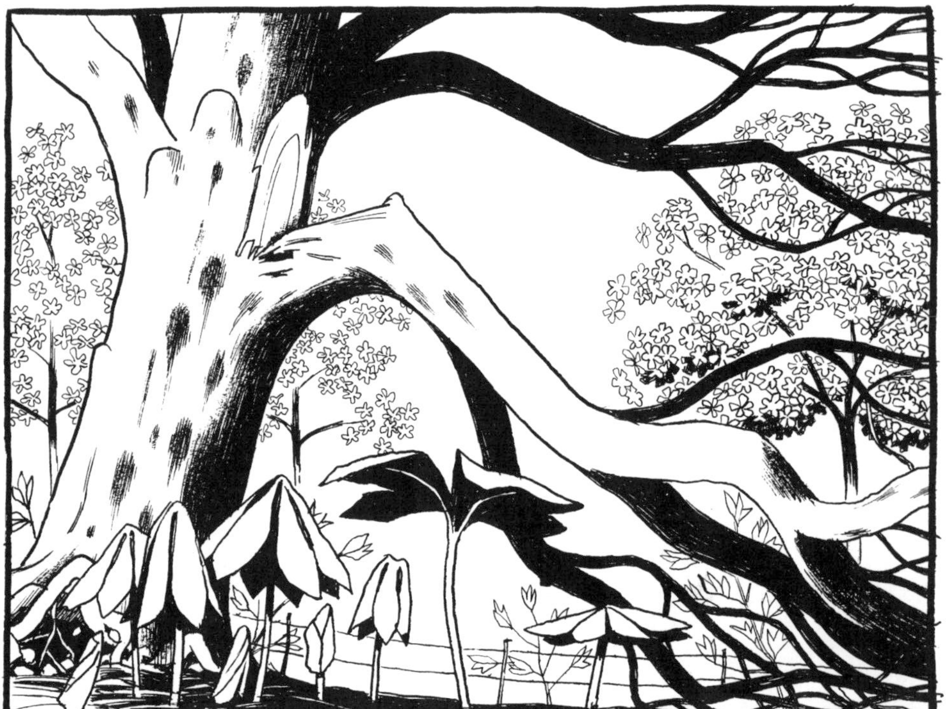

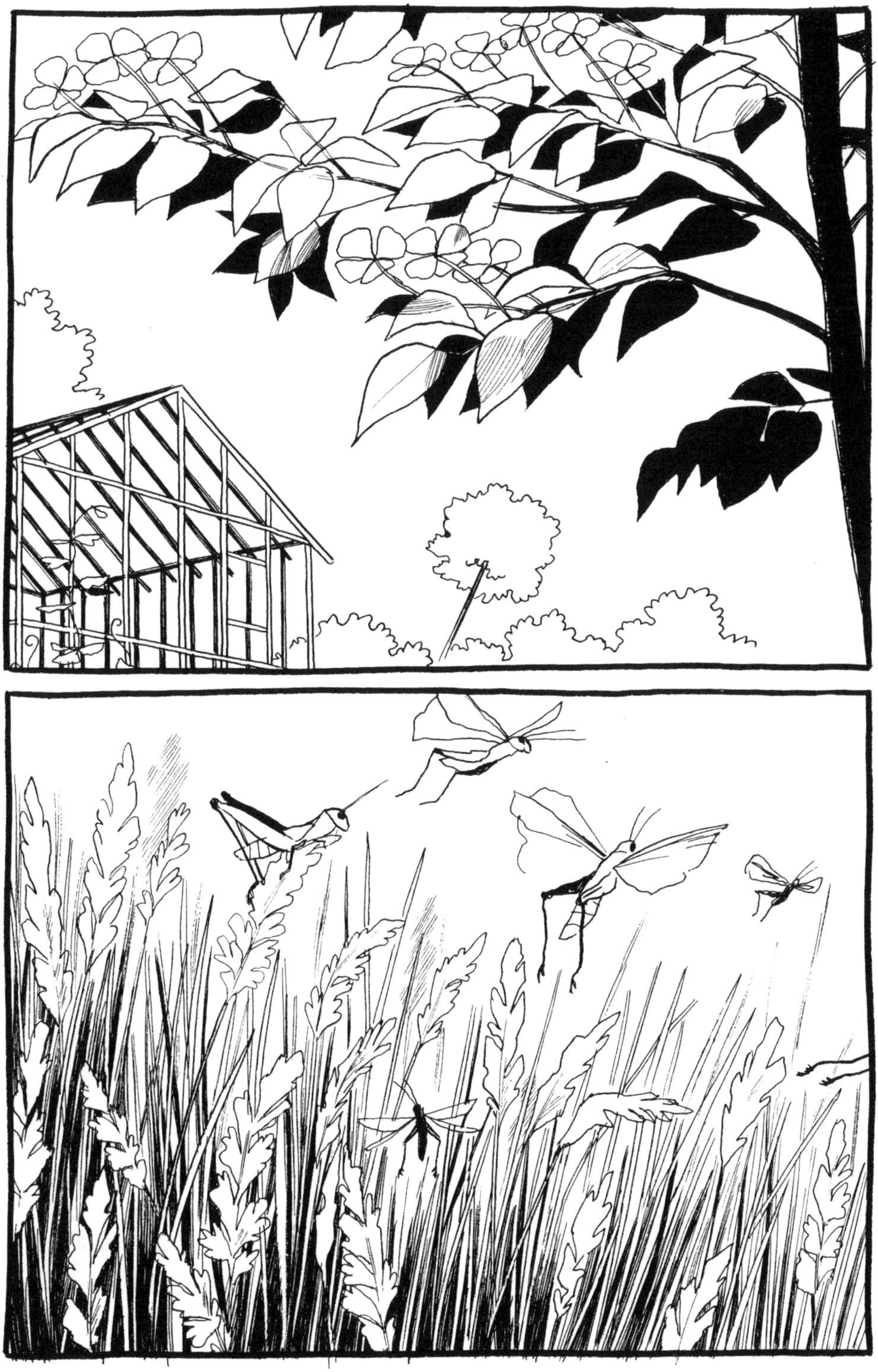

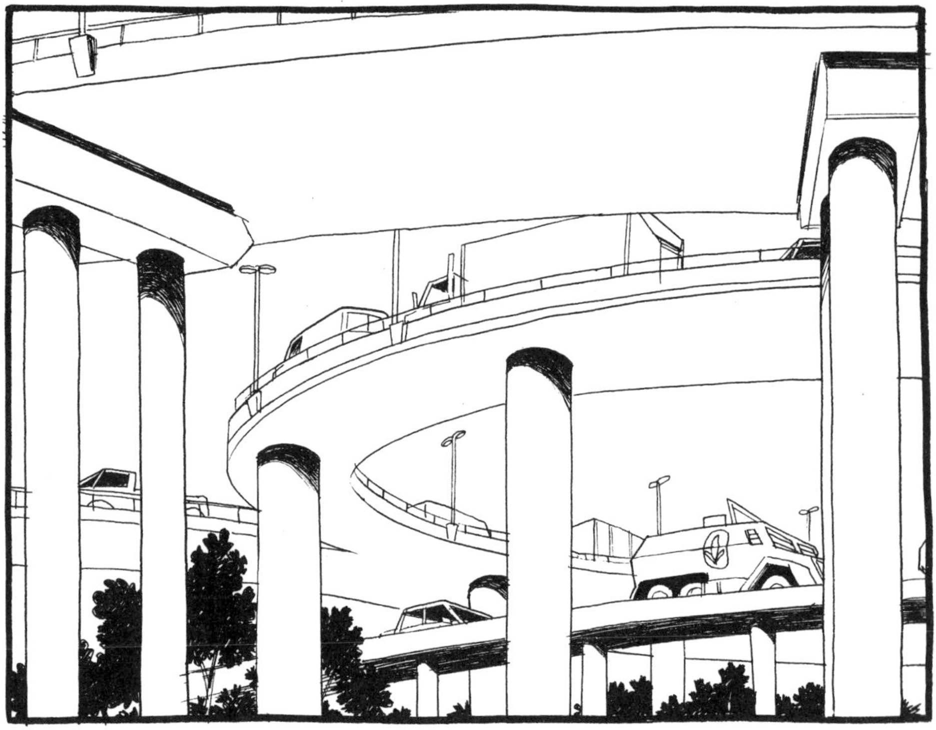

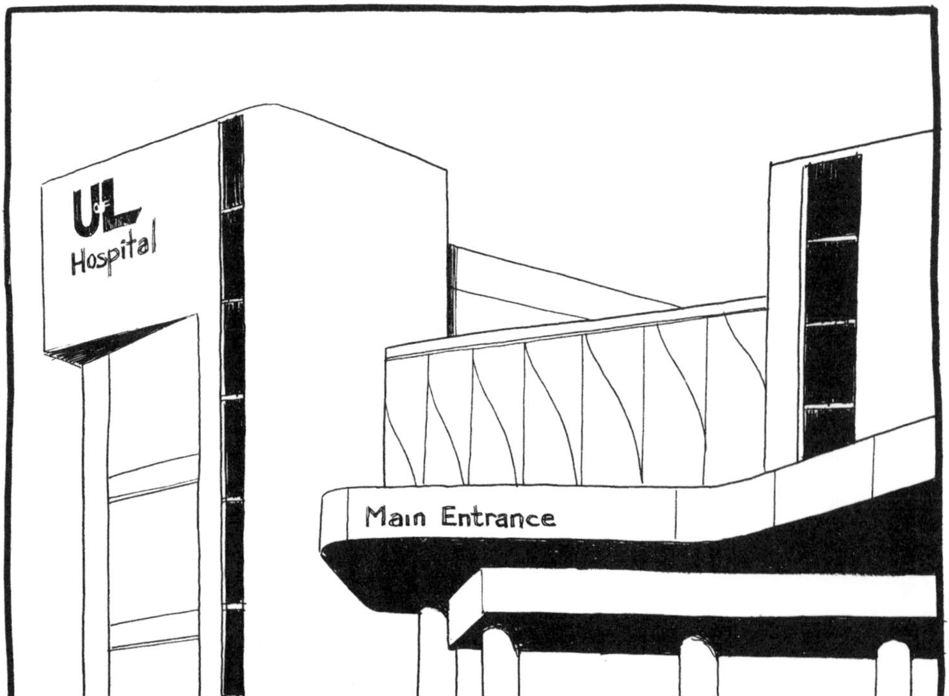
UofL
Hospital
Main Entrance

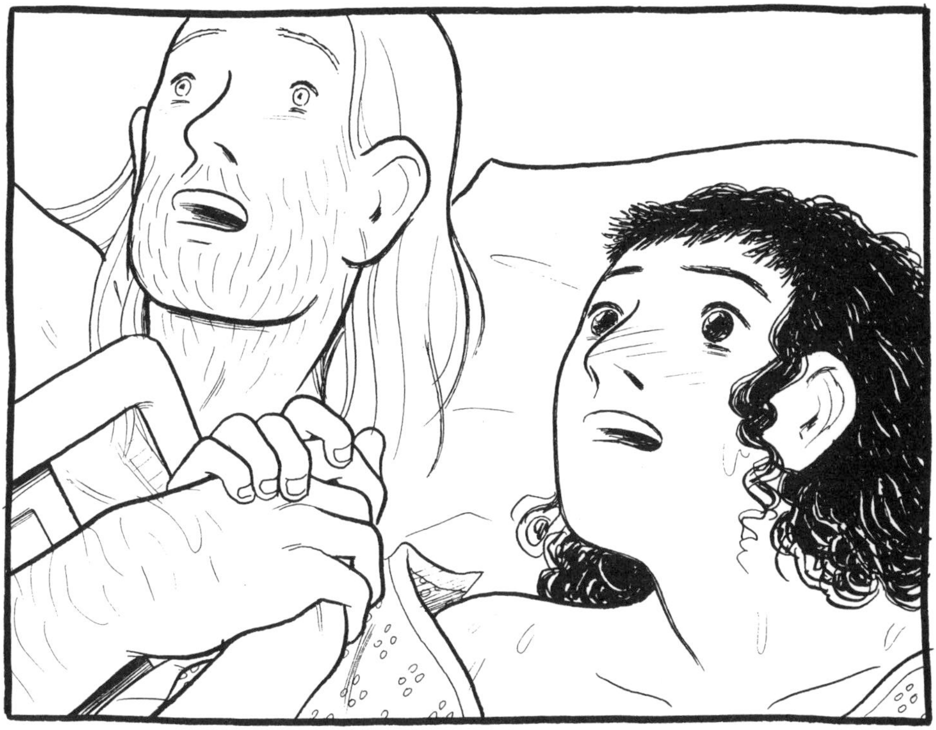

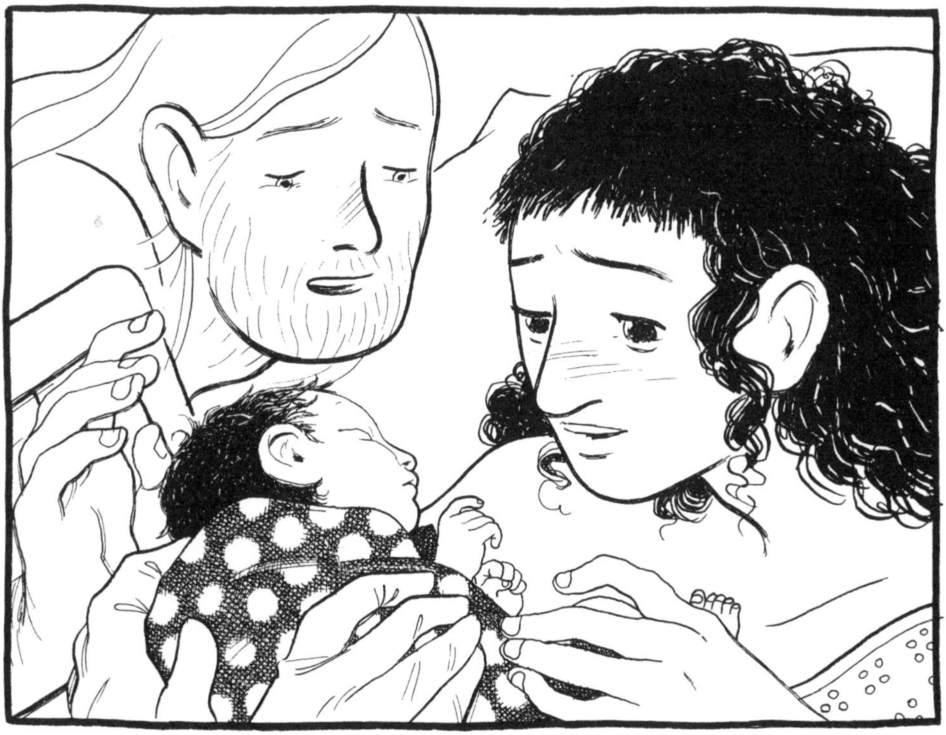

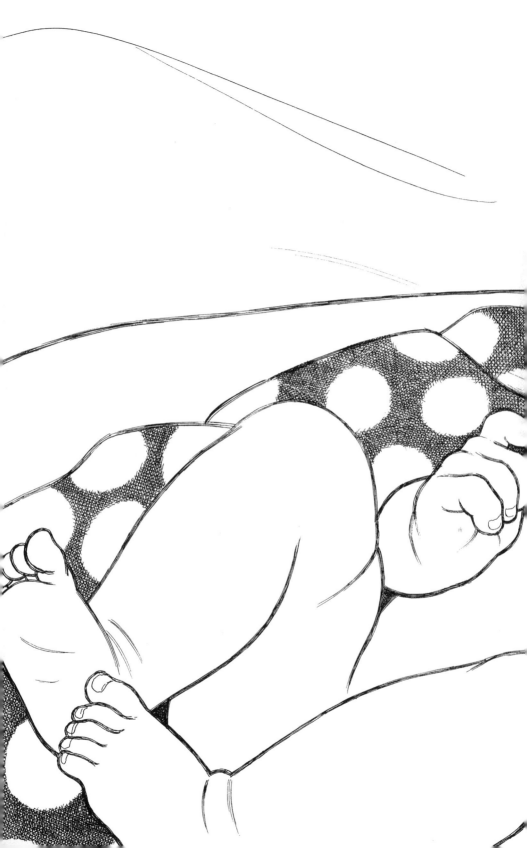

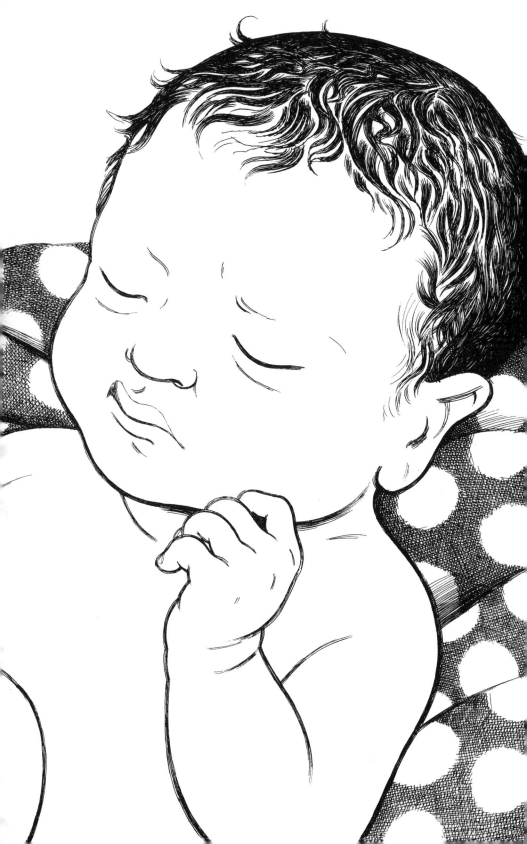

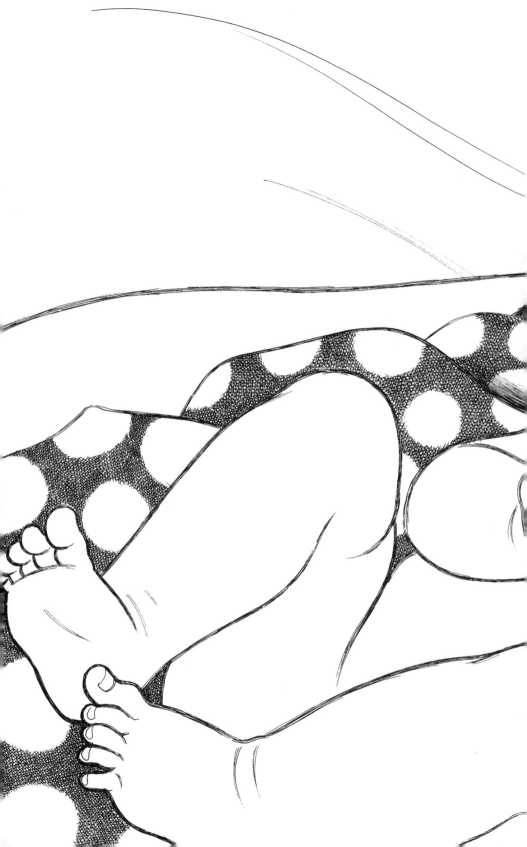

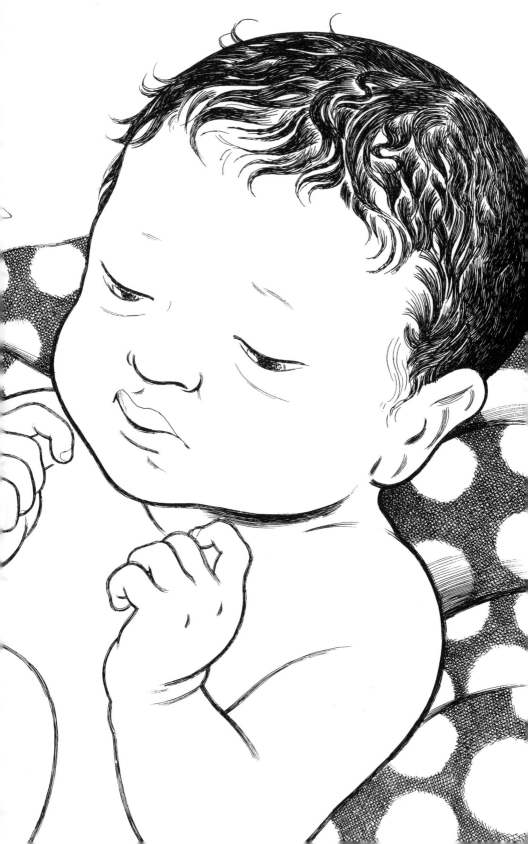

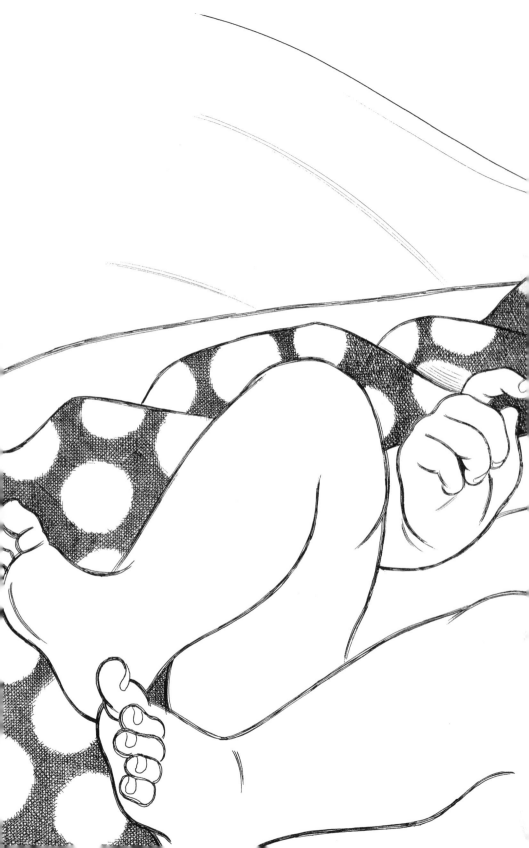

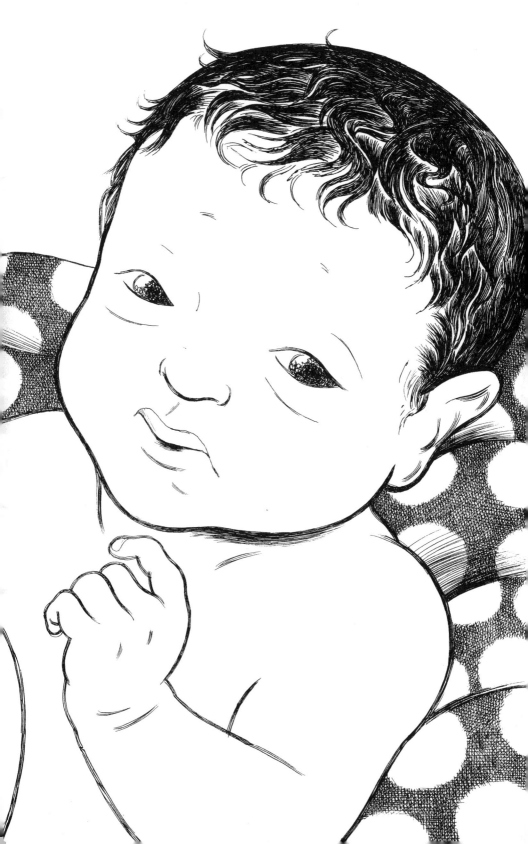

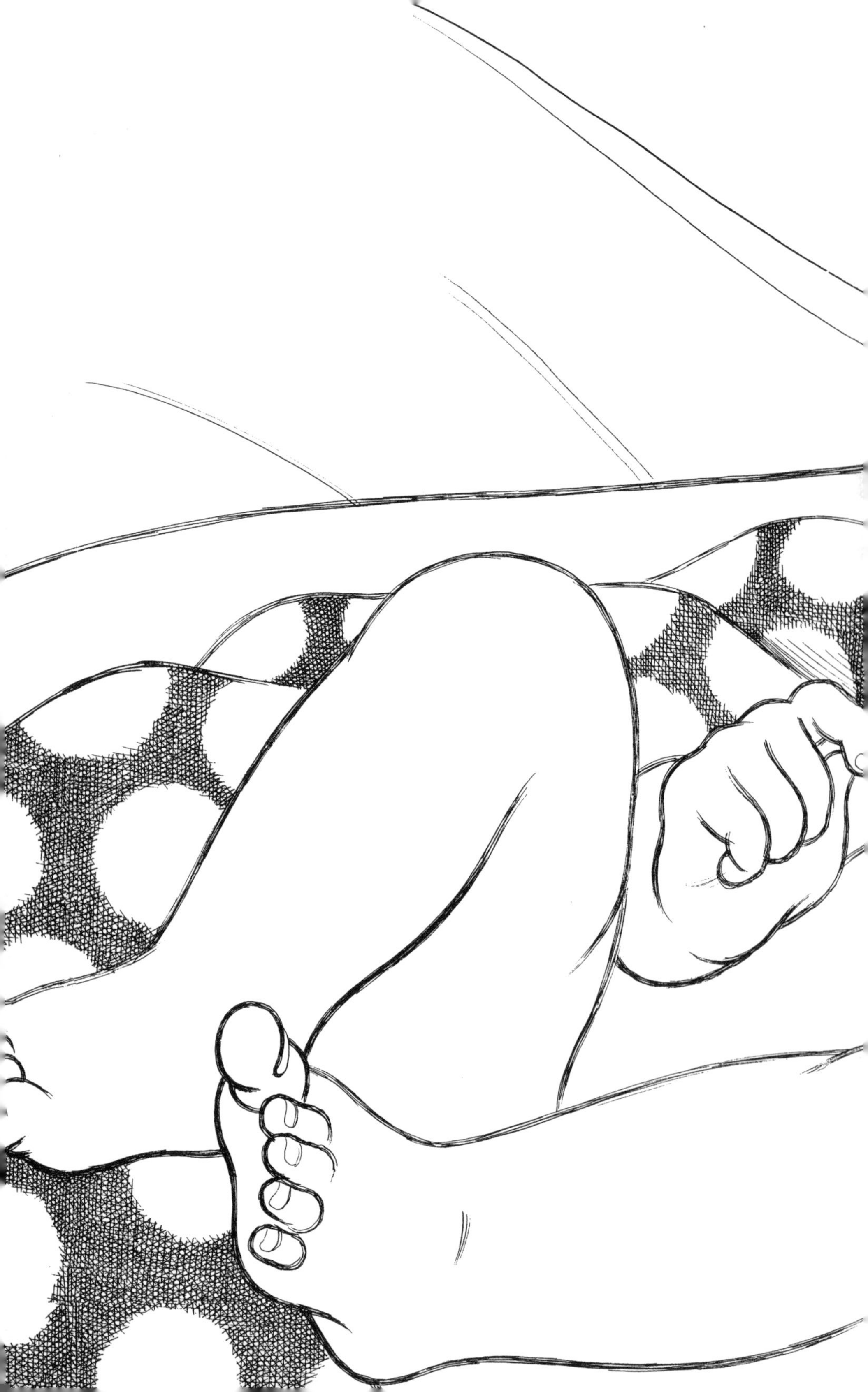

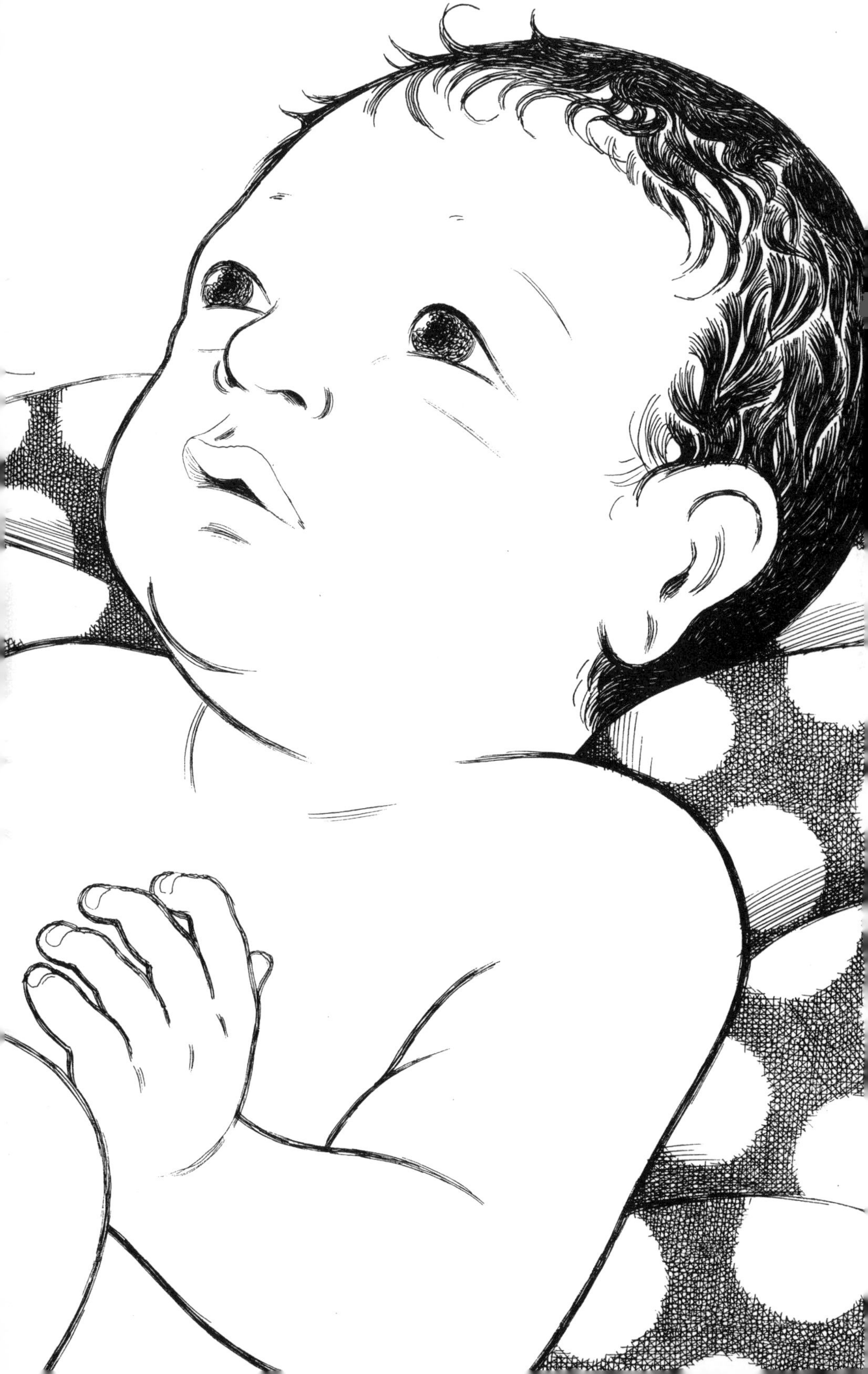

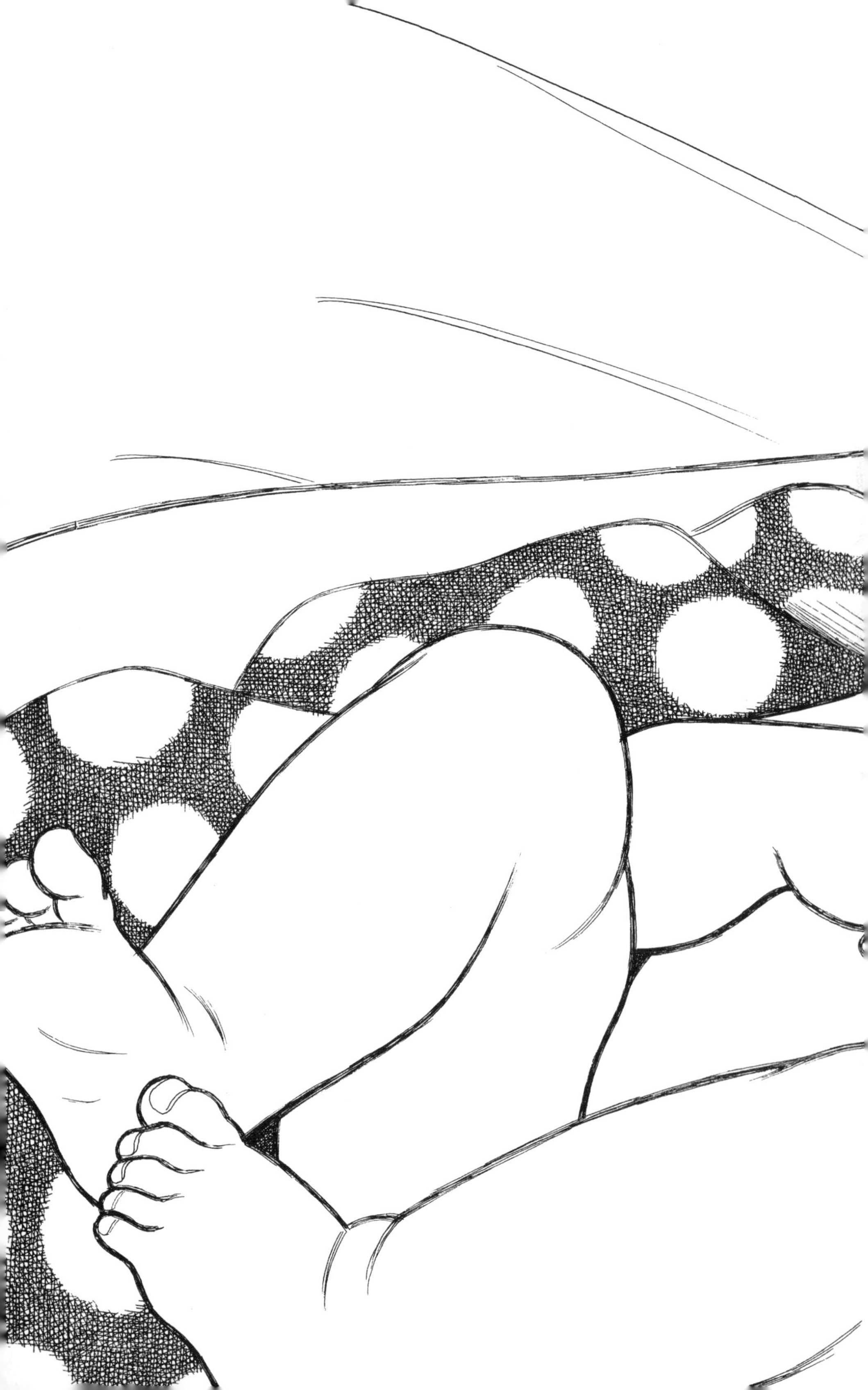

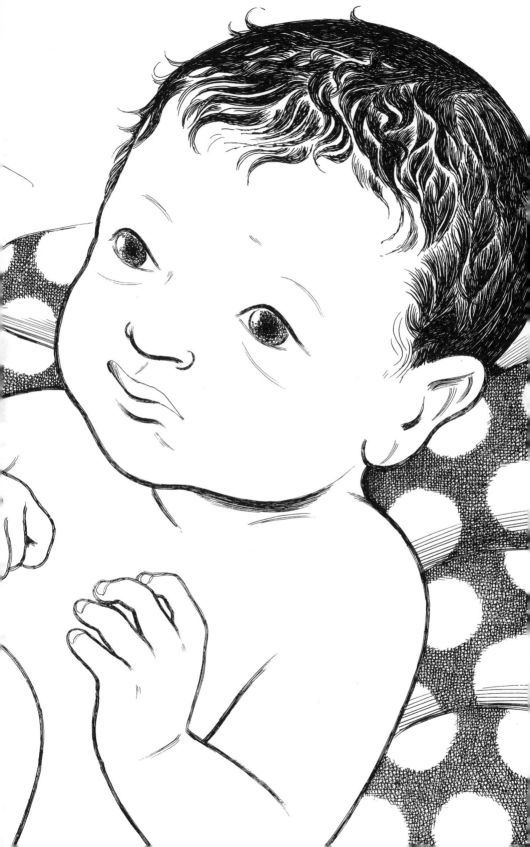

ELEANOR DAVIS is a cartoonist and illustrator. Her books for adults include *Why Art?*, *You & a Bike & a Road*, and *The New York Times* bestseller *How to be Happy*. She lives in Athens, Georgia, with her husband, fellow cartoonist Drew Weing.